ON THE MOVE

American Women in the 1970s

AMERICAN WOMEN IN THE TWENTIETH CENTURY

Barbara Haber, Series Editor

THE SCHLESINGER LIBRARY ON THE HISTORY OF WOMEN IN AMERICA, RADCLIFFE COLLEGE

Pulling together a wealth of widely scattered primary and secondary sources on women's history, *American Women in the Twentieth Century* is the first series to provide a chronological history of the changing status of women in America. Each volume presents the experiences and contributions of American women during one decade of this century. Written by leading scholars in American history and women's studies, *American Women in the Twentieth Century* meets the need for an encyclopedic overview of the roles women have played in shaping modern America.

Also Available:

Setting a Course: American Women in the 1920s
Dorothy M. Brown

Holding Their Own: American Women in the 1930s
Susan Ware

The Home Front and Beyond: American Women in the 1940s
Susan M. Hartman

Mothers and More: American Women in the 1950s
Eugenia Kaledin

ON THE MOVE
American Women in the 1970s

Winifred D. Wandersee

Twayne Publishers • Boston
A Division of G.K. Hall & Co.

*To my parents, Fred and Dorothy Wandersee,
who have lived, challenged, and interpreted the
decades of this century on their own terms and
allowed their daughter to do the same.*

305.42
WAN

On the Move
American Women in the 1970s

Copyright 1988 by G.K. Hall & Co.
All rights reserved.
Published by Twayne Publishers
A division of G.K. Hall & Co.
70 Lincoln Street, Boston, Massachusetts 02111

Copyediting supervised by Barbara Sutton
Production by Janet Zietowski

Typeset in Janson by Compset, Inc., Beverly, Massachusetts

Photographs copyright © by Bettye Lane
and reproduced with her permission.

First Printing

Printed on permanent/durable acid-free paper
and bound in the United States of America

Library of Congress Cataloging-in-Publication Data

Wandersee, Winifred D.
On the move : American women in the 1970s / Winifred D. Wandersee.
p.   cm. — (American women in the twentieth century)
Bibliography: p.
Includes index.
ISBN 0-8057-9909-5 (alk. paper).
ISBN 0-8057-9910-9 (pbk. : alk.
paper)
1. Feminism—United States—History.   2. Women—United States—
Social conditions.   3. United States—Social
conditions—1960–1980.   I. Title.   II. Series.
HQ1426.W35   1988
305.4'2'0973—dc19
87-29050
CIP

CONTENTS

ABOUT THE AUTHOR
PREFACE
GLOSSARY OF TERMS
INTRODUCTION

CHAPTER ONE
Good-Bye to All That: From Revolution to Liberation   1

CHAPTER TWO
Power through Politics: The Reformist Challenge to Democracy   16

CHAPTER THREE
Into the Mainstream: The National Organization for Women and Its
National Constituency   36

CHAPTER FOUR
Women-Identified Women: The Theoretical Basis of Radical
Feminism   55

CHAPTER FIVE
Out of the Mainstream, into the Women's Center: The Practical Application
of Radical Feminism   79

CHAPTER SIX
Scholars and Activists: The Gender Factor in Education   102

CHAPTER SEVEN
Making Choices: The Liberal Dilemma of Work and Family   127

CHAPTER EIGHT
"You've Come a Long Way, Baby": The Media and Women's
Liberation   150

CHAPTER NINE
The Spirit of Houston: Reformers, Radicals, and Reactionaries   175

EPILOGUE   197

NOTES AND REFERENCES   203
A NOTE ON SOURCES   239
INDEX   249

ABOUT THE AUTHOR

Winifred D. Wandersee is a professor of history at Hartwick College in Oneonta, New York, where she teachers courses in twentieth century American history and coordinates the Women's Studies program. She is particularly interested in women during the New Deal years. Her publications include *Women's Work and Family Values, 1920–1940* (Cambridge: Harvard University Press, 1981); "The Economics of Middle-Income Family Life: Working Women During the Great Depression," *Journal of American History* 65 (June 1978); "American Women and the Twentieth-Century Work Force," in *Women, Identity, and Vocation in American History*, edited by Mary Kelley (Boston: G.K. Hall, 1979); "Eleanor Roosevelt and American Youth: Politics and Personality in a Bureaucratic Age," in *Without Precedent: The Life and Career of Eleanor Roosevelt*, edited by Joan Moff-Wilson and Marjorie Lightman (Bloomington: Indiana University Press, 1984); and "A New Deal for Women," in *The New Deal Fifty Years After: A Historical Assessment*, edited by Wilbur J. Cohen (Austin: University of Texas, 1986). Her reviews have appeared in the *American Historical Review*, the *Journal of American History*, *Labor History*, and the *Journal of Social History*. She is currently working on a biography of Frances Perkins.

PREFACE

The history of American women in the 1970s is a history that is still alive and still a part of every woman who recognizes and accepts her connection with the past, present, and future. Therefore, this is primarily an attempt to make some sense out of what happened, or, as one participant said to me, "to write it down, before we all forget, because we didn't have time to write while it was happening." Many people did write, of course. And my debt to them is enormous, as indicated in the notes and bibliography to this volume. But just as important is my debt to those who contributed to my own unique experience in the 1970s: these include the Women Historians of the Midwest, especially Gretchen Kreuter and Susan Smith; my family and friends, especially Perry R. Bolin, and my children, Wes, Ben, and Andrea Bolin; my mentor, Clarke A. Chambers; and an entire women's softball team.

But this book was written in the 1980s—a decade that in many ways has been more challenging and exciting for me, at least, than even the previous one. Those who supported and sustained me, intellectually and emotionally, while I wrote this book include my colleagues and students at Hartwick College, my children, my friends in Oneonta, New York (especially at the Unitarian Universalist Society), and several close friends in Syracuse, New York: Mary Stanley, Suzanne Etherington, and most of all Carolyn Doughty.

Mary Stanley of Syracuse University was my most valued reader and friendly critic. I almost always understood exactly what I had written after she explained it to me. My editor, Barbara Haber of the Schlesinger Library at Radcliffe College, offered constant encouragement and many valued suggestions. Anne M. Jones of Twayne Publishers was similarly helpful and accomplished the rather nasty chore of cutting the manuscript down to size. Athenaide Dallett, also of Twayne, saw the manuscript through to its completion. Several friends—in particular, Suzanne Miller, and Joan Slepian—made their personal libraries available to me. Bettye Lane, feminist photographer, and perhaps the best visual recorder of women's experience in the seventies, was generous in allowing her photographs to be reproduced for this volume. In addition, the librarians at the Schlesinger Library were patient and resourceful in their efforts on my behalf. The librarians at Hartwick College and the State University of New York College of Oneonta were more than patient in their lending policies. My research was supported financially by grants from the Hartwick College Board of Trustees, the American Council of Learned Societies, and the Schlesinger Library. In addition, Hartwick College allowed me an early sabbatical in the fall of 1985, without which I could not have completed the manuscript.

Winifred Wandersee

GLOSSARY OF TERMS

AAC	Association of American Colleges
AAUW	American Association of University Women
ACE	American Council on Education
BMW	Battered Minority Women
BPW	National Federation of Business and Professional Women
CACSW	Citizen Advisory Council on the Status of Women
CCWHE	Coordinating Council for Women in Higher Education
DFL	Democratic Farmer-Labor party
EEOC	Equal Economic Opportunity Commission
ERA	Equal Rights Amendment
FAAR	Feminist Alliance Against Rape
FAP	Feminist Art Program
FCC	Feminist Counseling Collective
FSBC	Free Standing Birth Centers
FWHC	Feminist Women's Health Center
GLF	Gay Liberation Front
GSD	Graduate School of Design
ICSC	Interdepartmental Committee on the Status of Women
IWY	International Women's Year

LWV	League of Women Voters
MLA	Modern Language Association
NAACP	National Association for the Advancement of Colored People
NARAL	National Abortion Rights Action League
NCAA	National Collegiate Athletic Association
NCNP	National Conference for New Politics
NCRWED	National Coalition for Research in Women's Education and Development
NEA	National Education Association
NGO	Non-Governmental Organizations
NOW	National Organization for Women
NRLC	National Right to Life Committee
NWEF	National Women's Education Fund
NWP	National Women's party
NWPC	National Women's Political Caucus
NWSA	National Women's Studies Association
PCSW	President's Commission on the Status of Women
PEER	Project on Equal Educational Rights
PL	Progressive Labor
SDS	Students for a Democratic Society
SNCC	Student Non-Violent Coordinating Committee
SWP	Socialist Workers party
TFC	Task Force Coordinator (NOW)
UAW	United Auto Workers
WEAL	Women's Equity Action League
WHOM	Women Historians of the Midwest
WITCH	Women's International Terrorist Conspiracy from Hell
WLF	Women's Liberation Front
WONAAC	Women's National Abortion Coalition
YSA	Young Socialist Alliance

INTRODUCTION

The decade of the 1970s was a tumultuous and contradictory period in American history: a time when reform overlapped with reaction; when the most powerful military nation in the world was humiliated by smaller nations; when the most affluent society in history recognized its limits and vulnerability; and when the counterculture values of the previous decade crashed against a wall of reaction in the form of religious fundamentalism and a "profamily" movement.

A constitutional crisis created by Republican president Richard Nixon added to the moral confusion. Although the Democrats capitalized temporarily on Republican misfortunes with an electoral victory in 1976, the party was suffering its own crisis as a result of the Vietnam War and the internal battles of the late sixties. It was unable to rebuild the old Roosevelt coalition that had dominated the political climate for more than thirty years. The sixties had witnessed the greatest political upheaval and party realignment since the 1930s, and the seventies saw the consequences. Three presidents resided in the White House and departed ignominiously. The American people rejected their old party loyalties and turned to grass-roots organizations or adopted the stance of "independent voter," critical of their government and suspicious of their leaders. In the midst of political turmoil and economic decline, they grasped at personal solutions—everything from health foods to jogging, from psychotherapy to religious fundamentalism.

But one theme that stood out clearly throughout the decade was the rise of the women's movement and the repercussions it was to have upon women's lives and American society. For the first time in American history, women held at least a piece of the center stage, politically, culturally, and morally. They attempted to define themselves apart from men, but as equal participants in the American dream, although for many the dream itself had become sadly tarnished. The women's movement was a struggle for "liberation," but the definition of liberation varied, depending on the extent to which an individual or a particular group accepted the basic trends, values, and constructs that underlay American society in the sixties and seventies.

The 1960s had politicized the American people, and in the process they were fragmented into contending forces and ideals.[1] The women's movement was not exempt from that fragmentation. In fact, if one were to try to understand its history through the media coverage or through a reading of the ideological debates that appeared in the newsletters and periodicals of the movement, one could argue that its early momentum had quickly fallen victim to the splintering effects of internal dissension, as groups labeled each other and themselves according to political coloration, issues, and style.

That is one part of the story, but the advantage of studying recent history is that the participants are still alive, and they have their own view of events that does not always match the written record. There are, of course, so many women who were involved in the movement that it is difficult to interview a fair sample. And certainly those that I *have* talked to reveal its multifaceted character, as well as a wide range of perspectives. Yet even given these differences, a common thread runs through accounts of participants, activists, and leaders that is sometimes absent from the written accounts of internal struggle. Nearly everyone, in one way or another, attests to the reality of a movement that was based upon a consensus on the important issues and, as one early participant put it, on "an overriding sense of love—a burst of energy related to a sense of loving one another." As late as the National Women's Conference of 1977 there was broad agreement among movement people concerning social policies to benefit minority women, reproductive rights, free choice of sexual preference, and the Equal Rights Amendment (ERA). Throughout the decade, although radicals and reformers had contrasting styles and perhaps different long-range objectives, they tended to come together to support the immediate issue.[2]

This is not to say that there were no real differences, but they were differences of style, priority, personality, and ideology rather than substantial differences with respect to issues. This was particularly true for the early years of the movement, during which a sense of sisterhood prevailed, even if it was often imperfectly realized. The failure to achieve the goals of the movement were due not so much to problems within the movement as to the changing political climate of the mid to late seventies and the reluctance of most Americans to accept the radical implications of the feminist challenge, in whatever form it was presented.

The basic distinction often made by those who write about the women's movement is between the "reformers" and the "radicals."[3] The reformers are viewed as the first to identify with women's issues, although usually in the context of other social issues. In a sense, they had always been part of the American scene. These were the women who had been involved politically at one level or another for most of their lives. They were active in the major political parties, the Women's Bureau and other governmental agencies, the League of Women Voters (LWV), the National Federation of Business and Professional Women (BPW), the YWCA, and various church organizations. Most of them had acquired their feminist consciousness through professional and business careers that inevitably taught them the realities of sex discrimination.[4] The reformers began actively to identify with women's issues during the Kennedy administration, when some of them were appointed to the Presidential Commission on the Status of Women and others were active on the various state commissions that were subsequently established.[5]

The distinguishing characteristics of the reformers were their willingness to work within the system and their basic optimism about the possibilities of incremental change. Marlene Dixon, a Marxist feminist scholar, has called them the "bourgeois feminists" because most of them were white, middle-class, well-educated professionals who denied the need for—or the possibility of—a radical restructuring of the American political and economic system.[6] These liberal feminists were the people who organized the National Organization for Women (NOW), Women's Equity Action League (WEAL), Federally Employed Women (FEW), National Women's Political Caucus (NWPC), and International Women's Year (IWY). Although greatly influenced by the more militant participants of the women's liberation movement and nonplussed by the conservative backlash, the reformers have outlasted both, and they still prevail, albeit considerably subdued by the reactionary political climate of the 1980s.

The reformers, or liberal feminists, laid the groundwork and carried on the kind of mainstream activism that was to directly affect public policy. Their accomplishments in the fields of education, employment, and family policy exceeded those of any previous generation of women. But it was the women's liberation movement that stirred the consciousness of the American people and defined the women's movement in terms that went far beyond the women's rights issues of the moderate reformers. Betty Friedan had identified the "problem that has no name." Women's liberation named it. It was called "male chauvinism" or "the patriarchal system."[7]

What gave the women's movement of the 1970s its special character, in comparison with earlier movements, was that it emerged within the context of the liberal-left politics of the 1960s but was also deeply influenced by the radical politics of that decade. Thus, the women's movement had two sources: the liberal women's rights movement came out of the activism encouraged by the presidential and state commissions on the status of women; the women's liberation movement came out of the New Left.

Factionalism within women's liberation—reflecting differing political styles, organizational structures, races, classes, and sexual preferences—developed very early. But the range of issues and possible approaches to activism broadened the movement and made it accessible to women who might not have been attracted to a more traditional political movement.[8] The first basic division was between the New Left feminists, or the "politicos" (later called the Marxist feminists or socialist feminists), and the cultural feminists, who preferred the label "radical feminists." The politicos identified closely with the male-dominated New Left, and they saw women's oppression in the context of class exploitation that could be ended only through a socialist revolution. Thus they placed emphasis on a political solution through left-wing politics.

Although many radical feminists were also sympathetic to New Left politics and favored the communal social values of the New Left, they did not see a socialist revolution as the answer to women's problems. As radical feminists, they located the oppression of women, and indeed all kinds of oppression, within the patriarchal system. Thus, they placed women's issues ahead of all other political issues. In its extreme form, radical feminism advocated a lesbian/separatist solution in the face of what they perceived to be the overwhelming hostility of a patriarchal society.

The impact of radical feminism was impressive, leading to a new women's culture in the arts; attempts to establish communes and women's collectives; women's centers to deal with problems such as rape, wife abuse, and abortion; women's studies programs in colleges and universities; and other forms of alternative institutions. But the radical feminists offered an extreme critique of American society, which, because it did not allow room for compromise, encouraged the *possibility* of separatism rather than activism, and a search for personal solutions to political problems.[9] On the other hand, the approach of the politicos—that is, an alliance with the male-dominated Left in order to bring about a socialist revolution—became an increasingly remote possibility as the decade wore on and the political right wing within American society played a larger and more visible role in mainstream politics.[10]

By the early seventies, of the two factions, the radical feminists had contributed more successfully to the mainstream women's movement. By that time the distinction between "women's rights" and "women's liberation" had become blurred in the eyes of the public and among activists themselves. Instead, the "women's movement" became the acceptable terminology, encompassing a wide range of groups, styles, ideologies, and concerns. The radical feminists varied immensely among themselves with respect to the issue of activism versus separatism, and most of them combined the two to a greater or lesser degree. Their tendency to politicize the personal and to personalize the political caused them to introduce new issues into the body politic that had never before been addressed by the mainstream political system. The liberal feminists picked up on many of these issues—abortion, lesbianism, wife battering, rape—and they became part of the political-cultural debate of the 1970s.

The successes of the early women's movement, both in legislative gains and in the defining of new issues, contributed to the backlash that was part of the general reaction to the social and cultural revolution of the 1960s. But in the case of the women's movement, it was not so much a backlash as a "front lash"—the opposition had always existed. The movement never enjoyed the kind of broad moral support and sympathy that the civil rights movement had experienced during the sixties. Americans never felt a collective guilt for their sexism as they did for their racism; they never accepted collective responsibility for centuries of discrimination and the consequential secondary status of women within society.[11] Indeed, one of the major tasks of feminists was to convince women *themselves* that they had a right to their freedom, and that women's issues were justifiable political objectives.

The women's movement contributed to the conservative political climate that had emerged by the late 1970s, primarily by offering a focus that allowed the right wing to mobilize the forces of opposition. Two issues in particular—abortion and the ERA—led to organizational efforts among right-wing women who had previously avoided political activism.[12] No history of the 1970s would be complete without an evaluation of these women in terms that go beyond "false consciousness," and beyond the view that they were merely "tools" of the male-dominated establishment. One way to interpret the actions of right-wing women is to see them as part of the populism of the 1970s that was receiving such wide attention by the middle of the decade. In relation to the women's movement, they were experiencing a kind of status anxiety akin to that which afflicted the populists and progressives of Richard Hofstadter's work.[13] Andrea Dworkin argues that they feared the liberating effects of the women's movement, and for good reason—they had realistically assessed the power of male chauvinism and preferred to make a bad bargain with marriage and family rather than to risk the misogyny of the outside world:

The political Right in the United States today makes certain metaphysical and material promises to women that both exploit and quiet some of women's deepest fears. These fears originate in the perception that male violence against women is uncontrollable and unpredictable. Dependent on and subservient to men, women are always subject to this violence. The Right promises to put enforceable restraints on male aggression, thus simplifying survival for women.[14]

The women's movement had repercussions that went far beyond its immediate issues and intent. It *did* contribute to the political climate that was to sweep Reagan into the presidency in 1980, but it also opened doors for women that had always been closed, and it raised the consciousness of a nation with respect to a whole range of issues. The slogan "the personal is political" could well describe the whole decade of the seventies as much as the women's movement itself. Issues that were previously ignored or evaded—including sexual relations, sexual harassment on the job, child abuse, incest, wife battering, rape, and pornography—became public policy issues of the 1970s and 1980s, primarily because of the activism of women's groups.

One of the astonishing things about any social movement and any period of upheaval is the extent to which some people appear to be untouched. During a period of activism, it is natural to focus on the activists, but there is always a ripple effect that touches the lives of many who are unaware of or unwilling to acknowledge the impact. In the 1970s the lives of many women changed dramatically, especially in comparison to the standards of previous decades. The changes in sexual mores and family life, the opening up of educational and economic opportunity, the changing image of women in the media, and the visibility of women in places where they had previously been barred—these were all factors that had a direct and immediate impact on women's lives, whether or not they were feminists.

William Chafe had noted that during the decade of the 1950s social scientists debated the "women's question": what was to be the role of women in a modern, technologically advanced society? As Chafe points out, while scholars debated, ordinary women went about their business and resolved the problem themselves by combining jobs and family.[15] This was not the solution that feminists of the 1970s sought, but it was the way the public understood feminism, and it was the solution most often chosen by the women of that decade.

But the debate of the seventies was louder, more widespread, and more urgent than that of the fifties. If the scholars had debated in the fifties, women of all political and ideological hues debated in the seventies. Yet it must be acknowledged that many women ignored the debate and made their own choices reflective of their personal and family needs. There were more choices to be made—and more problems, too, of course—but there were also new options made possible by the activists of the women's movement. It is these choices, these options, that are the legacy of the seventies. How they became a reality—and the extent to which they did not—is a complex and challenging story.

CHAPTER ONE

Good-Bye to All That:
From Revolution to Liberation

In January of 1970, Robin Morgan, a poet, feminist, and former writer for the New Left journal *Rat*, received a call from Jane Alpert, a member of a radical underground group, the Weatherman, and worker on *Rat*. Alpert informed her that the women on the *Rat* staff had seized the paper to protest male chauvinist journalism and to devote an issue to women's liberation. Morgan responded quickly and brought with her about thirty women from all parts of the women's movement in New York City. They came from Redstockings, WITCH, (Women's International Terrorist Conspiracy from Hell), the New York Radical Women, and even NOW. Although they knew little about typesetting, layouts, advertising, printing, or distribution, they put out a paper that not only met the scheduled deadline but finally forced the male New Left to take women seriously. Morgan's contribution, "Good-Bye to All That," was, as one New Left journalist put it, "the shot heard round the Left." And Morgan herself claims that she intended the essay as her farewell to working with men in the New Left.[1]

It is tempting to view the *Rat* takeover and the Morgan essay as the watershed event that witnessed the demise of the New Left and the sixties, as it ushered in the women's movement of the seventies. But if this single incident was a watershed, it was only one of several. By January 1970, the women's movement within the New Left already had at least a two-to-three-year history, and the angry words of Robin

Morgan were symbolic of a deeply felt rage that had been germinating among women activists since mid-decade. To understand the intensity of that rage, one must understand the struggle of New Left women to be recognized by their male peers.[2]

A series of incidents had occurred during the last few years of the decade that raised the consciousness of women within the New Left and caused them to organize finally in response to their own oppression. The process had begun in the Student Non-Violent Coordinating Committee (SNCC) in 1964 when a small group of women led by Ruby Doris Smith Robinson presented a paper, "The Position of Women in SNCC." The paper elicited the famous comment from Stokely Carmichael, "the only position for women in SNCC is prone." In 1965 Casey Hayden and Mary King, SNCC activists, wrote another paper on the role of women in the movement, which was also greeted with scorn and ridicule by movement men.[3]

By the mid-sixties, however, the character of the civil rights movement was changing, and white activists were no longer welcome in SNCC. The whites shifted their attention to the antiwar New Left, led by Students for a Democratic Society (SDS). During the last half of the decade, the young people on the Left became increasingly disillusioned with the American political scene, the war policies of the Johnson administration, and the perceived bankruptcy of liberalism. Thus the rhetoric and the actions of the New Left took on a radical posture that was to culminate in the political adventurism of the Weathermen. It was in this atmosphere that the women's liberation movement was born, and the rhetoric and ideological struggles of the declining New Left were to shape the early years of the movement and to define several lines of conflict within feminism throughout the 1970s.

Women within the New Left, like those in the civil rights movement, found themselves ignored, put down, or ridiculed when they tried to participate in political discussions or exercise leadership. Finally, at a National Conference for New Politics (NCNP), which met in Chicago in September 1967, the tension between the women's issue and New Left politics escalated into an open confrontation. This event grew out of the actions of a Chicago women's group, which had met during the summer to discuss the possibility of presenting a list of demands to the NCNP. (This small group was the first independent radical women's group.) They joined with other women at the conference to present for general debate a resolution demanding a civil rights plank for women, similar to the twelve demands that had been presented by the black caucus and accepted by the conference.[4]

When the leaders of the NCNP rode roughshod over the women's plank, Jo Freeman and Shulamith Firestone, members of the ad hoc women's caucus, demanded a hearing. They were told that their issues were "trivial." Firestone was actually patted on the head and told to "calm down, little girl." The Chicago women left the conference and began meeting with each other on a regular basis. Freeman and Firestone became founders of women's liberation groups in Chicago and New York, respectively.[5]

By the mid-sixties, large segments of the Left had become disillusioned with activism within the system and started to withdraw from political activism into a "life-style revolution," in which emphasis was placed on how revolutionaries lived, their personal values, and their individual oppression. The ideal was to *live* the revolution by examining personal difficulties, developing alternative institutions, such as communes or collectives, and carrying out an individual act of revolution, no matter how irrelevant it seemed to the mainstream political system.[6] As one writer explained it, "They were going to surrender themselves to history, to make themselves into history's cutting edge, to become the catalyst of historical change."[7]

The new emphasis on living the revolution inevitably led women to examine their own oppression in relation to the men in the movement. In this respect, the New Left differed from the Old Left, which had emphasized an economic and political analysis of capitalism, excluding entirely the psychological dimension of oppression. Thus the women of the Old Left, although similarily oppressed, had neither the level of consciousness nor the ideological tools to confront their oppression. Women of the New Left, on the other hand, could relate their own experience to that of blacks and understand that, like the blacks, they would have to form their own group in order to deal effectively with their problems.[8]

Not all women of the New Left, however, accepted the primacy of women's oppression. Some belonged to political groups that retained the Old Left orientation, such as the Progressive Labor organization, (PL), the Socialist Workers' party (SWP), and the Young Socialist Alliance (YSA). These groups, along with a number of individuals in SDS and, later, in Weatherman, saw women's liberation as an organizing tool for the leftist revolution rather than a separate movement committed to ending the oppression of women. The split between the "politicos" and the "feminists" occurred very early and influenced both the intellectual debate and the activism of women in the movement.

The period between 1968 and 1970, then, was a time of intellectual ferment as women sought to define the ideological foundations of the women's liberation movement. A number of crucial essays was circulated in pamphlet form among women's groups or published in New Left periodicals. And women began to establish their own periodicals, which increased in number from two in 1968 to sixty-one by 1972. Although it is hard to estimate how many women actually read this outpouring of literature, it is clear that some members of the movement digested the new ideas and made them the focus of discussion in women's groups. By the end of 1969, women's liberation was nationally known. It had become a coherent, although many-faceted movement with its own ideology, a growing membership, and an informal but defined organizational structure.[9]

In the midst of this intellectual activity, the debate on the nature of women's liberation within the New Left took form. Ellen Willis, a writer for the *Village Voice* and a founder of the feminist group Redstockings wrote an article that appeared in the *Guardian* in February 1969; it lay the cornerstone of a radical feminist movement independent of the male-dominated Left. She rejected the idea of using feminist issues as an organizing tool for the Left, calling it antiwoman: "We have come to see women's liberation as an independent revolutionary movement, potentially representing half the population. We intend to make our own analysis of the system and put our interests first, whether or not it is convenient for the (male-dominated) Left."[10]

Willis argued that radical men were not willing to give up their power and that women had to develop group consciousness, recognizing that they might have more in common with reformist organizations like NOW than with radical men. Her article was met with an outpouring of letters, most of them favorable, although the *Guardian* chose to print those that were not. Willis responded to one critic in an unpublished letter in which she argued that although capitalism exploited women, the patriarchal family system predated the state and was therefore the primary oppressor of women. To overthrow the state was only part of the battle. Willis also made the analogy with the black power position. Women had to unite on their own in order to make clear to radical men the nature of their oppression and the seriousness of their resolve to end it.[11]

The internal split indicated by this exchange was acted out over several years. Several organizations were established that reflected the varying political stances. One group called the New York Radical Women was formed in late 1967 by Pam Allen and Shulamith Firestone. The group experienced internal conflict between politicos and feminists which intensified in January 1968, when it participated in an antiwar demonstration in Washington, D.C. The members joined a march for peace as part of a coalition of women's peace groups called the Jeanette Rankin Brigade, involving some five thousand women. The New York Radical Women's group planned a demonstration during the protest which they called the "Burial of Traditional Womanhood." Some three to five hundred women joined them in a torchlight parade at Arlington Cemetery and heard a speech delivered by Kathy Amatniek in which the slogan "Sisterhood is powerful" was used for the first time.[12]

The demonstration was called irrelevant and nonpolitical by radical women participating in the broader movement, and even the politicos within the New York group opposed the action. The differences intensified for several months, and in June 1968, New York Radical Women put together a mimeographed journal, *Notes from the First Year*, which included articles reviewing the Jeanette Rankin Brigade action and an essay that was to become one of the landmarks of the movement, Anne Koedt's "The Myth of the Vaginal Orgasm." The journal was distributed primarily in New York, but its influence was felt far beyond the city.

Seattle was one of the first places, after Chicago and New York, to form a women's group. Others came together in San Francisco and East Bay (Berkeley and Oakland). But the distinction between the politicos and feminists continued to divide the movement. The formation of WITCH was an example of an attempt to bridge this gap. Loosely organized, WITCH was an action-oriented subgroup within the New York group which based its activities on New Left–style guerrilla theater, engaging in "zap" actions, such as dressing up as witches and hexing the Stock Exchange or the telephone company and staging skits and antiwar protests.[13]

In 1969 the radical women's movement in New York underwent important changes that influenced the development of the movement in the rest of the country and reflected some of its organizational and theoretical problems. A new group formed by Ellen Willis and Shulamith Firestone, called Redstockings, was committed to the idea of small

group consciousness-raising. Although consciousness-raising was not a
new concept, Redstockings was the first group to articulate its function
and process, and to advocate its use as a means to liberation. Redstockings also advanced the "prowoman" argument, which stated that
women are not responsible for their own oppression and that men, not
women, must change their behavior.[14]

At the same time that Redstockings was being established, another
group was formed, led by Ti-Grace Atkinson, the president of the New
York chapter of NOW. Atkinson had walked out of NOW on 17 October
1968 and with several other discontented women, formed the October
17th Movement, later called the Feminists. The split within NOW,
caused by ideological conflicts over the meaning of feminism, indicated
the distance between the reformers and the radicals at this early stage
of the movement. The schism was based on differences over such issues
as marriage, abortion, family, and the class system. The philosophical
positions were perhaps most clearly illustrated by Betty Friedan's statement that her goal was "to get women into positions of power," and
Atkinson's statement that she wanted "to get rid of positions of
power."[15]

The struggle within NOW had climaxed when a proposal to eliminate
offices in the organization—reflecting the antistructure and antileader-
ship bias of some feminists—was ruled illegal under the bylaws. The
dissenting faction, made up of young radical women led by Atkinson,
then tried to diffuse the powers of the offices by increasing the number
of persons holding them. When this attempt was defeated by a 2–1
majority, Atkinson and her followers walked out. Most of the membership was not disappointed to see her leave. There had been objec-
tions to her appearance in court with Valerie Solanas, who was being
tried for the shooting and wounding of pop artist Andy Warhol. Friedan had been particularly upset by newspaper picture captions stating
that Atkinson was appearing in behalf of NOW. Conservative members
also objected to the young dissidents' support of Bill Baird, an abortion
crusader who used civil disobedience as a means of getting cases into
court.[16]

The October 17th Movement soon became the Feminists, a small
but influential group that considered itself a committed revolutionary
cadre, "á la Che Guevara." The Feminists set themselves up to destroy
the sex-role system and noted that it distorted the humanity of the
oppressor—man—and denied the humanity of the oppressed—woman.
All political classes grew out of this sex-role system, so that any new

class system would simply be used to reestablish the male-female system.[17]

The organizational principles of the Feminists differentiated them from other groups in the women's movement. The members viewed themselves as a highly disciplined action group in which attendance was required, participation was expected, and power was shared. Membership was a primary commitment that could not be superseded by anything else. Because the Feminists considered the institution of marriage inherently inequitable, and indeed a source of oppression, the group set a quota: no more than one-third of the membership could be involved in either a formal marriage or an informal living arrangement with a man.[18]

More interested in taking on other radical feminists, especially Redstockings, than in continuing the debate with the moderate reformers, the Feminists developed a theoretical critique of consciousness-raising and the prowoman position. The Feminists recognized consciousness-raising as a necessary step to teach women to see their oppression as political rather than personal, temporarily lifting the burden of self-blame. But there were dangers in the technique as well: the possibilities of inertia, boredom, dropping out, and a kind of internal oppression enforced by other women in the group. Called "prison guards," such women within the movement were perceived by other feminists to be acting for and in place of the male presence.[19] Thus a prison guard was someone who set a permissible standard of female behavior and used it to control the discussion and actions of a group: "There are always one or two guards around; at a party, in the office, in school, on the block. They are prettier, or nicer, or sweeter or sexier than other women, they know how to do things right."[20]

One group in San Francisco began a local paper, the *Women's Page*, which was created in reaction to the established politics of some groups. The paper attacked the prison guards for controlling the small groups and keeping them from progressing. Rather than providing a rationale for revolutionary change, the small group was actually preventing change. One such group, called Gallstones, was dominated by women who were or had been connected with leaders of the male New Left. These women had status within the group, as well as access to the underground press. But they were committed to their men, and the leftist male ideal of revolution, rather than to other women. Thus, they were more interested in the status quo than in change.[21]

The ideas expressed in the Women's Page coincided basically with the views of the Feminists, who critiqued not only the small group and consciousness-raising but also the prowoman line of the Redstockings. The latter argued that women's behavior did not have to change—only the external conditions under which they were oppressed. Whatever women did was "good," in the sense that it was always a reaction to oppression. The Feminists felt that this left no room for standards, no room for revolutionary change through the actions of women. The prowoman outlook was actually a "dangerous under-estimation of the potential of women and their capacity for revolution." It was dangerous because it kept women static and oppressed.[22]

Underlying the critique of the prowoman position, the small groups, the prison guards, and the general stultifying effect of consciousness-raising was the conflict between those who saw the women's movement as an auxiliary to leftist politics and those who saw feminism as their first and perhaps only concern. The division was not clear-cut: Redstockings was more interested in feminism than in leftist politics, for instance. But there was a strong difference between those who viewed women's oppression in class terms as opposed to those who saw it as a sex-role issue.

In December 1969, the New York Radical Feminists, a new group founded to replace the New York Radical Women, issued a manifesto that clearly stated its position on the issue of feminism versus leftist politics. Entitled "The Politics of Ego," the declaration took exception to the economic and class-based interpretation of women's oppression. Instead, the Radical Feminists argued that the purpose of male chauvinism was primarily to obtain psychological ego satisfaction, which was only secondarily manifested in economic relationships: "we do not believe that capitalism, or any other economic system, is the cause of female oppression, nor do we believe that female oppression will disappear as a result of a purely economic revolution." Thus, the "politics of ego" referred to men controlling women's egos in order to meet their own ego needs.[23]

Certainly many of the women who were the most actively engaged with the male New Left seemed to have a limited feminist consciousness that was more individualistic than sisterly. Their feminism tended to be submerged in their radical activism, their counterculture lifestyle, and their deep attachments to male lovers in the macho-style New Left.

On 6 March 1970, a Greenwich Village town house exploded,

resulting in the death of three young people, all of them members of the underground revolutionary organization, Weatherman. Among the members present were Kathy Boudin and Cathy Wilkerson, who escaped alive and disappeared, and Diana Oughton, who was killed.[24] By 1970 the New Left, as an effective political movement, had all but committed suicide. The Weatherman was an example of the extreme application of the New Left's revolutionary life-style, its disillusionment with the American political system, its emphasis on personal commitment and physical courage, and its fantasy of violent revolution in America. The only way to prove courage and commitment was to act whether it made good political sense or not. "They argued that an attack on the state was morally necessary. Once convinced of its necessity, the utility of such an attack became irrelevant."[25]

This kind of value, so repellent to some women—the macho style of the street fighter—brought about the formation of the Women's Liberation Front. And yet other New Left women, although they paid lip service to feminism, remained loyal to the male-dominated version of history which saw a socialist revolution—even if achieved violently— as an absolute moral necessity. The personal accounts of this commitment to the apparently irrational politics of violence indicated that some women internalized these values to the point that they no longer questioned either the rationale or the outcome. To question would be to challenge their life-style, their courage, their revolutionary ideology, their sense of history, their personal commitments—indeed, everything that they had become.

Diana Oughton, one of the young women who died in the Greenwich Village explosion, was an example of that kind of commitment. Born into a wealthy Chicago family, she had experienced a loving family life as a child. Her political beliefs were based upon a strong moral conviction that emerged during her college years and was intensified by her experiences in the Peace Corps. That moral conviction became more obsessive as she became heavily involved in movement activities and emotionally involved in a long-term on-again, off-again romance with Bill Ayers, a leading SDS activist.

Diana had a limited feminist consciousness. In March 1968, she helped found a women's liberation group. Most of the talk within the group centered on the subordinate role of women within the movement and their sexual oppression by macho men who thought of sex as a conquest. Although Oughton was willing to talk about the role of women in SDS, she was unable to see her personal oppression in her relationship with Bill Ayers. Like many women in the New Left, Diana considered women's liberation important because it gave women the right to be the revolutionary equals of men.

At a time when most women in the movement were touchy to the point of hysteria about their dignity, Diana was relaxed and realistic, one of the few SDS females who could be called a girl without starting a fight. All the others insisted they were women; Diana never insisted but was automatically considered one.[26]

This description seems to suggest that Oughton was what many feminists would call a "male-identified woman." Women's liberation really had very little to do with her personal and political style and commitment. This was true of other leading New Left women as well.

Susan Stern, an activist who wrote her own account of life underground, assumed a political stance that appears to have been primarily a gut-level reaction to personal circumstances and a search for belonging at an adolescent level.[27] Stern fit Kenneth Keniston's analysis of alienated youth[28] and was also representative of the extreme radical ("politics as theater") who typified certain segments of the New Left in its declining years. Stern, committed to experimentation in sex, drugs, and politics, was deeply insecure personally and sought political power within the movement for self-gratification. Although she seems to have been sincerely committed to a new revolutionary order, even to the point of risking her life and going to jail, she was unclear in her own mind as to her motivation. Her revolutionary ardor was apparently based as much upon a hatred of "Amerika," or more narrowly, "the pigs," as on a genuine love of "the people."

Stern took great pleasure in being "one of the boys," as when she was the only woman among the "Seattle Seven" arrested for revolutionary activity. But she did show occasional flashes of feminist consciousness. She was greatly impressed by Friedan's *Feminine Mystique*, which she read in 1968 at the age of twenty-five. She also met Flo Kennedy, the black lawyer and activist, who influenced her to set up a women's liberation group in Seattle. Stern, along with several other women, ran a series of weekly classes and organized a woman's group among the participants.[29] But her early experience in SDS and the Women's Liberation Front was soon overwhelmed by her commitment to Weatherman: "There was only one reality in my life. Weatherman. I fell in love with a concept. My white knight materialized into a vision of world-wide liberation. I ceased to think of Susan Stern as a woman: I saw myself as a revolutionary tool."[30]

Stern described her attempts, and those of other SDS and Weatherman women, to identify with and adopt the macho values of the male Left. "The vogue was to be tough and macho, and I was as overzealously aggressive and abandoned as a Weatherman as I had been timid and frightened prior to it."[31] The woman who was apparently most successful in matching the men for toughness, charisma, and revolutionary fervor was SDS leader Bernardine Dohrn, famous in leftist circles for her celebration of the Manson Family murders. Stern practically idolized this "high priestess" of the Left. "Whatever quality she possessed, I wanted it. I wanted to be cherished and respected as Bernardine was. More than that, I wanted to know Bernardine. I wanted to be an aristocrat too. I wanted to be part of that special, select group permitted to know her as a human being, rather than a mythological silhouette."[32]

Stern notes that although the New Left women continued to struggle with male chauvinism, they were very attached to SDS and decided to remain within the chapter rather than form a separate organization. The majority of SDS women in Stern's group supported Weatherman. On the other hand, they kept in constant contact with nonmembers through a women's caucus.[33]

One activist who is an extreme representative of the transition from New Left radicalism to 1970s feminism is Jane Alpert, the woman who played a large role in the *Rat* takeover of 1970. Alpert's autobiography, *Growing Up Underground,* describes her childhood in a middle-class family, her attendance at one of the better public high schools, Forest Hills, and her performance as an honor student.[34] But Alpert's family life was less than idyllic, and she felt alienated from other family members. As in the case of Stern, Oughton, Boudin, and others, there seems to have been no single reason for Alpert's becoming a leftist revolutionary. A large part of her conversion stemmed from her love for Sam Melville (SDS activist, later killed in the 1971 Attica uprising), another part from her emotional dependency, and another from her background in the context of the political climate in America. She studied Marxism as interpreted by Marcuse, Reich, and Paul Goodman and found that it fit her "like a new pair of glasses through which I seemed to see truth for the first time." She began to understand the connection between the personal and the political, and she applied movement ideas to every aspect of her life.

My beliefs were naive and rooted as much in rage as in idealistic hope. But I needed them. I could not have fallen so overwhelmingly in love with Sam if he had not given me such an ideology. Nor could I have accepted the ideology so wholeheartedly if I hadn't been so powerfully attracted to Sam. . . . The combination of sexual love and radical ideology was more than irresistible. It consumed me.[35]

As part of her New Left activism, however, Alpert attended consciousness-raising meetings where she met early feminist leaders like Robin Morgan and Ellen Willis. Willis was already, in 1968, urging a separate autonomous women's movement, but Alpert was not sure what women were demanding of men, and she informed Melville that she thought the idea of a separate political organization for women was stupid.[36] Six months later she attended a citywide women's liberation conference in which she met Kathie Amatniek (later Sarachild) and heard her and Robin Morgan discuss the future of women in the Left. Morgan went further than Willis. She thought that, rather than forming independent organizations, women should take over the Left and kick the men out of their leadership roles. Alpert found the idea electrifying and emotionally appealing, but an overreaction.[37]

At the time that Alpert and Morgan took over *Rat* in January 1970, the Left was in disarray, and Sam Melville was being held without bail for his part in several bombings, for which Alpert was also indicted. Much of the radical Left was going underground. (Alpert, in fact, was about to go underground herself, which she did in May 1970). The emotions and the rationale behind the *Rat* takeover were complex, and they were both personal and political. The long-range anger was directed at Amerika, a nation they looked upon as not only capitalist, imperialist, and racist but also patriarchal and male chauvinist. There was an immediate situation, too, that was triggered by Alpert and picked up by Morgan.

Alpert, fresh out of jail and still awaiting trial, felt that the New Left movement had become moribund. Her faith in the reality of a revolution began to fade, as she saw that the radicals really had no army, no unity, no national organization. At a time when she could not break her own commitment to the movement, her eyes were suddenly opened to its weaknesses. In particular, Alpert became disillusioned with *Rat*, which she felt was deteriorating from a lively radical journal into a sophomoric joke sheet. Her fears were confirmed when the male staff members at *Rat* turned out a "sex-and-porn special" that angered Alpert and other female staffers so much that they decided to put out a women's issue.[38]

Alpert herself admitted that the issue was not particularly impressive journalistically. But Morgan's essay "Good-By to All That," was an exception that was soon to become a feminist classic. It was a scathing indictment of the male Left and a call for revolution led by women. It was written in the language of the New Left—highly emotional, intense, accentuated by obscenities and leftist rhetoric. Alpert was impressed, but also somewhat puzzled by Morgan's version of feminism. Nonetheless, she and several other women were inspired enough by Morgan's militance to take over the paper permanently, carrying on its publication for two more years.[39]

The *Rat* issue and the Morgan essay exposed the split between the male-dominated New Left and the Women's Liberation Front, but the incident was primarily symbolic and its clarity an illusion. In fact, WLF had been in the process of breaking away for at least two or three years. Only by understanding the efforts of the New Left women to communicate to the men their anger at being ignored and trivialized can one understand the intensity of feeling that lay behind this split.[40] On the other hand, many women in the movement continued to place New Left politics first, and their commitment continued into the 1970s, even after the New Left itself was defunct. The debate between the politicos and the radical feminists continued to have an impact on the women's movement, but by the mid-seventies, the debate had become a sideshow in which the star performers were radical activists and intellectuals.

An example of this continuing debate surfaced in 1973 and again involved Jane Alpert. *Ms.* magazine published a feminist manifesto, "Mother Right: A New Feminist Theory," in its August 1973 issue. The statement had been written by Alpert in a long personal letter to Gloria Steinem at a time when the former was living underground as a legal fugitive. It was meant as an appeal to her "Dear Sisters in the Weather Underground," begging them to recognize the male chauvinist basis of leftist politics and practices. But Alpert also hoped to reach a far wider feminist audience, which was why she sent it to Steinem.

My own politics demand that I share with all women my knowledge of the sexual oppression of the left. . . . the experiences that I am going to relate may speak more effectively to women involved in other branches of the left, from

McGovern organizers to Socialist Workers Party members . . . [and may] persuade you to leave the dying left in which you are floundering and begin to put your immense courage and skills to work for women—yourselves.[41]

Alpert argued that the politico-feminist split would continue as long as leftist women were unwilling to accept themselves as women first of all and to recognize their own oppression so that they could work together for their own liberation. She gave firsthand accounts of male attitudes among the Left, presenting damning anecdotes about Mark Rudd and Sam Melville as representative revolutionaries who were also representative sexists.[42]

Alpert's article, combined with her surrender in November 1974 and the arrest of three underground radicals the following spring, polarized the women's movement in New York. Three petitions were circulated by supporters and detractors: one specifically charged Alpert with informing on her former underground colleagues, one was indirectly critical of her, and a third strongly defended her.[43]

Those who signed the petition defending Alpert, calling her "a woman of great integrity and strong feminist commitment," were some of the leading lights of the women's movement—Gloria Steinem, Kate Millett, Rita Mae Brown, Phyllis Chesler, Karen DeCrow, Jill Johnston, Grace Paley, and Margaret Sloane. On the other side stood a number of leftist and feminist organizations, including New York Women's Union, New York Women's School, Women's Health Forum, East New York Alliance, National Lawyers Guild, and the Prairie Fire Distributing Committee. Another anti-Alpert petition was signed by four women—Susan Sherman, Ti-Grace Atkinson, Joan Hamilton, and Flo Kennedy. This petition saw the Alpert surrender, and her conversion from radicalism to feminism, as a kind of betrayal that reflected the injustices of America's class system. The Alpert incident, they thought, represented a movement based on class privilege and on white privilege.[44]

But other feminists saw it very differently. A letter to Charlotte Bunch, long-time activist and editor of *Quest: A Feminist Quarterly*, expressed the view that male values were again being used to divide women and that there was a need to discover an ethics, a way of living, that would keep women connected. Jane Alpert had been diminished from the status of leftist and feminist by the single word *informer*, when in fact there was no evidence that she had informed.[45]

Clearly the issue was not Alpert, but rather the relationship between feminism and leftist politics. It was to continue to be an issue throughout the 1970s, and it was the focus of much of the feminist writing of the period. But most radical feminists moved away from the male-dominated Left and toward an alliance with the more radical and even liberal elements of the reform feminists, thereby moving the reformers further to the Left. As Jo Freeman has pointed out, the terms *radical* and *reformer* do not do justice to the complexity of the women's movement in terms of ideology, structure, and strategy. And activists of the period have themselves attested to the overlapping and networking that occurred among different elements of the movement.[46]

By 1970, the women's movement had become a national movement that was to have a dynamic impact on the decade of the seventies and on women's lives. Much of the political success it was to experience was the direct result of organizational efforts, mainstream politicking, and institutional reform carried on by reformist women all over the country. But the Women's Liberation Front, emerging out of the New Left, lent a special flavor to those efforts. It introduced new and controversial issues and offered support for a whole range of activities at the national and grass-roots levels. Without this input, the women's movement might have happened, but it would have been a much tamer and less impressive phenomenon.

CHAPTER TWO

Power through Politics:
The Reformist Challenge to Democracy

Long before the Women's Liberation Front became the feminist conscience of the New Left, a few women reformers were beginning to understand oppression in their own terms and to recognize the potential within themselves to bring about change. Whereas the WLF was a reflection of women's disillusionment with the male-dominated New Left, the reform branch of the movement was a product of the liberal optimism of the early sixties that characterized Kennedy's New Frontier and Johnson's Great Society.[1] This optimism also led, inevitably, to disillusionment but never to a desertion of the mainstream political system.

Perhaps the most important landmark on the way to greater political influence and a new feminist consciousness for the reformers was the establishment of the Presidential Commission on the Status of Women, (PCSW) in 1961, which was chaired by Eleanor Roosevelt and dominated by Esther Peterson, assistant secretary of labor and director of the Women's Bureau. The commission was intended to explore and document problems of sex discrimination, but its goal was not equal rights for women but rather the old progressive goal of protection—particularly the protection of working women. It was also intended to fulfill an obligation to women who had worked on the Kennedy Campaign. Peterson's influence on the commission was to steer it away from advocacy of what she called "that awful Equal Rights Amendment situation."[2]

Catherine East, a career civil servant who was transferred from the U.S. Civil Service Commission to the staff of one of the seven committees working on the commission's report, attested to the moderation of the Kennedy administration with respect to women's issues. East found that attending committee meetings was a "liberal education in the pervasiveness of sex discrimination." She felt that the evidence of discrimination was so strong that the recommendations of the PCSW seemed too temperate. Nevertheless, the commission was important in that it changed discussions of women's roles and status "from ridiculous to respectable" and opened the door to stronger recommendations in the next few years.[3]

Perhaps the most far-reaching consequence of the Kennedy Commission was the establishment of various state commissions, which provided a significant number of women with a forum at the state level. By February 1967, an extensive women's network had been built around these commissions, with all fifty states and the District of Columbia involved. The commissions played a major role in promoting reforms through national, state, and local legislation. They also became an important source of leadership to the emerging women's movement.[4]

The state commissions were charged with gathering data on women and documenting their discrimination. Through this process, the members of the commissions and their staffs came to know one another and to share common concerns. Furthermore, the data they gathered provided an example of what feminist Jane O'Reilly would later call the "click" of feminist consciousness. Finally, the process of data gathering drew other groups into the activities of the commissions and created a women's constituency and a climate of expectation that something would be done.

The Kennedy-Johnson years were a time of great confidence in the power of the federal government to identify and resolve problems. Therefore, once the PCSW had issued its report identifying the sex inequities in American society, it was assumed by many women activists that the government would take steps to remove those inequities.[5]

To some extent, that is what happened—at least at the level of enactment. For instance, President Kennedy issued a directive reversing an 1870 federal law that had barred women from high level civil service jobs. Also, after almost twenty years of lobbying, the Equal Pay Act was passed in 1963. A year later the Civil Rights Act of 1964 was passed, including Title VII which forbade discrimination based on sex.[6] But the Equal Employment Opportunity Commission (EEOC) was not interested in the issue of sex discrimination. Its commissioners made open jokes about the topic, and in any case, EEOC had little enforcement power. In June 1966, delegates to the conference of state commissions on the status of women presented a resolution demanding that EEOC enforce the sex clause of Title VII, but conference officials refused to let it come to the floor for a vote. Two dozen angry delegates, including Betty Friedan, Pauli Murray, Mary Eastwood, and Kathryn Clarenbach, decided that the time had come to form a separate organization for women—NOW.[7]

The National Organization for Women established itself as a nongovernmental organization, but many women reformers continued to work within the government and the two-party system during the late sixties and early seventies. They knew the political ins and outs of the Washington scene, but at the same time they were sensitive to the increasing importance of a feminist constituency that lay outside the centers of national power. Two groups that were formed very early during the Kennedy administration came directly out of the recommendations of the PCSW. They were the Interdepartmental Committee of the Status of Women (ICSW) which was made up of secretaries of those departments concerned with women's interests and other government officials, and the Citizens' Advisory Council on the Status of Women (CACSW), which was composed of twenty private citizens appointed by the president. According to Catherine East, the council in particular acted as a liaison between government agencies and women's organizations. Because it was located in the Women's Bureau, it was able to distribute CACSW recommendations and position papers to state commissions, women's organizations, and individuals, thereby strengthening the emerging national network.[8]

The CACSW pinpointed several key issues that were to become major concerns of the women's rights movement. For instance, the council's first project was the preparation of a policy paper on the section of Title VII dealing with sex discrimination. In 1966, when retiring senator Maurine Neuberger became chair, the CACSW set up four task forces to review and update the recommendations of the Kennedy Commission. The Task Force on Family Law and Policy formulated a progressive report, which recommended a fundamental study of family property law and the preparation of a model law to protect the rights of married women in common-law states. Other issues it addressed were alimony, grounds for divorce, child custody, and married women's domiciles. The task force also examined the issues of abortion and birth control, recommending the repeal of laws making abortion a criminal offense and restricting access to birth control devices and information. Finally, the task force declared that illegitimate children should have the same rights as legitimate children.[9] At a time when the personal had not yet become political, even among New Left women, the CACSW Task Force on Family Law and Policy took a surprisingly progressive stance on many issues that were to become the focus of feminist activity in the 1970s. But the constituency that would respond to these issues had not yet emerged.

In the spring of 1969, another Washington group came into being when Arvonne Fraser, wife of Representative Don Fraser from Minnesota and long-time political activist, invited twenty of her women friends to join in a discussion of the new women's movement. The group called itself "the Nameless Sisterhood" to emphasize the women's reluctance to identify with their husbands' careers. It soon became the foundation for Washington chapter of the Women's Equity Action League (WEAL), established by Fraser, Bernice Sandler, and several other Washington activists for the purpose of focusing on women's legislative needs. It acted as a pressure group and also tried to build nationwide support for specific legislation. The WEAL published a report—the *Weal Washington Report*—that listed all bills introduced in Congress dealing with women's issues.[10]

At the national level WEAL had developed out of a disagreement within NOW over its platform. Elizabeth Boyer, an Ohio lawyer and one of the founders of NOW, felt that NOW had become too militant in its stance on a number of issues—especially abortion—and that its leader, Betty Friedan, was too controversial. Also, in the opinion of Boyer, NOW was becoming too diffuse in its goals and organization. So WEAL developed differently, with a more selective membership and a relatively narrow focus on the legal, educational, and administrative inequities facing women. Although the organization's base was located first in Ohio, it soon moved to Washington when Arvonne Fraser became the fourth president. It remained relatively small, but it was an excellent example of knowledgeable women's ability to exert influence and lobby effectively for changes in federal policy. The organization was often successful in affiliating with other women's groups with similar goals, since the differences between them were more often a matter of style than of issues.[11]

One major reform that occurred in the 1960s that was to have an impact on the women's movement of the seventies was political party reform, particularly in the Democratic party. The opportunities for reform were enhanced considerably by the activism of the 1960s; in fact, the sixties was a turning point for the American party system. The previous decade had been one of consensus politics in which Democratic congressional leaders, such as Sam Rayburn, Lyndon B. Johnson, and Hubert Humphrey, worked with a popular president to maintain a moderate political climate which steered a safe, middle-of-the-road position on issues such as civil rights, defense spending, and social programs. The national leadership of both parties saw no urgent need to identify new problems or look for solutions.[12]

But the presidential politics of the 1960 election campaign altered that pattern of consensus. Kennedy's New Frontier, with its challenge to the American people—"Let's get the country moving again"—was a reflection of the optimism of the intellectuals who pervaded Washington and the nation during the early years of the decade. And Kennedy's legislative program defined the major themes of the conflict that was to emerge in the areas of foreign and social policy. The election of 1964, in which the Republican candidate, Barry Goldwater, offered the American people "a choice, not an echo," emphasized the new importance of issue politics. National television brought alive and intensified the debate between Goldwater conservatives and Kennedy-Johnson-type liberals.[13]

Women political activists played a large role in the evolution of the national debate of the sixties, not only in the anti-war and civil rights movements and on the presidential and state commissions, but also in the area of party politics. One of the most important developments of the late sixties was the movement for party reform, particularly within the Democratic party which established the McGovern Commission in response to the bitter division that emerged dramatically in the Chicago convention of 1968. What one scholar has called "the Quiet Revolution"—reform in the manner of choosing delegates for democratic national conventions—became a foot-in-the-door for women and other underrepresented groups, particularly youth and minorities.[14]

By September 1969, the McGovern Commission had adopted a set of guidelines that eliminated unit rules at all levels and recommended that delegates be chosen through some kind of election rather than by caucus. In addition, affirmative action guidelines specified that women, youth, and minorities were to be encouraged to participate "in reasonable relationship to their presence in the population in the state." On 19 February 1971, the Democratic National Committee adopted these guidelines and included them as part of the preliminary call for the 1972 convention.[15]

One of the ironies of the reform movement within the Democratic party is that it occurred at a time when the rest of the country was becoming more conservative and many old-line Democrats were wavering in their loyalty to the party. Herbert S. Parmet, in his study of the Democratic party during these years, points out that in 1968, nearly 68 percent of the American people chose either Nixon or Wallace. Humphrey received only 38 percent of the white vote. This was also the time when, according to Kevin Phillips, a new "emerging majority" could be discerned.[16]

The effect of the party reforms was to further alienate the old Democratic constituency by diminishing the power of special interest groups, especially organized labor, who would no longer be assured of the dominant role within the party councils that it had held since the 1930s. Moreover, old and established leaders—the party regulars—faced the prospect of being challenged by the new breed of reformers who were intent upon opening up the party. The reformers included the antiwar branch of the party, as well as other activist contituencies, such as blacks, Hispanics, and homosexuals. In addition, the "good government" advocates, students, suburbanites, and intellectuals who had always been part of the traditional progressive force in the Democratic party became heavily involved in lobbying for reforms in all fifty states. They created statewide caucuses called the New Democratic Coalitions (NDCs) that were used to elect delegates for the reform candidate Sen. George McGovern.[17]

Political feminism must be understood within this context of reform and reaction, and indeed, the two developments were to shape the history of the women's movement throughout the 1970s. Women rode the crest of the reform wave of the sixties, but they also had to struggle with the reactionary tide that was already emerging. Few of the feminist reformers were conscious of this danger in the early seventies, however. From their point of view, even the liberal politicians were too conservative when it came to women's issues, and women themselves had no real political power. In spite of the activism of New Left women and the establishment of NOW and a women's network, women were badly underrepresented at all levels of the political process. For instance, at the 1968 Democratic convention, only 13 percent of the delegates were women, and at the Republican convention, 17 percent were women. Only 1 of the 108 Democratic delegations was chaired by a woman—Rep. Edith Green who led the Oregon delegation. By 1970, when women constituted over 52 percent of the population, there were only twelve female representatives, one senator, and no governors. Women held less than 3 percent of all the elective offices in the United States.[18]

It is no wonder that reform feminists saw increased political participation as a major objective on their agenda. The most important feminist organization that focused on this goal was the National Women's Political Caucus. The NWPC was established in July 1971, when about three hundred women held a conference in Washington, D.C., in order to develop a political strategy for the rapidly emerging women's movement. Betty Friedan was the originator of the idea of a permanent caucus, and Bella Abzug was a motivating force; obviously it had been in the air for some time. Throughout 1971 there had been discussions among several leading reform feminists, including Friedan, Abzug, Gloria Steinem, and Shirley Chisholm, about the nature of the women's political movement, and on 22 May, Abzug gave an account of a difference of opinion between Friedan and the others. Friedan felt that they should support women for political office no matter what their views, but the others felt that their obligation was to build a political movement of women for social change. A few days later another meeting was held in which other women were included, and Abzug reported a kind of reconciliation between herself and Friedan, although Abzug still felt that Friedan did not really understand politics: "You know, it's nice to say that by 1976 we're gong to have two hundred women in Congress, but do we want the kind of women who are going to vote for missiles and Vietnam wars? Or do we want the kind of women who are going to put our tax money into housing and health and child care centers and abortion clinics and things like that?"[19]

Another meeting was held in June to "hash out the differences," and a wide range of women attended. After a great deal of arguing back and forth, it was finally agreed that a more representative conference had to be held. The conference on 10 July in Washington included women from all over the country, of all ages and all races, and embracing a wide range of political views. To Bella Abzug, it was the women's movement's coming of age—a way of mounting a radical critique against the male-dominated system:

This moment requires women to lead the movement for radical change, first, because we have the potential of becoming the largest individual movement; second, because our major interests are in common with other oppressed groups: and third, because we've never had a chance to make mistakes in government and so we have no mistakes to defend. Men have made the world the way it is.[20]

Thus, the NWPC was established basically to support women's advancement in politics. It was bipartisan and multidimensional, but its main concern was women's rights issues and the support of candidates of either major political party who supported those issues. The caucus pledged itself to oppose racism, sexism, institutional violence and poverty through electing women to public office, reforming the party, and supporting women's issues and feminist candidates across party lines.[21]

The NWPC made an immediate impact on the public and on the media, perhaps because of the celebrity status of several of its founders. But the real significance of the organization was felt in the inner circles of party politics. In mid-October of 1971, the Democratic National Committee held a meeting in which it adopted the entire reform package of the Party Structure and Rules Commission (McGovern Commission), and the only thing that remained problematical was the interpretation of these reforms that were passed so easily. The original intent was that they were to be used as *guidelines*, but owing to pressure from several constituencies within the new politics, in particular, the NWPC, there was a major reinterpretation of the guidelines that specified demographic representation and proportionality. The NWPC was at the heart of an effort to convert the language on demographic balance into explicit numerical targets or, in other words, demographic quotas.[22]

Bryon E. Shafer who has made a thorough and scholarly analysis of the reform process and its impact on party politics, argues that the chain of events that led to reinterpretation began with the founding of the NWPC in July. The caucus consolidated itself with superb timing on 19 September 1971, made its presence felt at the mid-October meeting, and put pressure on National Committee chairman Larry O'Brien at a meeting in November. Rep. Don Fraser, who had succeeded

McGovern as chairman of the Party Structure and Delegate Selection Commission, advanced a prima facie argument, meaning that if a particular state delegation did not meet the demographic guidelines, the burden of proof was upon that state to prove that it had not discriminated in its delegate selection process. Even Doris Meissner, executive director of the NWPC Task Force on Delegate Selection, was startled by this turn of events.[23]

The key figures in this victory, according to Shafer, were Bella Abzug, who had exerted great pressure on the party regulars, and Arvonne Fraser, who was a charter member of NWPC and of its original policy council. She had served as an informal connection among Washington activists concerned with feminist issues since the establishment of the Washington chapter of WEAL, and she used her connections to set up several meetings during the fall and summer on the issue of delegate selection. Another important participant was Phyllis Segal, who had done some early research that led Abzug to focus on the possibilities of delegate politics. She also helped Meissner draw up the resolution that made delegate selection a priority issue for women's caucus, and she served as an important link between the caucus and the Party Structure Commission.[24]

The consequence of party reform on the makeup of the Democratic National Convention was revolutionary, and there was even a fall-out effect on the Republican party. The Democratic convention went from 13 percent women delegates in 1968 to 40 percent in 1972; the Republican convention moved from 17 percent women delegates in 1968 to 30 percent. But, as Shafer points out, the reforms had an equally important impact on the structure of the traditional Democratic party system over the next decade and into the 1980s. The party regulars were essentially superseded by the New Democrats, which allowed for two insurgency candidates to emerge—the liberal George McGovern in 1972 and the conservative Jimmy Carter in 1976. Neither of these two candidates, both of them outsiders, could have won the nomination had the party regulars been in control.[25]

Whatever the longe-range effect on national politics, the combination of party reform and feminist activism vaulted women into a new position of high visibility at the 1972 national convention. How they used this visibility and the power that it supposedly reflected has been analyzed and evaluated by journalists, scholars, politicians, and the women themselves. For women, 1972 was a peak year politically, but it had its share of disappointments along with the successes. Gaining the trappings of power—representation, high visibility, and influence—did not necessarily translate into actual power in terms of policy. The degree to which the convention of 1972 was a triumph for women is subject to interpretation.

The relationship between the McGovern camp and the political feminists at the 1972 convention was, in a sense, the archetypal conflict between politics and idealism. The difference was that McGovern, as the candidate of the new politics, supposedly embraced idealism, and the feminists were, in a sense for the first time, actually playing politics—that is, they were trying to use the political strength they had amassed through the past year of organizing to gain certain objectives, real and symbolic, within the mainstream party system. And although they made a mighty splash, the judgment of the old-time political observers, like Theodore White, was that they hurt McGovern with his broader constituency and, therefore, hurt themselves.[26]

Feminist observers, on the other hand, felt that the women sold out, allowed themselves to be co-opted, or simply appeared to be satisfied with the trappings of representation rather than the reality of power. Just being there was enough.[27] What really happened was ironic: their idealism caused them to stress issues that may have been harmful to McGovern, and yet they did not successfully utilize their full strength to win victories on those issues.

A contributing problem was that the NWPC leaders were still divided among themselves as to their goals and methods. Did they want to advance feminism as a women's issue, which was Friedan's approach; or did they want to relate the women's movement to the broader social issues of the day, which was Bella Abzug's stance?[28] And then there was the highly touted diversity of the movement. In January 1972, a national convention of the NWPC was held in Houston, Texas. "Black women, rich women, poor women, politically sophisticated women and neophytes, radical feminists, and women from almost every state in the union expressed their views; all went home more politically sophisticated than they had come."[29] The diversity of the women's movement was one of its strengths, but it also led inevitably to differences of opinion and approach, as the movement tried to be all things to all women.

For instance, Shirley Chisholm's presidential campaign raised a certain amount of displeasure among NWPC leaders because they did not feel the time was ripe for a woman candidate. Abzug expressed her concerns in August 1971, when she heard that Chisholm had sent her supporters to several states, testing the political waters. Abzug felt that for the NWPC to throw its support behind a woman candidate would simply divert energy from "reasonable goals" that, once attained, would inspire other women to join the movement. Chisholm, for her part, was confused by Abzug's ambivalence about her candidacy.[30]

Chisholm was a messianic campaigner who emphasized her central position as the logical candidate for her times: "I am part of the new politics in this country. I am a peace candidate. I am a woman's candidate. I am a black candidate. I mean, you name it and I am the one person that is in a very unique position today in America.[31] Although she received no direct support from women's political organizations, such as NWPC or NOW, several individuals gave her their personal support. Wilma Scott Heide, president of NOW, endorsed her personally and worked long and hard giving speeches, setting up appearances, and wearing at least fifteen Chisholm buttons wherever she went.

Liz Carpenter, who owed her loyalties to Hubert Humphrey, nonetheless helped in other ways. She used her considerable influence with the press to encourage coverage of the Chisholm campaign, and she called Ben Bradlee, managing editor of the *Washington Post*, to suggest that *Post* editors hold a background session with Chisholm as they had with other candidates. She allowed her name to be used in several Washington-area fund-raising efforts and attended some of the events herself. Jo-Ann Evans Gardner, a Republican member of the NWPC board from Pittsburgh and a long-time activist in the women's movement, joined with Alma Fox, a black woman active in Democratic politics, the NAACP, and other civil rights groups, to organize a Chisholm for President chapter in Pittsburgh.[32]

Chisholm's candidacy never posed a serious threat to McGovern, but it did offer feminists an alternative that might have been pushed to greater advantage. Instead it merely increased their ambivalence. Betty Friedan urged Chisholm to run even before Chisholm had actually announced her candidacy, but she also supported Eugene McCarthy whom she had worked for in 1968. And Gloria Steinem was similarly ambivalent.[33] Steinem, a well-known and highly visible media figure, was also an astute politician who had supported McGovern since the 1960s. But she saw in the Chisholm campaign the opportunity to bring pressure from the left at a time when all the pressure on McGovern was coming from the right. Furthermore, in spite of Steinem's admiration for McGovern, she felt that he still fell short on women's issues.

Went to my district meeting and became a Chisholm delegate after all. I think it was the surprise in McGovern's voice that did it: surprise at the strength of women's issues in New Hampshire, or that one benefit speech in Florida could bring ten thousand dollars in ticket sales into campaign coffers. He still doesn't understand the women's movement.[34]

Essentially, what Steinem was saying was that McGovern devalued women, their political ability and potential power. This was a significant, though intangible factor behind the conflict that occurred at the convention, resulting in the feelings on the part of the McGovern staff that the women were ungrateful and unrealistic, and on the part of the feminists that McGovern sold them out to realpolitik. Yet most women politicos, including Steinem and Friedan, and certainly Abzug, were unwilling to give wholehearted and enthusiastic support to the Chisholm candidacy because they say it was a lost cause, and this time they wanted to win. Minority women, on the other hand, more accustomed to lost causes, were among Chisholm's strongest supporters.[35]

But the NWPC was determined to go with McGovern, and in the end, their unqualified support weakened their cause. A meeting between McGovern and a group of NWPC leaders, held in Washington in June 1972, revealed some of the tensions. Betty Friedan voiced a concern about the underrepresentation of women on the McGovern staff. Actually, there were a number of women in key positions, including Shirley MacLaine and Jean Westwood. But it was pointed out that women were seldom in decision-making positions, and they were not treated with respect by male staff members. Gloria Steinem had observed this problem much earlier when she had campaigned in New Hampshire. The women were workers, not decision makers, at least in the eyes of the arrogant young men running the campaign.[36]

By the time of the Democratic convention in Miami, women were impressed with their own numerical strength, and they were determined to turn it into significant victories. But as one interpretation put it: "For the women a sort of domino theory of betrayal seemed to have been operative, as they watched McGovern renege on a series of promises." For instance, many feminists felt betrayed when McGovern's earlier promise of a cochairperson turned into support for the traditional male chairman–female vice-chairperson. The issue was symbolic, but that made it no less important. And it made the women determined to make their power felt on other issues, symbolic and concrete. In 1968, and every previous election year, women had been barely existent as a political force. In 1972 they were determined to make their presence known.[37]

But for McGovern and his staff, the question was, what could the women do for him? He had made it possible for them to be there in the first place. He had the best record on the peace issue and the best stand on women's issues. Rick Stearns, a top McGovern aide, noted that the McGovern campaign had no intention of collapsing its identity into the women's movement—which he felt the NWPC leaders expected.[38] In fact, what happened was just the opposite. The women ended up being co-opted into the McGovern campaign, even though they lost on every important issue.

The first significant event was the battle over the credentials of the South Carolina delegation, which had only eight women. The McGovern forces, along with the feminists, had the votes to win on this issue, and McGovern had promised his support. But during the actual roll-call vote, McGovern pulled back his forces, fearing that too large a victory would lead to a challenge on the California delegation, and if McGovern lost delegates in California, he might lose the nomination.[39] That was the strategy of McGovern's campaign manager, Gary Hart. Bella Abzug reacted with a violent verbal attack on Shirley MacLaine, who was the liaison with women's groups, accusing the McGovern staff of selling women down the river. MacLaine was in an awkward position. She was not popular with the women leaders because, although she was politically sophisticated, a hard campaign worker, and devoted to McGovern, she was seen as a "movie actress" by the feminists. They would have preferred a serious woman politician, such as Sissy Farenthold. MacLaine later admitted that Abzug's accusation was right: "The McGovern strategists had gotten nervous too soon" and sacrificed idealism on the altar of pragmatism. But her primary goal was to nominate McGovern, no matter what the cost.[40]

The loss on South Carolina made the feminists more determined than ever to have a victory on their most important issue—abortion, which had become the litmus test of feminism in their eyes. It was a test that McGovern was unable to pass. During the June platform hearing, he had met with twenty NWPC leaders to work out a compromise on this issue, but the Democratic party was to find out in 1972 what the rest of the country would find out subsequently. There was no compromise position on abortion. This was the first time that it had really emerged as a full-blown political issue, and although it was certainly seen as a dangerous, or hot issue by most politicians, few were able to perceive how important it would become in the shaping of women's politics during the 1970s and beyond.

Quite apart from the political ramification, McGovern was personally uncomfortable with the morality of abortion. Shirley MacLaine was aware of his discomfort; even if the polls had reported 100 percent of the people favoring abortion on demand, McGovern was not for it. Whenever he talked about it, he always brought up the number of weeks. Therefore, MacLaine felt the need to protect him on that issue: "McGovern would have trapped himself. . . . He trapped himself every time he opened his mouth about abortion. First he would say it was up to a woman and her doctor. Then he would say it was a state's rights problem. . . . These are totally contradictory statements."[41]

At the platform meeting McGovern wanted a statement that made only the most general reference to abortion. The NWPC leaders, however, wanted much stronger language. Steinem offered up what she and other feminists considered a modified resolution: "non-governmental interference in the sexual and reproductive freedom of the American citizen." The wording was temporarily accepted, but MacLaine was troubled by its implications and came to the conclusion that it put McGovern in an impossible position with respect to the whole issue of sexual freedom. She cut the proposal on abortion out of the platform (violating her own personal beliefs, she later claimed) because she saw it as an issue that threatened McGovern's candidacy and introduced abortion into the campaign as a partisan issue that would help elect Nixon and hurt the cause of abortion over the long run.[42]

But for the feminists, abortion represented what Bella Abzug called a "transcending point of view." That is, the freedom of women to control their own fertility was an issue that had to be discussed, regardless of its political volatility. A minority resolution was put into the platform, and on the third day of the convention, it came before the body. The minority plank lost after a passionate floor fight in which MacLaine spoke against it and a right-to-lifer advocate took the podium, bringing feminist anger to a peak. Gloria Steinem, usually cool and collected, the image of elegance, wept in frustration and verbally attacked Gary Hart, McGovern's campaign manager: "You promised us you wouldn't take the low road, you bastards."[43]

The issue divided women against women, and even husbands against wives. The intensity of emotion that was aroused by the abortion issue foresaw the intensity that was to characterize the abortion debate throughout the decade. At this point there was no *strong* right-to-life-movement, no New Right, no Moral Majority. Although politicians were reluctant to take a stand on the issue, the antiabortionists element did not fully mobilize until after the Supreme Court decision, *Roe v. Wade* of 1973, which established women's legal right to an abortion.[44]

Most prochoice feminists felt that they had the public on their side, and indeed the polls seemed to indicate that. Shana Alexander, in a *Newsweek* editorial, argued that MacLaine at the Democratic convention and Jill Ruckelhaus at the Republican convention "each sold her sex down the river in the name of political expediency." The irony, according to Alexander, was that the majority of Americans supported abortion on demand, and a strong abortion plank would have been politically expedient.[45] In fact, what Alexander and other feminists were unable to see at this early date was the beginnings of a cultural reaction. Like many leftist liberals who had put the best interpretation on the social movements of the sixties, they had a somewhat naive faith in liberal institutions and a progressive view of history. They were not yet aware of the backlash vote that was to contribute to a Nixon landslide and McGovern's defeat.[46]

In spite of several defeats on the floor, the women still had numerical strength, and that was expressed most visibly in the Sissy Farenthold bid for the vice presidency, a fairly spontaneous draft that shocked the McGovern forces and held up convention proceedings so that McGovern had to give his acceptance speech at 2:48 A.M. instead of during prime time. Even the feminists were surprised with the size of Farenthold's vote. She received 420 votes, as opposed to 1,741 for McGovern's candidate, Senator Tom Eagleton.

Farenthold had first come to national attention in a Texas gubernatorial primary in which she made an unexpectedly strong showing. She was a liberal state legislator who called herself "Den Mother of the Dirty Thirty," referring to thirty rebellious Texas legislators who had unearthed a major financial scandal involving the Texas speaker of the House, the governor, and the lieutenant governor. Her bid for the vice presidency originated with three students who had worked for her campaign in Texas. At first she took it lightly, but others, including John Kenneth Galbraith, picked up on it. Galbraith soon backed out, not wanting to oppose McGovern on his choice of Eagleton, but by this time Chisholm had decided to withdraw, and the women's caucus was ready to endorse Farenthold. This was one issue on which the women were able to unite much more effectively than they had on abortion. Even Shirley MacLaine was delighted with their strong showing. And the Arkansas delegation, in spite of its anti-ERA stance, cast a large majority of its votes for Farenthold.[47]

Although she made a strong showing, Farenthold was never considered as a replacement for Eagleton by the McGovern staff during those troubled days after the convention. Also, her bid was treated with contempt by the media and political pundits. Walter Cronkite commented disdainfully, "A lady named Farenthold wants to be Vice-President." The CBS network then blacked out Sissy's nominating and seconding speeches with commercials.[48]

The convention of 1972, with the Chisholm and Farenthold candidacies and the high visibility of women delegates, was a remarkable achievement for the political feminists. The Democratic party took a strong stand on the ERA, and Senator McGovern was supportive of social issues important to women, in spite of his problems with abortion. Yet not all observers saw the event as a victory for women. One of the most scathing critics was the British feminist Germaine Greer, who argued that the women's caucus was never really a caucus at all— that the McGovern machine had pulled the rug out from under them: "They were used in Miami as cards in McGovern's hands, to be played or discarded as he wished. . . . they would vote him to the nomination because they had no alternative. . . . Womanlike, they did not want to get tough with their man, so womanlike they got screwed."[49]

Greer was writing in the aftermath of a debate that just a few years earlier could not have been a part of presidential politics. Women's entrance into the mainstream of the Democratic party was nothing short of dramatic. It was not just the size of the delegation, the organizational skills of the NWPC leaders, or the introduction of new issues; it was also the impact that all these factors had upon the party platform. In 1968, the platform had barely mentioned the word *woman*. In 1972 it called for a "priority effort" to ratify the ERA, elimination of discrimination in jobs and public accommodations, extension of the jurisdiction of the Civil Rights Commission to cover women; establishment of educational equality, extension of maternity benefits to all working women, elimination of tax inequities and permitting deduction of housekeeping and child-care costs as business expenses, extension of the Equal Pay Act to cover all workers, and appointment of women to top government positions.[50]

To have a major party make such a dramatic commitment to women's issues—even though its candidate was to lose resoundingly in November—marked a new era in presidential politics. Women had become a new element, and with their entrance into national politics, new issues were introduced that were to remain a factor throughout the seventies.

The NWPC also had an impact upon the Republican convention. Led by Jill Ruckelshaus, the group presented to the convention most of the same items that had been presented to the Democrats including a demand for equal representation of women on all delegations and party committees, a plank on abortion, and a resolution for day-care legislation, which Nixon had vetoed earlier in his term. They also had a petition signed by forty liberal and conservative Republican women for feminist changes in the party. The platform committee adopted the whole NWPC plank, with the exception of abortion, which had caused such turmoil at the Democratic convention.[51]

The most significant change in the Republican party was in the arrangement for the future selection of delegates. Under pressure from the NWPC and other liberals, the convention agreed to amend the party's Rule 32(a) to define broadly the participants in the Republican party as "women, young people, minority and heritage groups, and senior citizens." Rule 32(c) specified equal representation of men and women. But the meaning of these reforms had yet to be determined, and a struggle between liberals and conservatives was already underway as to whether the 1972 changes were rhetorical or substantive.

These were significant procedural changes, but the national press gave little attention to the potential liberalizing impact of the reforms. Also, the NWPC was pressuring for change within the party at the same time that the party was undergoing other kinds of changes that were pulling it in opposite directions. The Republican party had almost completely lost its black constituency during the 1960s and instead was picking up the conservative, lily-white South and the newly emerged "silent majority." Within the next several years an internal party struggle would force the liberal elements out of the party and make it much less appealing to feminists.[52]

But the significance of 1972 was felt throughout the seventies, whether measured as a progressive influence or as an indicator of reaction. Of course, the changes did not happen overnight at the national conventions or in one election campaign. Women's groups had put their issues on the political docket during the 1960s, but it had taken the emergence of the feminist movement—which included both an organizational structure and a mass constituency—to get their agenda implemented and to achieve increased political representation. The key to the emergence of women as a mass constituency has been analyzed in Ethel Klein's study, *Gender Politics*. Klein describes the interplay of several aspects of women's roles that had changed during the twentieth century—labor force participation, fertility, and family life. The interaction among these trends led to the growth of consciousness that supported the emergence of a women's movement.[53]

Most of the women who ran for public office during the 1970s knew campaign politics from the inside and had earned political equity in their communities through years of active service. Whether they started at the bottom or moved directly into races for more powerful positions, women candidates of the seventies were converting years of political activity and voluntary participation in civic affairs into political credibility. But the women's movement publicized the acceptability of running for office. For years organizations like the League of Women Voters, the Federation of Business and Professional Women, and the American Association of University Women had urged women to play a leadership role in public affairs, but it required a new social consciousness to get women to stop "licking and sticking" for the election of men and to start working for their own campaigns and those of other women.[54]

Yvette Oldendorf, a political activist in St. Paul, Minnesota, explained how that had happened in her state. By the late 1960s, women activists in Minnesota were beginning to recognize that they shared a feminist perspective on many issues, but that the male candidates for whom they worked were dividing them. It was the male candidate who provided a vehicle for women to be active because they could not be active on behalf of themselves or other women. Yet this same candidate would often trivialize women's issues. Between 1968 and 1972, women in the Democratic Farmer-Labor party (DFL) of Minnesota launched the DFL Feminist Caucus, which was based upon a set of progressive feminist principles. The most controversial was the fourteenth: the caucus would not support any candidate who by public record of voting or intent would not support the principles of the caucus.[55]

Thus, the NWPC and its success at the 1972 conventions essentially highlighted a national network of women that had been active for several years. The NWPC gave a focus to this network by establishing a national board and a Washington office where women could exchange information and develop political strategies. The NWPC held its first national convention in Houston in January 1973, where it drew fourteen hundred women from almost all states; they were Republicans,

Democrats, Catholic nuns, blacks, Indians, Chicanos, and labor union-
ists. It was a timely show of progressive spirit and militant activism
that attracted a great deal of media attention and presented to the
American public an alternative to the conservative policies of the Nixon
administration.[56]

In many ways, this was the most important role of the political feminists in the early 1970s: they offered an alternative, and they encouraged other women to follow their lead. Two organizations were
established to advance the candidacy of women. The National Wom-
en's Education Fund (NWEF) was the brainchild of Margot Polivy, a
former administrative assistant for Bella Abzug, and Ellen Sudow, who
was working for the House Democratic Study Group and had edited
the *Weal Washington Report*. Their idea was to use tax-deductible money
to prepare women for political participation and to provide information
about women in politics. The NWEF was active throughout the decade,
providing regional training seminars and a national information service.
In addition, the Women's Campaign Fund, an idea spearheaded by
Sandra Kramer, a Washington activist, was designed to raise money for
women candidates, especially at the congressional level.[57]

Finally, between 1972 and 1976, women were increasingly effective
in influencing federal appointments through a subgroup of the NWPC
the Coalition for Women's Appointments. This group was active during the Nixon and Ford administrations, but was even more effective
during the Carter administration, when more women were appointed
than at any previous time. "The crucial elements in all of this feminist
political activity were the intimate friendships and working relationships between Republican and Democratic women, and the understanding that individuals in both parties had a common goal—the
inclusion of women in the political process.[58]

The leadership at the top was reflected at the state level as more and
more women began to challenge male-dominated state legislatures.
Throughout the 1960s, the number of women who served in state legislatures across the country hovered around 300, but that changed dramatically in 1972–73, when the figures went from 344 women
legislators to 441, a 28 percent increase. Three times as many women
ran for state legislatures in 1974 as in 1972, and the total number of
women state legislators rose from 441 in 1973 to 587 in 1974. This was
still less than 10 percent of all state legislative seats, but it was nonetheless an indication of a new willingness on the part of women to
engage in politics in a direct and forceful way.[59]

In these early years of the decade women pursuing political office were more likely to be from the political Left than from the Right. Bella Abzug is the most prominent example. She was far ahead of her party on the peace issue and on women's rights, and even her approach to feminism was based upon a very broad racial and class constituency. Similarly, Shirley Chisholm was outspoken on race and social issues, as well as on the peace issue. Carol Bellamy, who won the city council presidency of New York City in 1977, had worked for one of the largest Wall Street law firms and was a principal organizer of Wall Street Lawyers against the Vietnam War. Patricia Schroeder, a congresswoman from Colorado, ran on a campaign platform stressing social issues and opposition to the Vietnam War.[60]

And yet not all the newly elected women of the seventies belonged to feminist organizations, nor did they necessarily draw on their resources in order to gain public office. Rep. Elizabeth Holtzman of New York found that individual women were the backbone of her campaign, but that the women's movement—in particular, the NWPC and the movement "stars"—gave her no help at all. Certainly the NWPC made a significant contribution in many cases, but they were more likely to concentrate their attention on known candidates, and they did not serve as the main base for most women candidates. By the mid-seventies, when the rate of increase in women legislators was the greatest, these women were more likely to have come out of the LWV than out of NWPC or NOW.[61]

Although the early impact of women's activism was clearly progressive, there was an underlying irony. Feminists, both within the mainstream and beyond, were addressing issues the American public would have preferred to remain private, and these issues were finding their way into the mainstream debate. If there was an awakening feminist consciousness in the 1970s, it was countered by an awakening conservative consciousness, and the feminist reformers were providing the focus for a conservative mobilization. The rest of the decade was to prove that liberal feminists were not the only women willing and able to organize in pursuit of social and political goals. But meanwhile, the liberal reformers who had established NOW found themselves pulled to the left by the newly emerging women's liberation movement.

CHAPTER THREE

Into the Mainstream:
The National Organization for Women
and Its National Constituency

One way of defining the nature of the women's movement of the 1970s is to envision it as an attempt to establish political legitimacy. Barbara J. Nelson, in a *Signs* article on women and citizenship, notes that the ideology of liberal theorists excluded women from the public sphere, particularly with respect to politics. Even after women acquired the vote with the passage of the Nineteenth Amendment, their status as citizens remained tenuous, owing partly to their precarious economic position and partly to a long-held philosophical belief that women lack a sense of public justice because their commitment to their families confines them to the private sphere.[1]

One of the most effective strategies for acquiring legitimacy in a pluralistic society is through organization. The range and diversity of organized groups in the women's movement created a grass-roots constituency focused on a large number of issues, but it also led to considerable confusion and divisiveness over goals and methods of achieving them. No other organization in the women's movement better reflects this diversity than the National Organization for Women (NOW). Criticized by radicals for being too conservative and perceived by most Americans, even reformers, as being too radical, NOW was neither and both during the decade of the seventies. Its conservative reputation was no doubt due to its origins within what Jo Freeman called the "older branch" of the movement, sometimes automatically perceived to be conservative by New Left feminists.[2]

In its early years NOW definitely set itself apart from the Women's Liberation Front, but by the early 1970s, the distinction had become blurred, especially with respect to issues and even with respect to structure and organization, at least at the local level. But NOW was always an organization in the process of becoming. The definition of *what* it was to become constituted a source of conflict within the National Board, as well as between the national organization and its various constituencies—the national task forces, and the state, city, and local chapters. For this very reason, NOW is the organization that best represents the women's movement—its diversity, philosophical differences, and power struggles. Although NOW tried to be too much for too many women—its reach far exceeded its grasp—it articulated and gave form to the dissatisfactions of thousands. Unfortunately, it was also representative of the shortcomings of the movement in its inability to shape a consensus and its failure to map a long-range plan that went beyond the immediate need to end discrimination.

It is difficult to label NOW because the women's movement itself, and the issues that it raised, were outside of the traditional left-to-right political spectrum. For instance, the 1980s debate over the censorship of pornography illustrates the difficulty of labeling feminists as "radicals" or "conservatives." Some feminists favor the sexual libertine position on this issue and see those who are opposed to pornography as aiding and abetting the right-wing conservative reaction. But feminists who oppose pornography have redefined the issue to be a matter of women's oppression and "woman-hating" rather than freedom of the press or personal freedom. Neither of these two groups can be easily placed within the traditional political spectrum.

The "average American" (that is, nonactivist, nonfeminist) believed NOW to be radical for several reasons. First, NOW was militant in its approach to women's issues—much more militant than any women's group since the early twentieth century when Alice Paul led the National Women's party in the fight for women's suffrage.[3] Second, the controversial image evoked by Betty Friedan, the founder and first president of the organization, projected a much more radical position to the media and the general public than was actually the fact. Finally, although NOW's roots and background were middle class, its implications were radical in two ways: first, the issue of sexual equality was radical in and of itself, and second, NOW represented an emerging social movement that had no real legitimacy within the existing system.[4]

The organization originated out of the state commissions on the status of women which created a network of feminists that was to lead the political activism of the seventies. In June 1966, the third national conference of these state commissions met in Washington, D.C., in an atmosphere of intense frustration caused by the Equal Economic Opportunity Commission's (EEOC) lack of interest in women's rights, and its failure to respond to discrimination in help-wanted ads. On the last day of the conference, a group of women met over lunch and established NOW, appointed a temporary chair, Kathryn Clarenbach of Wisconsin, and agreed upon their main purpose, which was hastily written out by Friedan: "to take action to bring women into full participation in the mainstream of American society now, assuming all the privileges and responsibilities thereof in truly equal partnership with men.[5]

In spite of the agreement on a "main purpose," there were, even at this early date, some tensions among the founders of NOW, and much of it centered on Friedan, who was outside of the circle of government activists and state commission people. As Hole and Levine described the situation, "Friedan's avowed feminist position coupled with her flamboyant and combative personal style had made her extremely controversial and, in some corners, greatly feared."[6] Nevertheless, when NOW announced its incorporation on 29 October 1966, Friedan was elected president.

It is ironic that Friedan's image, even among her feminist colleagues, was that of a radical. It is an apt commentary upon the general attitude that prevailed toward outspoken women and toward the whole issue of women's rights. In fact, Friedan's analysis of the women's issue was very much within the mainstream of American political thought, and it was eventually accepted by the very elements who first saw her as radical—the media, the public, and the mainstream feminist reformers. Zillah R. Eisenstein, in her study *The Radical Future of Liberal Feminism*, points out that the ideals that Friedan voiced were the ideals of liberalism—equality of opportunity and individual fulfillment within the existing capitalist system. These were goals that appealed not only to the middle class but to *most* American women, regardless of race or class, because, like most Americans, they had no alternative form of political reference. Friedan herself had no alternative to liberalism because she had no self-conscious theory of women's oppression. She did not admit to a patriarchal system nor did she believe that women were oppressed by men as a sexual class.[7]

The key to Friedan's analysis, according to Eisenstein, lies in the theory of liberal individualism. Women are robbed of their individuality through the "feminine mystique" which encourages them to ignore the question of their own identity by submerging it in their femininity, defined only in relation to others. Friedan does not really explain the social and economic origins of the mystique; she argues instead that once social, legal, and economic barriers are removed, women will move beyond the mystique to find their own identity. Thus, the oppression of women is, to some extent, self-inflicted. "I think all these resistances are not that great. Our own self-denigration of ourselves as women and perhaps our own fears are the main problem."[8]

Friedan envisioned a changing consciousness on the part of women that would enable them to move into the mainstream of the existing society. This was the underlying ideology of NOW—a form of liberal individualism that was embraced by its founding members. If the founders were correct in believing that full sexual equality could be achieved without significantly changing the prevailing social and economic system, then indeed, feminism in the 1970s would have been simply a moderate reform movement, and NOW could have successfully attuned itself to the reform climate of the late sixties and early seventies. To some extent, this is what happened. But there was a strain within NOW that mirrored the more radical elements of the women's movement. Not all feminists, even in NOW, believed that equality could be achieved within the existing patriarchal capitalist society. And some did not want to achieve equality at the cost of accepting that system.

From its early inception, NOW was militant in pushing for an end to sex discrimination. The tactics that it used were modeled along the lines of the civil rights movement, and its main target was the executive branch of the federal government, which was pressured directly by petition, picketing, and letters to President Johnson.[9] Given the political climate of the sixties, with its focus on the federal government, and the liberal reformist faith in a strong presidency, this approach was entirely logical for NOW activists. As Hole and Levine have noted, it was surprisingly successful. The impact was impressive, largely because nothing like it had ever happened before: "NOW scared the wits out of the government," according to one founding member. In an interview shortly after its formation, Friedan declared that NOW would use every political tactic available to it to end sex discrimination: "We don't even exclude the possibility of a mass march on Washington."[10]

Certainly these were words that lent support to the public view of NOW's radicalism. Furthermore, NOW proceeded to take stands on several issues that were considered radical within the context of sexual relations in the 1960s, and yet they were issues that were essential to women's pursuit of individual equality, even within the liberal capitalist system. One was abortion, and the other was the Equal Rights Amendment.

In November 1967, at its second national conference, NOW drew up a Bill of Rights for Women for 1968. It was to be presented to the platform committees of both political parties and to major candidates running for national office. The first right was an Equal Rights Amendment to the Constitution. The last of eight was "the right of women to control their reproductive lives." Both of these principles were included only after long and bitter debate that led to a major splintering of the group.[11]

Some reformers viewed the ERA as a dead issue, and they preferred to work toward the specific legislation that seemed more attainable. Others belonged to organizations that opposed the ERA. For instance, the women from United Auto Workers (UAW) were not personally opposed to the ERA, but their union was still on record in opposition to it. They threatened to leave NOW if the amendment was voted support. When that occurred, the UAW women did not resign, but they did withdraw their clerical services from NOW, which caused a significant inconvenience for the next year.[12]

The principle of reproductive rights was even more controversial than the ERA. Essentially it meant the repeal of all laws restricting women's access to birth control information and devices, as well as the repeal of abortion laws. Opponents argued that abortion was not a women's rights issue and that to take a stand on it would be damaging to NOW's public image, which was already subject to ridicule. But the resolution was passed, making NOW the first women's rights organization to argue for abortion in civil libertarian and feminist terms: women had a *right* to control their own bodies. By taking this stand, NOW incorporated abortion into the newly emerging women's movement, but in doing so it lost the conservative wing of the organization. A year later, in the fall of 1968, those who were opposed to NOW's broader definition of women's rights formed the Women's Equity Action League (WEAL), which was to have a narrower focus on the legal and economic rights of women.[13]

By this time NOW was also beset by opposition from the Left. Given its militant public image, it is ironic that NOW was attacked by leftists for its conservative, middle-class orientation. But this apparent anomaly is understandable, given the political polarization of the late 1960s. The year 1968 saw two political assassinations, mass antiwar demonstrations, the destruction and chaos of the Democratic convention, the backlash of the Wallace campaign, and the spiraling hostility of blacks and youths expressed through militant leftist organizations. It was a time when political labeling was in itself a weapon, used with little regard for truth or accuracy by all segments of the political spectrum. If NOW's actions were perceived as too militant by establishment feminists, it was perhaps because they feared an escalation of militancy similar to that experienced by other reformist groups of the sixties. If radical feminists saw NOW as too conservative, it was because they recognized its basic commitment to the established order, its reluctance to go to the root of women's oppression, which, according to the New Left interpretation, lay within the patriarchal capitalist society.

As a reform organization, NOW applied militant sixties-style tactics to achieve what its *leaders* perceived to be moderate and logical reforms. In fact, these moderate reforms had radical implications if they were actually achieved and implemented, and some NOW activists recognized that. But the radical critics could not see it because they did not believe that women's liberation could occur without a social and economic revolution. They saw reform efforts as ameliorative rather than as a potential first step toward a different social order.

The attitude of the radical feminists toward NOW was one of disdain, even contempt, and there was a tendency to lump the organization rather carelessly with other reformist groups, such as the state commissions, WEAL, NWPC, or even the LWV and the BPW. Although there may have been a certain logic to this categorization at the time of its founding, NOW was definitely on the cutting edge of the women's movement, and by the early seventies, it was becoming radicalized by the Women's Liberation Front at the same time that it was trying to hang on to its more moderate base.[14] As a consequence, from its earliest years, NOW suffered from a split personality in which the liberal goal of bringing women into the mainstream conflicted with the militant rhetoric of the newly emerging radical constituency, which eventually led to open conflict and a major split in the organization.

When Ti-Grace Atkinson left NOW in 1968, Friedan reacted with a warning on the dangers of radicalism, or what she called the "pseudo-radicalism" of "infantile deviants" who advocated the abolition of marriage and family. "We can't have these, our brightest and most spirited young women turning their backs on society, . . . That is an awfully old-fashioned hang-up."[15]

But indeed many radical feminists *did* turn their backs on society, at least as it was traditionally defined to circumscribe women's roles. Atkinson was only one of a large number of activists and intellectuals who took their stance outside of the mainstream and tried to bring about feminist goals in nontraditional ways.[16] These were the women who approached NOW with a certain scorn, an interesting phenomenon because for the most part, the radical feminists were also white, middle class, and either professionals or students. Their differences seemed to be a matter of style, although they also held differing philosophical beliefs.[17]

On the other hand, there were some young activists who did find a place in NOW, and some of them approached its possibilities from a radical perspective. Lois Galgay Reckitt, who became vice president–executive of NOW, was essentially "an activist looking for a cause," when she heard newly elected NOW president Wilma Scott Heide speak at the University of Maine in 1971. The next day Reckitt and ten other women organized the first NOW chapter in that state. To Reckitt, there was no real difference between NOW and women's liberation—at least not in Maine: "NOW was the only game in town. . . . In my head I'm still a radical. I would much prefer to change the way the world operates than integrate women into that system." Reckitt remained active in NOW throughout the seventies, attending the national conference in 1973 and each succeeding year. When she became a national board member in 1976, she brought with her an interpretation of NOW's purpose that put her on the side of the "radicals" on the board.[18]

The terms *radical* and *conservative* do not make much sense in the context of NOW politics. One member reflected on the overlap of membership between NOW and the women's liberation groups of the early 1970s:

You were a radical if you thought philosophy, ideology, and lifestyle were more important, and you became a NOW member if you thought political action and organizing for change was more important . . . but the overlap was *enormous*. An awful lot of NOW members, especially in major cities, have been radicals and still belong to a radical group or collective or something. . . . I don't think there's much of a dichotomy. People tend to see these two groups as very split, but I don't think they are.[19]

An attempt was made by NOW to establish a liaison with the more radical branch of the women's movement in November 1969, when the first Congress to Unite Women was held in New York City. Several others were held elsewhere during the next year, but they were not a success. Having become aware that the movement was much too diverse to be contained under one umbrella organization, some NOW leaders began to accept this diversity as a strength rather than a weakness. On the other hand, Friedan's colorful description of the "sexual shock-tactics and man-hating, down-with-motherhood stance" of the radical feminists revealed the gap between the women's liberation movement and the women's rights movement. But it also revealed Friedan's inability, and presumably that of many of her colleagues, to recognize the potential significance of the issues raised by the radicals.[20]

What was different about NOW in comparison to the small women's liberation groups that sprang up in the late sixties and early seventies was that it very early commanded a national identity and a corresponding hierarchical structure. In addition, although it had definite links with the establishment, it also had the potential for building the kind of mass movement that the radicals could only envision in theory.

The appeal of its liberal, equal-rights approach was first made apparent in a surprisingly successful national demonstration which occurred on 26 August 1970—the Women's Strike for Equality. This was another Friedan brainstorm, which came out of her frustration with the rhetoric and the shock tactics of the radical groups. Friedan believed that the liberal women's movement had a broad potential, but that many women were becoming alienated by the radicals. Also, the issue of lesbianism was beginning to emerge as an indication of what Friedan viewed as a new "sexual ideology" that could only discredit the movement and frighten women away from it.[21]

The issue of credibility was an important one because the media was still treating the women's movement as a joke and the fear of ridicule inhibited many potential feminists from identifying themselves as such. Friedan felt that a major action was needed to reveal the breadth and the strength of the movement so that it would finally be taken seriously by the public, the politicians, and the media. Her colleagues on the NOW national board were not as sanguine, and their reaction to her bold call for a "strike for equality" in her last presidential address at the 1970 conference was met with serious misgivings. In 1970, NOW had about three thousand members scattered throughout thirty cities. To pull off a nationwide strike was a task of considerable magnitude. If the effort failed, it would be an embarrassment to NOW and a setback to the movement.[22]

But the Strike for Equality, held on 26 August to commemorate the fiftieth anniversary of the passage of the Nineteenth Amendment, was the largest demonstration ever held for women's rights. Friedan estimated the crowd at Central Park at about thirty-five thousand, but the action was nationwide, involving women (and men) of all ages, social classes, and occupations. According to one scholar, this event marked the beginnings of the women's movement as a mass movement. Friedan saw it as an opportunity for NOW to take the lead in organizing a permanent ongoing political coalition of women reflecting the diversity that was represented in the strike. The exhilarating effect of 26 August certainly made the public aware of women's potential political power, but it also created a false sense of unity. The women's movement was already deeply divided, and NOW was both a part of and a victim of these divisions.[23]

The presidency of Aileen Hernandez, Friedan's successor, was in part an attempt to address some of the divisions. Hernandez was a minority woman from California, a founder of NOW, and a former EEOC commissioner. An able administrator, Hernandez kept a low profile in comparison to Friedan, but she was almost immediately faced with a critical issue that had been brewing for several years and would continue to affect the internal politics of the movement and of NOW. By 1970 the gay liberation movement had developed, and homosexuality had become a publicly discussed issue. Lesbians within women's rights organizations began to demand open acceptance and public support from these organizations, and a few NOW members spoke out in support of their civil rights. Other members reacted fearfully and took the position that lesbianism was not a women's rights issue. Hernandez issued a statement that was generally supportive, but she tried to play down the significance of the issue, arguing that the media was applying a kind of "sexual McCarthyism" that was diverting the movement from the real issues of sexism. Her position was attacked by both conservatives and lesbians, causing the latter to frame a resolution on the issue for presentation at the fifth national convention in September 1971.[24]

That convention passed a resolution declaring a woman's right to her own sexuality and acknowledging "the oppression of lesbians as a legitimate concern of feminism." The NOW resolution did not indicate that the organization was being taken over by lesbians, nor did it mean that most, or even many, NOW members were lesbians. What it did mean was that the general membership was having its consciousness raised by the more radical feminists, and lesbianism was defined and accepted as both a civil rights and a women's issue. By the 1973 convention, NOW had established a National Task Force on Sexuality and Lesbianism, which was directed toward developing legislation to end discrimination against lesbians.[25]

The convention of September 1971 was important also in that it saw the election of Wilma Scott Heide to the presidency. Heide was to play a significant role during the two and a half years that she served—years that saw NOW's most rapid growth as well as its adaptation to the new feminism. Heide was both an intellectual and an activist who combined feminism and humanism in a way that made a tremendous impact on her colleagues and contemporaries in the movement.[26] The years of her administration were troubled by divisions within the national board and a lack of communication between the national organization and the broadening constituency. Heide was unable to resolve these problems, but she made a heroic effort to address them, and she was a force for unity within a divisive political environment.

Although Heide's presidency was much less flamboyant than Friedan's, she took a strong position on the new feminist issues and therefore led NOW in a more radical direction. For instance, she was much more comfortable with the issue of lesbianism than Friedan had been. Friedan gave lip service to the principle of sexual freedom, but she viewed lesbianism as counterproductive, a form of "pseudoradicalism" that was paralyzing the movement. To some extent, her view of its impact on the movement was correct in that it was a great source of division and conflict. But Friedan's attempt to trivialize its importance and to deny its centrality to feminism made it impossible for her to play a leadership role on an issue that had to be resolved, and this failure made her increasingly irrelevant to many feminists and led to a decline of her influence within NOW.[27]

Another significant source of division that Heide had to deal with during her presidency was the influence of the left-wing feminists who were members of Marxist organizations such as the Socialist Workers Party (SWP) or the Young Socialist Alliance (YSA). For NOW feminism came first, ahead of any political party or ideology, and the NOW lead-

ership was suspicious of any infiltration from the Left that might divert
the organization from its main purpose.

That Heide and other NOW members viewed the leftist presence as
a threat reflects the very real tension between Marxist feminists and
other feminists that was a continuation of the conflict of the late sixties.[28] But the Left was not a major concern for NOW in the early seventies. The problems were primarily internal, and they centered in
particular on tensions between the NOW leadership and the various
parts of the organization that it tried to represent.

Almost as soon as Heide became president, Ann Scott, NOW's legislative vice president, wrote to her about NOW's organizational problems, which she viewed to be at a crisis level. The group had
experienced tremendous growth and would see even more growth in
the next several years. Scott was addressing a chronic problem of the
organization, and that was structure, and communication within that
structure. As legislative vice president, she was particularly concerned
about the national task forces and the role they played in developing
and supporting NOW's legislative program. Her concerns reflected her
dedication to the political objectives of the women's movement. She
was convinced that changes in legislation were essential if feminists
were to attain the cultural changes they advocated. She, along with
Lucy Komisar, another NOW activist, created a national NOW lobbying
network and worked to secure passage of both the 1972 Equal Employment Opportunity Act Amendment and the ERA.[29]

But the biggest problem during the Heide administration was NOW's
enormous and rapid growth, not only in terms of membership but also
in terms of the number of issues it was trying to address. Jo Freeman,
in her analysis of feminism as a social movement, saw the problems as
structural, not ideological. The organization had to combine grass-roots
activity with national coordination; it had to develop a national policy
that did not alienate its diverse membership; and it had to allocate limited resources. As is true of many social movement organizations, the
hierarchical structure necessary to change social institutions conflicted
with the participatory style necessary to maintain membership support
and the democratic nature of the movement's goals. But NOW did not
completely succumb to the process of bureaucratization that usually
occurs when a reform organization accommodates itself to its conservative surroundings and focuses upon maintaining itself. Because of the
ideological pull of the younger branch of the movement, NOW, during

the early seventies, accommodated itself to the new feminist environment rather than to the broader society.[30]

The organization applied pressure in behalf of feminist goals from the top through the offices of Scott and Heide and other board members, along with the work of the national task forces, and from the bottom through the work of the local chapters and their task forces. Whereas Scott was involved in organizing and coordinating legislative and lobbying efforts, Heide used the direct personal appeal to major public officials. For instance, when Senator George McGovern invited Heide to be a member of his Women's Rights Advisory Council, she declined because if she accepted such a position it would be interpreted as a wholehearted endorsement by herself and by NOW. But she took the opportunity to urge him to act as advocate for the ERA, and she also requested a letter of intent from him with respect to his position on women's issues.[31]

In January 1973, Heide wrote to President Richard Nixon, inviting him to NOW's Sixth National Conference, on 17–19 February 1973. The president, said Heide, needed the insights of feminists who spoke for the potential of over half the population. Nixon did not leap at this opportunity, and Secretary of State Henry Kissinger also declined.[32]

In her communication with government officials, Heide stressed the importance of NOW as "the largest unequivocally feminist organization in the world." According to her, it was differentiated from the other more conservative women's groups by its style and philosophy. Heide's conception of NOW was that it was a radical feminist organization attempting to bring about change by applying pressure to patriarchal society. Her goals were radical and her style was militant, but she was committed to working within the system.[33]

Whereas Heide and others were working at the top, NOW activists at the state and local level set their own agendas and were not always able to see the importance of the national board. By late 1973, NOW had over six hundred chapters, most of them in the United States, but a few overseas. There were twenty-seven national task forces, and countless ad hoc and continuing committees and chapter and state task forces touching on almost every area of the human experience. For instance, at the national level, there were task forces on poverty, minority women and women's rights, labor unions and working women, the image of women, textbooks, marriage and divorce, employment, sports, child care, and sexuality and lesbianism, among others too numerous to list.

Basically, any member who had an idea could take the initiative to organize a group around an issue.[34]

Such a diverse and free-wheeling style was attractive to the feminist principles of grass-roots democracy and a nonhierarchical structure, but it often created problems. Communication was one such problem, primarily owing to the rapid organizational growth and the inability of NOW's founders to support the staff and basic secretarial help needed to keep on top of this growth. The problem existed between the national and the locals, but it also existed at the local level.[35]

At the national level, board members tried to keep in touch with memos, telephone contacts, and quarterly board meetings. There were also two newsletters: *NOW Acts* was published approximately every quarter, and it was supplemented by a monthly newsletter, *Do It NOW*. The latter was intended to suggest specific timely actions for NOW members on a local and national level. Newsletters supported by the chapters were also very important in maintaining a local network, since only about one-tenth to one-third of the membership might attend monthly meetings.[36]

A major part of the problem in maintaining communication was financial. The organization suffered from a chronic shortage of funds, its major source of income being membership dues supplemented by a few small contributions and fund-raising efforts. Expenses increased dramatically in the early seventies, going from $26,000 in 1970 to $100,000 in 1972 and about $240,000 in 1973. Local chapters' budgets ranged from a few dollars to $18,000, depending on the size of the chapter and the level of its activism. But the real budgets, at both the local and national levels, were much larger than the stated amount because of the unpaid time and incurred expenses contributed by members.[37]

Since membership dues were the most important source of income to national NOW, the board was understandably jealous of its dues-collecting power, and it resisted any efforts by local or state chapters to change the dues-paying formula. It was stressed that members belonged to national NOW first and foremost, and that the chapters existed at the pleasure of the board to serve as a liaison between the national organization and the individual member. To put the interests of the local chapter ahead of the national would negate the value of belonging to the only national feminist organization in the country.[38]

The local chapters were apt to see it differently. They felt that their money was being misused, that policy at the top was being determined without their input, and that activities at the grass roots were not always given recognition by the national organization. Often these complaints were voiced in terms of the ideals held by the more radical feminists, who resented what they viewed as the "elitism" of the board members and the board's preoccupation with its own activities at the national level.[39]

The organizational problems, along with philosophical and personal differences among board members, contributed to a major crisis in the national organization that lasted for several years. It was exacerbated by a regional split between the Chicago NOW and the Pennsylvania NOW, which reflected changes in the organization. Some members of the board wanted to respond more vigorously to the grass-roots criticisms of elitism by taking NOW in a new direction and, to some extent, changing the philosophy and style of the organization. Most of these people were on the East Coast—in Pennsylvania or New York State.

Wilma Scott Heide had acknowledged the need for a new direction, or at least a revision of NOW's statement of purpose, in her February 1974 presidential report. Although she refused to run for a third term in 1974, because of poor health and general weariness, Heide was sympathetic to the idea of broadening NOW's concerns and deepening its commitment to minorities, lesbians, poor women, and older women.[40]

Three candidates vied for the presidency at the 1974 national conference in Houston, making this the first competitive presidential election in NOW's history. Mary Jean Collins, an early NOW member, president of the Chicago chapter, and a national board member, was representative of the ins. That is, she was part of the slate chosen by the nominating committee. A second candidate, Karen DeCrow, was also an early NOW member. She was eastern regional director and had been membership chairperson for several years. She emerged as leader of the opposition party, or what DeCrow herself has characterized as the "young Turks." The third candidate was Anne Lange, active in the Pittsburgh chapter of NOW.[41]

The DeCrow faction represented the dissatisfactions within NOW that had been simmering under the surface ever since its inception, but were now to break out in the open. DeCrow wanted to move beyond the "well-educated, white, professional woman image of NOW" and reach out to minorities and blue-collar women. She wanted not to "shy away from gay rights." And she very much wanted to make NOW a two-gender organization with a two-gender board. "We weren't going to make changes in the U.S. without involving men."[42]

Chicago NOW, Collins's group, issued a statement that indicated its recognition of the need for change as well, if for no other reason than to meet the opposition. In a paper entitled "Chicago NOW POWER NEW Directions," the chapter acknowledged its own organizational problems and outlined methods for resolving them: an orientation training program for new members; establishment of direct action priorities; and the hiring of a paid staff person to handle administrative responsibilities and thereby free Chicago NOW leaders to lead.[43] The Chicago directive addressed one of the major causes of tension within NOW—the conflict between the hierarchical bureaucracy that had inevitably emerged with the rapid growth of the women's movement and the grass-roots organizational structure that demanded action and results on the issues. It was, as noted earlier, the classic dilemma of a social movement organization. Growth inevitably led to internal conflict.

DeCrow won the highly contested election, 512–448, but her election did not end the conflict. The literature released from the conference was upbeat, calling attention to a "dynamic and far-reaching program" based on the conference theme, "You Can't Stop NOW!" Priorities were established in employment, marriage and family, women's right to choose (abortion), women in sports, and international feminism. But the issues themselves were not really new, and although the new faction tried to characterize itself as the "radicals" and their opponents as "conservatives," neither the programs nor the long-range consequences could be labeled (nor could the Heide administration be considered conservative).[44]

If the DeCrow presidency was intended to close the gap between the board and the membership, or to reverse the process of bureaucratization, these intentions were not realized. DeCrow's style of leadership was very different from that of Heide's. She was a more flamboyant personality—a speaker, a catalyst, rather than administrator—and the activities at the NOW national office were not among her top priorities. DeCrow felt that the job of liaison with the membership was critical and that travel was essential if the national organization was to improve its profile with the chapters and the individual members.[45]

DeCrow's attempt to improve communications between the national and the grass-roots groups led to a breakdown in communications at the top. For whatever reason, she failed to maintain contact with her executive officer, Jane Plitt. During the summer and fall of 1974, relations between the two women became seriously strained, as Plitt tried to connect with the elusive DeCrow.[46] The communication gap be-

tween the president and her executive office intensified and was exacerbated by personal and policy differences. Perhaps the underlying
problem was that Plitt represented the "old order," and DeCrow
throughout her first administration felt frustrated in her attempts to get
her program through what she perceived to be a hostile board.[47]

By November, DeCrow had decided to have Plitt removed from her
position as executive director on the grounds of incompetency and un-
professionalism. The December board meeting, held in New Orleans,
confronted this issue, and the discussion quickly erupted into an open
split. DeCrow and twelve other board members (out of thirty-eight)
walked out and formed the "Majority Caucus," claiming that in spite of
their minority position on the board, they represented the majority
opinion in NOW. Although there were attempts by a group of independents to bring about a reconciliation, by the time of the Philadelphia
conference in the fall of 1975, the organization was still strife-ridden at
the top and suffering a financial and organizational crisis that was intensified by criticism, and near rebellion, from below.[48]

In the months before the Philadelphia conference, a struggle was
waged for the loyalty of the membership. A written forum, *Electric
Circle*, was established by the Majority Caucus, as a means of publicizing its radical feminist vision of revolutionary change. The conference
slogan was "Out of the Mainstream, Into the Revolution."[49]

The NOW platform adopted at the Philadelphia conference was a testimony to "revolutionary" ideals. The conference called for a constitutional convention to rewrite the bylaws in a way that would
democratize the organization. And a direct action—an "Alice Doesn't
. . . Day"—was set for 29 October when a nationwide strike by women
would emphasize the support women give to a system "that continually
ignores, oppresses, rapes, brutalizes, imprisons, confines and restricts
Alice and her potential."[50]

DeCrow was reelected president at the Philadelphia conference, and
she was successful in getting a sympathetic board composed primarily
of Majority Caucus people. But the cost was high in terms of the polarization of the organization through the use of questionable methods.
Furthermore, for the first time, a NOW conference was a media event;
the public was interested, and the election received world press coverage. This was perhaps the peak of the women's movement in terms of
nationwide interest, but it was an unfortunate time for NOW to go public. One participant called it "absolutely a disaster. The whole conference was an embarrassment." Another NOW member declared that the

conference drove hundreds of members out of the organization—primarily because of such campaign tactics as personal attacks and political labeling, or, in other words, "trashing."[51] Wilma Scott Heide, distraught by the acrimony and strife, went home early. Most embarrassing of all, the American Arbitration Association had to conduct the election because no one in NOW trusted anyone else.[52]

Although NOW was not destroyed by the internal battles of 1975, neither was it radicalized, as a Majority Caucus had envisioned. Frances Kolb, activist and NOW historian, looked back from the perspective of 1985: "Was it really more radical? I wonder. A lot of people do. It didn't work out that way. It didn't lead to more radicalism in NOW. . . . the issue was power; who would run the organization. Change was not meaningful at all."[53]

The internal fighting continued for several years, and membership declined dramatically. It was not until January 1977 that NOW was able to pull itself together with the ratification of a national constitution and bylaws. The new bylaws actually made the organization *less* democratic because they concentrated power into fewer hands. But NOW united behind the election of Eleanor Smeal at the national conference held in Detroit in April 1977.

Although NOW eventually recovered from its internal struggles, it had been nearly incapacitated by dissension for three critical years. These were years during which the ERA momentum was reversed. In 1975 through 1976, only one state ratified the proposed amendment. Meanwhile opposition to the women's movement was mobilizing and using the key issues of abortion and the ERA to develop a conservative profamily movement that directly challenged the feminist program. Supposedly at the peak of its power, NOW had fallen into disarray and failed to meet the challenge.

Smeal, the new president, had been one of the leaders of the Majority Caucus and chairperson of the board under DeCrow. She had a similar charismatic style, but her presidency, which lasted for more than five years from April 1977 to October 1982, was very different. Smeal made ratification of the ERA the focus of NOW's activities, and this concentration on one issue had a varied and debatable impact on the organization. First of all, it was an extremely effective organizing device; it gave NOW a focus and a goal. The ERA campaign, and especially the campaign for extension of the ratification deadline, brought in new members and large contributions, and it drew national attention to the women's movement. But it also led to the exodus from NOW of many radicals who found the women's rights focus too narrow. Some of these feminists were suffering from burn-out, weariness and disillusionment with organizational politics, but certainly the single-issue approach to the ERA was not keeping with NOW's past history, from its inception through the DeCrow presidency.[34]

The organization's political position by the late 1970s was as close to being mainstream as it had even been, and this approach was to continue into the early eighties, with the presidency of Judy Goldsmith. The issues, the structure, and the methods were basically reformist. The Left was gone—from NOW and from the whole political scene of the late seventies and early eighties.

In 1979, Kay Whitlock, a former NOW activist, board member, and task force coordinator, wrote a critique of NOW from the leftist perspective. She accused it of reproducing internally "the same form of power relations and hierarchical domination that characterizes a patriarchal society." This was hardly a new complaint, but it was a revealing analysis of the trends of "recent years"—the consolidation of power at the top, the reproduction of an "old boys' political network," institutional racism, oppression and ghettoization of lesbians within the organization, and the commitment to "women's rights" for white, middle-class, heterosexual women, through the singular attention given to the passage of the ERA. Prioritizing the ERA above all other issues meant that NOW had finally achieved organizational unity of purpose, unity of policy, and unity of priority. But from this writer's point of view, there was a price to pay: " 'We are the mainstream' the President of NOW declared, to thunderous applause of NOW delegates attending the 1979 conference. And damn if it didn't feel just that way."[55]

One of the significant issues of the 1979 election was the defeat of Arlie Scott, vice president–action and an avowed lesbian. It was never clear whether Scott was defeated for her sexual preference or her politics, since she opposed the slate of officers chosen by President Eleanor Smeal. But Charlotte Bunch pointed out that in either case, the result was the same—a loss of diversity within NOW that weakened the organization and alienated many women in the movement. "We can only hope that the NOW leadership will evaluate the costs of such expedience and move toward a more inclusive view of feminism in the future."[56]

Minority women were similarly slighted by the 1979 election results. Sharon Parker of Washington, D.C., chair of the NOW Minority Task Force, lost her race for secretary to the white incumbent. Black women politicians and activists in California—members of a newly organized

Black American Political Association of California (BAPAC)—expressed their dismay and endorsed a strong resolution introduced by Aileen Hernandez, former NOW president. The black women were "appalled that the recent conference of NOW, billing itself as the 'largest feminist organization of the world,' failed to direct its attention to the elimination of racism and failed to take even the 'token' step of electing the one minority (black) woman running for national NOW office." The black women rejected membership overtures from NOW and urged other black feminists to do the same.[57]

By the late 1970s, those who considered themselves radical or cultural feminists no longer had the political impact that they had had in the early days of the movement. Partly this was due to the hostile political climate, but also there were fewer radicals, politically and culturally. The seventies' generation of young people was not moved by the rhetoric and the ideals of the late sixties. And the older cultural feminists were dropping out of the political scene—they were living feminism as a life-style outside the mainstream. Thus, there was no politically active radical constituency to push NOW to the left. The consequences of this new political reality were mixed: NOW's reformist mainstream tactics did not bring a victor on the ERA. But the visibility and credibility of the women's movement was, in large part, created by NOW's activism, along with that of other mainstream women's organizations, in particular, the NWPC. It was this kind of activism that made possible for the first time, in 1984, the nomination of a woman to the second highest position on a major party ticket.

But the question of NOW's political and cultural identity remained to be resolved. As a social movement organization, it continues to struggle with the dilemma posed by two contradictory goals—credibility versus revolutionary change—a dilemma that has always characterized social movements in a pluralistic society. And the issue of women's political legitimacy, whether that is perceived as acceptance into the mainstream or as a revolutionary revision of patriarchal values, still remains in doubt.

CHAPTER FOUR

Women-Identified Women: The Theoretical Basis of Radical Feminism

The inability or unwillingness of NOW to escape the mainstream contributed to its relative success, as well as to its internal divisions. But many feminists sought change in ways that went beyond the mainstream, and beyond the hierarchical structure of a national organization. The reformers sometimes argued that the "radical feminists"—that is, those who emphasized life-style rather than politics—were actually more conservative than the political activists who challenged the system on its own terms. The radical feminists tended to eschew power, remove themselves from the "real world," and expend a great deal of energy in consciousness-raising. "*Nothing* could be more conservative than consciousness-raising," declared one prominent NOW activist.[1]

The mainstream activists saw the radical feminists as dropouts, in part because their own interpretation of political reality was based upon a traditional male view of a hierarchical society with power concentrated at the top. Radical feminists defined gender as the root cause of all oppression. They envisioned a gender-free society in which women were *empowered* horizontally rather than hierarchically.[2] And their empowerment of women, albeit on a smaller scale, *did* have a radicalizing effect on the women's movement, as well as upon individual women.

Underlying the values, life-style, and activism of the radical feminists was a theoretical framework that evolved out of a debate carried on by intellectual feminists in academia, in literary and religious circles, in the counterculture and separatist communities, and through the journals and periodicals that bloomed in the early years of the decade. The feminist engaging in a social critique that operated at an intellectual level was able to go much further than the political activist in thinking the unthinkable and asking what Carol Christ called "non-questions"—that is, questions that probe such deeply felt convictions it is difficult for others to even hear the questions.[3] This kind of social critique was necessary to the process of societal consciousness-raising. Consequently, the radical feminists raised issues that most liberal reformers resisted at the same time they were attempting to formulate a conceptual framework for a nonhierarchical, nonpatriarchal society.

Finally, the radical feminists were much more than mere visionaries.[4] Many of them were true activists on a small scale, creating communities committed to an alternative life-style and establishing women's centers that focused on a whole range of issues affecting women's lives at a direct and personal level. The seventies saw a proliferation of rape crisis centers, health collectives, battered women's centers, child-care centers, food cooperatives, alternative education programs, women's studies programs, and feminist journals and newsletters. Although this mode of activism did not result in a direct frontal attack on the system, it contributed to the new consciousness of alternatives that was so much a part of the early seventies. The basic premise of this consciousness, in feminist terms, was a woman-centered alternative. For the radical feminists, women's experience is the central human reality with respect to their intellectual work, their political activism, and their personal life-styles. Women became the focus of goals and the measure of achievement. The male-dominated society became, in a sense, irrelevant.[5]

This women-centered consciousness emerged out of the reforms of the sixties, and it was a strong presence within the movement by the early seventies. But it did not occur overnight: radical feminists usually went through several stages—from a reformist position to a more radical critique of society and then, for some at least, to a separatist position. Religion offers one example of this kind of metamorphosis, as women theologians moved from a reformist critique within the traditional church to female spirituality. The debate over religion and sexism was a product of the intellectual controversy that shook the

Catholic church in the mid-1960s and that in its first stages had little to do with feminism and much more to do with the reform climate that was characteristic of the early sixties.

The major turning point for the Catholic church was the Second Vatican Council, 1962–65, during which nearly every aspect of Catholic doctrine was questioned.[6] An intense discussion in the Catholic press about the status of women raised the consciousness of several women theologians who were to contribute to a new feminist theology during the 1970s.

These religious feminists varied widely in their critique of traditional religion, but they held certain basic beliefs in common. First of all, they agreed that religion is deeply meaningful in that it involves the constant search for meaning and direction in human life. Second, they all thought that the Judeo-Christian tradition had betrayed women through its sexist theories, practices, language, and symbols. Finally, they said, religion must be reformed or reconstructed if women are to attain their full human dignity.[7]

But beyond these three basic premises, the feminists differed widely on their approach to the issue of reform versus revolution. The reformists spoke for women in the church by attempting to reinterpret and transform tradition from within, whereas the revolutionary thinkers were not interested in reconstructing tradition. For them, the essential theological task was to explore the dimensions of women's experience free from the constraints of the past. The women's movement had convinced them of the value of women's experience as a potential starting point for theological reflection.[8]

The first open challenge to traditional religion by a woman came in 1960, when Valerie Saiving began an essay with the statement: "I am a student of theology; I am also a woman." Saiving's essay established the basic premise of feminist theological scholarship—that the vision of the theologian is affected by his or her experiences as a man or a woman; that gender does, indeed, make a difference.[9] Her essay preceded the women's movement by almost a decade but it established a point of takeoff for a more radical and thoroughgoing critique of traditional religion in subsequent years. Two women who led the attack were Rosemary Radford Ruether and Mary Daly, who represented the two strains in feminist theology—reformist and revolutionary.

In 1971, women scholars organized the Women's Caucus within the American Academy of Religion. Ruether and Daly presented papers that were ground-breaking attempts to challenge traditional religion and its subordination of women. Within the next few years, several anthologies were published, raising issues of women's ordination, the need to transcend Scriptural traditions about women, and the inadequacy of male-created theological terms and symbols.[10]

Much of this work was reformist, in spite of its radical implications. Rosemary Ruether, for instance, was a long-time activist in the antiwar, feminist, and civil rights movements. Her theology challenged the church by describing the nature of sexism, which she felt was deeply rooted in Christianity. But Ruether also believed that the Christian tradition had a liberating core that could be used to transcend oppression. And she was not a separatist. She argued that women had to look beyond their own liberation from oppression to that of the oppressor as well.[11]

Other reformers within graduate schools and seminaries focused their efforts on the struggle to win ordination for women. This was in large part a civil rights issue, which involved trying to establish equal job opportunities for women within the church. But the issue was complicated by religious orthodoxy and deeply felt emotions, especially in the religious groups that refused to ordain women—the Episcopal and Roman Catholic churches, and the Conservative and Orthodox branches of Judaism.[12]

Carter Heyward, an Episcopal priest, recounts in her autobiography, *A Priest Forever*, her determination to challenge sexism in the church but at the same time to cling to her faith that a reformed church *did* have room for women and that, indeed, it *needed* women's energy in a new way. "I see women as the single most creative force within the Christian Church," she wrote. "We, as a group, are those challenged most immediately with the task of *renewal*—of making new what is old—within and beyond ourselves in the Church and elsewhere.[13]

Heyward also attached deep personal meaning to the struggle for her ordination. It was important to her that she, as a woman, should have had since birth the right to be eligible for ordination and the right to choose and shape her own life and to take responsibility for it. This was the essence of the personal struggle out of which would come a new order to the church. The present order would change because women were agents of transformation, not because they had powers inherent to their gender, but because they were symbols of *difference*—they offered a different ethic derived from a collective exclusion.[14]

On 29 July 1974, the feast day of Mary and Martha, eleven women were ordained priests of the Episcopal church. Carter Heyward and her colleagues saw women's potential contribution to religion as radicalizing, but basically, reformist. Most feminists within the church took this reformist approach which was, in a sense, a focus on civil rights, but with far broader implications.

On 20 August 1970, the Joint Committee of Organizations Concerned with the Status of Women in the Roman Catholic Church presented a statement to the National Conference of Bishops. The Joint Committee accused the church of discriminating against women, thereby denying them the fulfillment of their personhood and betraying its own mission. It proposed a nine-point program of corrective action, including opening enrollment at Catholic seminaries and universities to women and the ordination of women to the priesthood. One of the more interesting proposals was that women's studies courses be included in the curriculum of all seminaries, "in order to ensure that future priests will have a correct understanding of women."[15]

Religious feminists, whether reformist or revolutionary, placed women at the center of their analysis. Where they differed was in the extent to which they believed that traditional religion could change to meet the demands of the new women-centered consciousness. Mary Daly, radical Catholic theologian, is perhaps the most striking example of the revolutionary approach. She began her pilgrimage to a women-centered theology confident that a re-reading of the Scripture and reform of the church was possible, but she ended by creating a whole new theology—metaphysical feminism. Daly's first book, *The Church and the Second Sex*, was published in 1968, before the women's liberation movement had emerged. According to Daly's own account, the book would never have been written at all had it not been for the Second Vatican Council—"the time/place where the Catholic Church came bursting into open confrontation with the twentieth century." Daly described "an ebullient sense of hope" as theologians, students, journalists, and lobbyists came together and found that their secret thoughts about the church were shared by others. Their hope was based upon the belief that the church could and would reform itself.[16]

Daly finished her book while she was teaching at the Jesuit-run Boston College. In the spring of 1969, she was given a terminal contract with the college, which set off a major cause célèbre. This was a year of nationwide student unrest, and Daly became a symbol of academic freedom at Boston College. Hundreds of students demonstrated, signed a petition, and held a teach-in. Self-declared local witches came and hexed Boston College, the president's house was picketed, and the

administration building was decorated with brilliant red graffiti. The
campus became a focus of the media, and the case received wide publicity.[17] Daly eventually received tenure and a promotion, but she had
lost respect for the "academic freedom" of herself and her colleagues.

Daly moved quickly beyond her own reformist critique to a more
radical interpretation. By the early seventies she had been stirred by
the emerging women's movement to new dreams of a women's revolution. In March 1971, she published an article in *Commonweal*, "After
the Death of God the Father: Women's Liberation and the Transformation of Christian Consciousness." This essay represented a stage in
her personal journey away from the church, and it also contained a
crucial breakthrough for feminist theology. First of all, the community
out of which Daly spoke was no longer the church but the women's
movement. Daly argued that women in the movement were in a unique
position to examine and challenge the oppressive tendencies of traditional religion. Second, she argued that the core symbolism of Christianity had been warped by a male perspective. The maleness of God
and Christ provided images of the rightness of male rule, and reinforced
and legitimated the powers of males in society. Either the symbolism
had to be transformed entirely, or it had to be abandoned.[18]

Daly's most important breakthrough was contained in her second
book, *Beyond God the Father* (1973). Here she took the final step outside
of Christianity by refusing to accept the male God of Christian tradition or the possibility of a male messiah. Instead, she identified the rise
of a new religious tradition within a community of women. Daly
grounded her new theology solidly within the women's movement and
within their experience, arguing that the new wave of feminism had to
be ultimately religious in its vision in order to reach outward and in-
ward, beyond the gods that had stolen women's identity.[19] This, in
turn, would have a revolutionary impact on society. She wrote: "Beliefs
and values that have held sway for thousands of years will be questioned as never before. This revolution may well be also the greatest
single hope for survival of spiritual consciousness on this planet.[20]

Daly's "Post-Christian Introduction" to *The Church and the Second Sex*,
which was reissued in 1975, was a scathing attack on her own earlier
reformist approach and underlined her commitment to a radical, separatist solution. The species "Catholic Feminist" was virtually extinct,
as far as she was concerned. In 1975, to speak of a partnership with
men implied an "unspeakable poverty of imagination." Women and men

were not coming from the same place, and it was impossible to engage in dialogue on equal terms with the oppressor.[21]

By 1979, with the publication of *Gyn/Ecology*, Daly had carried her separatism to its logical extreme. She proclaimed that patriarchy itself was the prevailing religion of the entire planet, and that women had to undertake the perilous journey of "self-becoming." She documented the history of men's atrocities to women and invited every woman to "leave behind the deadly patriarchal universe to create her own self within a community of similarly searching selves." As one reviewer noted, Daly's analysis of the connection between phallocratic society and religion posed a systematic challenge not only to the church itself but to the women who were attempting a reformation of traditional religions.[22]

Daly ran counter to the reformist scholars, such as Ruether, Letty M. Russell, and Elisabeth Fiorenze, who were attempting to liberate tradition from its patriarchal bias without carrying their critique to the separatist extreme. But she *did* represent the rise of feminist spirituality within the women's movement. The literature of women and spirituality that came out of this period is immense in range and diversity. By the late seventies nearly every major feminist magazine had featured an issue on women's spirituality, and two feminist journals specifically concerned with spirituality and its implications for feminist politics had emerged: *Woman Spirit* and *Lady-Unique-Inclination-of-the-Night*.[23]

Women's spirituality, as a theological phenomenon, rose in response to the recognition that feminism was a new worldview that could be applied to religion as well as other aspects of the human experience. Feminist spirituality was women-centered, but its reach was broad and inclusive, in contrast to the narrow and exclusive tenets of patriarchal religion. For some feminists it has involved the search for the Goddess, for others, a search for meaning in other kinds of women's rituals— witchcraft, sisterhood, healing, expanding personal power through meditation, futurism, and images of women's spirituality in literature or other aspects of culture.[24]

Amanda Porterfield has noted that "spirituality refers to personal attitudes toward life. . . . But spirituality covers a larger domain than that staked out by religion because it does not require belief in God or commitment to institutional forms of worship." Another scholar, Eleanor Humes Haney, sees the framework of feminist spirituality in terms of community: "The vision is one of community, indeed of a new heaven and earth. It is a vision of women in all areas of life. . . . Feminist vision, and thus feminism, is a values—a moral—revolution."[25]

Women's spirituality, then, like feminism itself, had both personal and political implications. Sometimes there was a tension between the two, and this was reflected in the dialogue between scholars. Those who wanted to reform patriarchal religion tended to see feminist spirituality as a kind of apolitical copout. Ruether wrote an essay, published in the *Christian Century*, 10–17 September 1980, that argued that feminists who were involved in postpatriarchal spirituality were countercultural and peripheral. Responses from theologians Carol Christ, Z. Budapest, Naomi Goldenberg, and others appeared in various publications, reflecting the tension between a women-centered reformist approach and a more radical women-centered separatist approach that existed within cultural feminist thought of the 1970s. What these feminists shared was a sensitive consciousness of themselves as women, *different* from men in terms of their values and experiences, which therefore made them perhaps "superior"—or at least possessed of the potential to create a superior culture and life-style based on women-centered values. For some this could be done within existing institutions, but for others it meant creating new institutions.[26]

This women-centered consciousness was also characteristic of the radical feminists who came out of the New Left of the 1960s, roughly during the same years that Mary Daly and other radical theologians were moving from reform to separatism. New Left women became increasingly conscious of themselves as women, with a different identity from men, because of the emphasis on sexuality in the political New Left and the counterculture movement of the sixties. Although women have been traditionally defined in terms of their sexuality, it was not until the women's liberation movement that sex was analyzed politically and openly as an aspect of the power relations between men and women. Earlier analyses of sexism included the sexual dimension, but it was the open climate of the sixties that provided an audience able to accept sexuality as a political issue.[27]

The connection between sexuality and politics was first made in the consciousness-raising groups of the late sixties. These groups met regularly to discuss the effects of male supremacy upon women's public and private lives, and they resulted in a great outpouring of emotion against the way women were used sexually. The women who expressed these feelings did not feel liberated by the sexual revolution; they felt victimized by it. They were expected not only to perform the usual women's work—typing, mailing, coffee making, and the like (usually referred to as "shitwork")—but also to sleep with the radical men they worked for without making any demands in return. "Their own feelings, their needs for affection, recognition, consideration, or commitment did not count.[28]

Conscious-raising groups emphasized the interconnectedness of feelings, events, and disparate lives in a way that led radical feminists to take direct actions, such as picketing the Miss America contest in September 1968, an obvious political reaction to women's sexual status. For the women's movement as a whole, the link between politics and sexuality opened up a whole range of issues that the more moderate reform feminists did not immediately address because the issues were the "non-questions" of the secular world. Anne Koedt's essay "The Myth of Vaginal Orgasm,"published in 1968, argued that women did not need men to experience sexual pleasure: heterosexuality was only one option, not a necessity.[29] Ti-Grace Atkinson developed the analysis further, noting that orgasm is not necessarily the most important component of a sexual experience, and Dana Densmore urged women to consider the possibility of celibacy, since it was sexual love that kept women enthralled and justified their exploitation.[30]

Not all radical feminists were willing to give up heterosexual relations, of course, but the logic of this position for those who had arrived at a radical understanding of women's oppression within a patriarchal society created a great deal of tension within the movement, and within the lives of individual women.

Robin Morgan, a writer, poet, New Left activist, and feminist theorist, exemplifies the kind of personal struggle that some women undertook in their effort to resolve the tensions between radical feminism and heterosexuality. In *Going Too Far,* Morgan recounts the early years of her marriage, which she recorded through a series of letters to herself, her husband, and her child. The letters express the ambivalence and the love, the tensions and the emotional dependency that is typically part of a heterosexual relationship, particularly marriage. The early letters of the mid-sixties were written out of a prefeminist consciousness, in which Morgan sought solutions to problems that she thought were uniquely her own.[31]

A few years later, Susan Braudy, a writer for *Newsweek,* the *New York Times,* the *Village Voice,* and eventually, *Ms.,* struggled with the consequences of a failed marriage. By this time (the early seventies), she was operating within the context of the new women's movement, to which she was able to relate her feelings and experiences as she moved out of a six-year marriage and into the complexity, excitement, and loneliness of self-reliance. "But I am not alone." she wrote. "Today, in a self-conscious explosion of intimate talking and writing, many young women are re-educating themselves with new negative formulas about their relationships with men. . . . Many have decided . . . to be lonely, self-reliant adults rather than protected child-wives."[32]

Some chose loneliness, but others sought community with women. One of the most important developments of radical feminism was a women-centered life-style that combined social and political values with an intense emotional and sexual commitment to other women. The result was a redefinition of lesbianism in the broadest possible and most positive sense of the word. The feminists of the 1970s reclaimed the historical tradition of female same-sex love, which had held an accepted place in nineteenth-century America, by redefining it in new terms that were liberating rather than constraining. Before the 1970s, such a redefinition would have been impossible because the climate of opinion, controlled by medical experts, literary venerables, and the mass media, had created an image of love between women as sick, perverted, and even evil. But the sexual revolution that accompanied the rise of feminism permitted widespread experimentation, so that the notion of lovemaking between women no longer created automatic horror and aversion, especially for women who were beginning to seriously explore alternatives to male exploitation.[33]

Lesbianism as a feminist issue was a striking illustration of the connection between the political and the personal. It involved a highly personal sense of self, yet it became a political force within the women's movement, even as it provided a personal alternative for women whose feminism had made the imbalance of a heterosexual relationship unattractive, if not impossible. For women who were already lesbians, opening up the issue to public discussion, at least within the movement, meant a tremendous liberation of old restraints and the hope for moving beyond guilt and self-hatred that was so much a part of the image of the old-style lesbian.

Beginning in 1969, a series of events occurred that crystallized the importance of lesbianism within the movement. Originally resisting identifying itself with lesbianism, NOW had heeded Betty Friedan's early warning of the dangers of the "lavender herring."[34] But from the beginning, lesbians were able to become members of NOW. They were permitted to work behind the scenes and even occasionally occupy top offices if they could pass for straight and if they kept silent about their life-style. But that was a big "if." As NOW became increasingly open to consciousness-raising and the connection between the personal and the political, active gay women found it difficult to conceal their sexual preferences.[35]

The issue was forced into the open within NOW by Rita Mae Brown, who had joined New York NOW in mid-1969 and immediately announced that she was a lesbian. An able and outspoken activist, as well as a talented writer, Brown soon became newsletter editor and a member of the board of the New York chapter, where she both influenced and antagonized other members of NOW. Pressures to downplay the issue of lesbianism brought about Brown's resignation in January 1970. She became a founding member of Radicalesbians, a collective that drew its membership from the women's movement and the Gay Liberation Front (GLF).

The collective circulated a position paper among straight feminists, explaining the relationship of lesbians to the movement. The paper, "The Woman-Identified Woman," clarified the political meaning of lesbianism and its role in the movement and explained why gay women belonged in the women's movement *first*, rather than in GLF.[36] The essay also expressed in stark terms the rage of lesbians and, by extension, that of all women: "What is a lesbian? A lesbian is the rage of all women condensed to the point of explosion." The rage, or at least its honest expression, was positive in that it meant that energies flowed toward other women, rather than toward the oppressor. It declared that "It is the primacy of women relating to women, of women creating a new consciousness of and with each other, which is at the heart of women's liberation, and the basis for the cultural revolution. Together we must find, reinforce, and validate our authentic selves."[37]

A woman-identified life-style gave women the strength, collectively and individually, to find alternatives to what they perceived to be an oppressive patriarchy. But it also led to a period of intense internal conflict within the movement. Historically "lesbian-baiting" had been the most effective way of keeping "uppity" women in their place, and the threat of being labeled a lesbian was a powerful control over even the most dedicated feminist. Martha Shelly noted that when members of women's liberation picketed the 1968 Miss America pageant, they were able to stand up to the hostile taunts that they were "commies" and "tramps," but some of them broke into tears when they were called lesbians.

The lesbian constituency wanted to address this issue, and to move all women, both gay and straight, beyond the irrational fears created by a homophobic society. And gradually, many feminists, whatever their sexual persuasion, began to see the necessity of dealing with the issue in order to prevent sabotage of the movement from outside. This was the basic theme of the "Woman-Identified Woman" essay: "As long as the label 'dyke' can be used to frighten a woman into a less militant stand, keep her separate from her sisters, . . . then to that extent she is controlled by the male culture. . . . As long as male acceptability is primary . . . the term lesbian will be used effectively against women."[38]

In their efforts to overcome the undermining effects of lesbian-baiting, some lesbian feminists began to play a more open and confrontational role within the movement. In May 1970 at the second annual Congress to Unite Women, they carried out a "zap action" intended to raise consciousness and bring home the reality of their presence within the movement. In an auditorium filled with three to four hundred women, the lights suddenly went out. When they came on again, the wall blossomed with posters: TAKE A LESBIAN TO LUNCH. SUPER-DYKE LOVES YOU. THE WOMEN'S MOVEMENT IS A LESBIAN PLOT. Twenty women in lavender T-shirts emblazoned with the message "Lavender Menace" were standing at the front of the auditorium and began a dialogue with the audience. Other women contributed to the discussion, some of them coming out about their sexual preference for the first time. One of these women was Kate Millett, a professor at Columbia University, founding member of Columbia Women's Liberation, and chairman of the Education Committee of New York NOW.[39]

Millett was a relative unknown in May 1970, but by the end of the year she was a literary celebrity, anointed by the media as the foremost theorist of the new women's movement. Millett's brilliant critique of patriarchal literature, *Sexual Politics*, was widely read and reviewed and was probably the first feminist study to have a major impact on mainstream culture and social criticism. But Millett's downfall came almost immediately after her rise to glory. In November of that same year she appeared at a forum on sexual liberation, sponsored by Gay People at Columbia University and attended by many gay activists as well as Columbia students and professors. Millett was challenged by a radical feminist to state openly her sexual preference, and a *Time* reporter picked up her response on a tape recorder. *Time* magazine ran a story in December that was in effect an attack on Millett and, through her, an attempt to discredit the women's movement through the familiar tactic of lesbian-baiting.[40]

From Revolution to Liberation: Anti-Nuclear Demonstration, New York City.

The Reformist Challenge to Democracy: Shirley Chisholm, Democratic National Convention in Miami.

The National Organization for Women and Its National Constituency: NOW conference, Philadelphia.

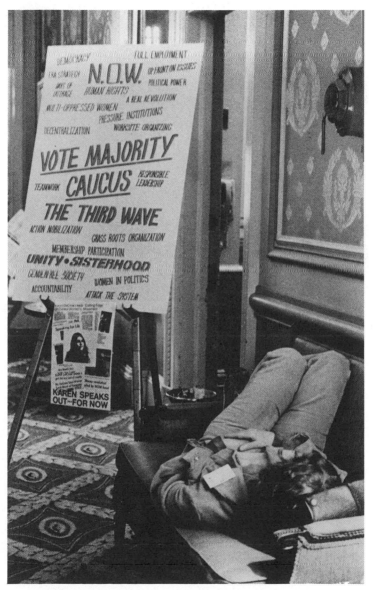

NOW conference, Philadelphia.

The Theoretical Basis of Radical Feminism: Artist Janie Washburn.

The Millett incident, along with the growing tension between straights and gays within the movement, finally forced feminists to deal openly with the issue of lesbianism. A press conference was held on 17 December in which a large number of theorists, writers, and activists showed their support for Millett. Participants included Ti-Grace Atkinson, Gloria Steinem, Flo Kennedy, Sally Kempton, Myra Lamb, Susan Brownmiller, Caroline Bird, NOW President Aileen Hernandez, and chair of the board Wilma Scott Heide. Media coverage was very good and quite fair. According to at least two lesbian feminists, the event virtually ended media lesbian-baiting.[41]

But it did not resolve the tensions within the movement. The ideological rationale for a lesbian life-style seemed the logical extension of a women-centered identity, and for that reason, some lesbian feminists began to perceive their position as politically more correct than one that allowed for heterosexuality. The internal politics of the movement were colored by the intense ideological significance that was placed on this issue. Although there were those that tried to play down its importance, arguing that it did not speak to the concerns of the majority of women, or even the majority of feminists, it became crucial to a redefinition of women's autonomy and to the independence of the movement from other social movements: "On a gut level, the women's movement has to be about sexuality. Otherwise, it's just another civil-rights movement and that's not dealing with the problem women have to face. If sexuality is at the base, then Lesbianism is totally relevant."[42]

To become a lesbian was, for most feminists, much more than a sexual preference. It was a personal and political choice in which the individual announced to herself and to her peers in the movement the degree and the intensity of her commitment to other women. Lesbianism was supposedly synonymous with love for other women, but ironically the issue stirred up hatred and bitterness within the movement, partly because it was perceived as a threat by straight feminists and partly because of the ideologically purist stance of many lesbian feminists. Sidney Abbott gives a description of NOW's struggle with the issue, but she ends on an upbeat note: "It was finally decided then not to let the Lesbian issue split N.O.W. down the middle, which in a larger sense was a victory of all Feminists, and not just for Lesbians." But the history of NOW for the rest of the decade indicates that lesbianism continued to be a divisive issue.[43]

The group's official policy position on lesbianism was good, but lesbian activists still felt that it was not receptive to their presence in top leadership position. At the twelfth annual NOW convention, a slate was

elected that consisted of five white straight women in an apparent shift
in the name of political efficiency. The 1979 election was a reflection
of NOW's attempt to move into the mainstream and, in particular, to
gain broad support for the passage of the ERA—a reform that was perceived by many radical feminists, as well as minorities, to be a white
middle-class objective. Whether or not the organization was sympathetic to lesbians, it appears that the reformist leaders were not placing
a high priority upon either lesbian rights or minority issues.[44]

If lesbians had difficulty attaining full recognition within the reformist movement, they were apt to turn the tables on heterosexual feminists in the more radical women's liberation groups. Robin Morgan
attested to the depth of feeling that created division within the movement when she delivered a keynote speech at the West Coast Lesbian
Feminist Conference in Los Angeles, August 1973. In a nervous, but
inspired, effort to pull the issue out of the closet, she pointed to the
incongruities on both sides: "A funny thing happened to me on the way
to the Feminist Revolution: both Betty Friedan and Rita Mae Brown
condemned me for being a 'man-hater.' Both *Ms.* magazine and *The
Furies* began to call for political alliances with men, *The Furies* at one
point implying that lesbians should band together with gay *and* straight
men (preferably working-class) in a coalition against the enemy:
women."[45]

The point that Morgan made was that women were allowing themselves to become divided again, fighting with each other rather than
with the men. The act of turning on each other—"trashing"—had become a serious problem by the early seventies, and it continued to be
so throughout the decade.[46]

The tendency toward trashing was more prevalent among radical
feminists who stressed personal change than among reform feminists
who stressed institutional change. The movement's emphasis on "the
personal is political" made it easier for trashing to flourish because it
seemed to be saying that personal behavior or life-style was a reflection
of political belief and commitment. "This legitimated for many the idea
that the Movement could tell us what kind of people we ought to be,
and by extension what kind of personalities we ought to have."[47]

There is no doubt that the women-centered consciousness that characterized radical feminism created some political problems for the
movement and led to unfortunate personal experiences for individual
women. Yet its positive aspects balanced, and perhaps outweighed, the
negative. The achievements of radical feminism were manifold: there

is no doubt that the attempts at sisterly bonding often succeeded, if not in bringing about the millennium, at least in greatly enriching many women's lives. Moreover, the lesbian alternative was a necessary and valuable step in the direction of sexual liberation for all women, both heterosexual and lesbian. It gave some women, at least, the freedom to openly love other women either sexually or nonsexually.

The women-centered consciousness in general, and lesbianism in particular, had a creative impact upon American culture that encompassed feminism but also went beyond it to the mainstream culture in the areas of art, music, literature, and film. An important debate opened in the seventies and continued into the eighties on the relevancy and viability of a feminist perspective, a women-centered analysis, and the accuracy of genres such as women's literature or women's music. Never before had the role of women in intellectual and cultural life been given the serious criticism and consideration it received in the 1970s.

Themes that underlay the "women's renaissance" of the seventies in cluded egalitarian relationships; choices in love, sexuality, and family life; respect for women's experience; women's control of their bodies; and a new women's consciousness. The renaissance, like radical feminism itself, emphasized the *differences* between men and women as well as the unique contributions of a woman's perspective. The literature of the seventies was directly affected by an outpouring of work by new women writers, including Marge Piercy, Marilyn French, Alice Walker, Adrienne Rich, Toni Morrison, and Gail Godwin. Although their feminist credentials were varied, their writings both reflected and spoke to a new women-centered consciousness. Increased attention was given to already established women writers, such as May Sarton, Joyce Carol Oates, and Doris Lessing, as well as Kate Chopin, Harriet Arnow, and Zora Neal Hurston who were rediscovered.[48]

One of the major literary events of the decade occurred in 1970 with the publication of Millett's *Sexual Politics*. A devastating and witty critique of male literature—in particular, the writings of Norman Mailer, Henry Miller, and D. H. Lawrence—Millett's work combined political passion with a brilliant literary analysis. Her later works, in particular, an intensely personal lesbian novel, *Sita*, put her in disrepute, even with many feminists. But *Sexual Politics* announced to the literary world the arrival of feminism as a serious critical perspective.[49]

The title of Millett's best-seller presaged a major theme of women's writing of the seventies. One critic draws a parallel between the fem-

inist novels of the seventies and the "confessional novel" in contemporary fiction. A confessional novel, such as J. D. Salinger's *Catcher in the
Rye* or Kingsley Amis's *Lucky Jim*, is structured around the voice of a
principal protagonist and tends to focus on the experience of adoles-
cence and young adulthood with particular emphasis on the sexual experiences that characterize this stage of life.[50]

A number of commercial successes in the seventies fit the general
category of the women's confessional novel. One of the wittiest and
most audacious was Erica Jong's *Fear of Flying* (1973), the saga of a
married woman in search of the "zipless fuck." Her relentless quest was
as much a comment on the sexual restlessness of the seventies as upon
feminism, but putting a woman at the center of such an uninhibited
odyssey marked a decidedly new way of thinking about women.[51] Others that fell into this genre, such as Lisa Alther's *Kinflicks* (1975), which
added a lesbian dimension, Sara Davidson's *Loose Change* (1975), and
Alix Kates Shulman's *Memoirs of an Ex-Prom Queen* (1972), enjoyed similar success.

In 1973, the publication of Rita Mae Brown's *Rubyfruit Jungle* did for
lesbian sexuality what *Fear of Flying* did for women's heterosexual es-
capades. Molly Bolt, undoubtedly the most self-confident gay in literary history, was dirt-poor and smart-ass, beautiful and brilliant,
irrepressible and apparently irresistible to males and females alike, but
especially females. Perhaps her only fault was that she had none. Thus,
whereas Molly was utterly comfortable with her own identity (which
went beyond mere sexuality), most lesbian feminists were a tad more
timid about embracing her brand of gusto. But Brown, like Jong, Alther, and Shulman, combined humor and sexuality in a direct appeal
to women's new sensitivities and acceptance of these topics.

But a bitter, cynical view of sexuality was also very much a part of
the writings of the seventies. Perhaps the most revealing look into the
state of heterosexual relations in contemporary America was Marilyn
French's best-seller, *The Women's Room* (1977). The novel's reception and
the sales and discussion it generated indicated that many Americans,
women especially, could relate to this story of early marriages, early
motherhood, dissolution of marriages, and struggles for identity. As
one critic noted, French's novel was an expression of an instrumental
bond between the sexes that was in the process of decay. The women
slept with their husbands to get the job of wife, and they had children
to keep the job.[52]

One of the most important feminist writers of the 1960s and 1970s was Marge Piercy. Her early novels, *Going Down Fast* (1969) and *Dance the Eagle to Sleep* (1970), reflected the politics of the sixties, and had no real feminist consciousness. Piercy was a New Left activist who was made to feel by other movement people that political work took precedence over creative work. Writing was self-indulgence. But this changed as the women's movement encouraged cultural work and provided a home for a new kind of creative consciousness. "For the first time in years of being politically active, I found myself respected for the work I did, even though what I write always remains controversial within the movement as well as outside."[53]

Piercy's next two novels, *Small Changes* (1972) and *Women on the Edge of Time* (1976), were testimonies to her new sense of support within the intellectual milieu of the women's movement. *Small Changes* attempts to reproduce a fictional equivalent of the consciousness-raising group. It is a long and detailed narrative of two women as they struggle to make changes in their everyday life. As the title indicates, the protagonists are able to make only small changes, and in the end, they are both forced to retreat in the face of tradition: "women have little choice: they have no stories of their own and can only slightly change the stories written for them by the patriarchy."[54]

The sense of a universal oppression of all women expressed in this passage was an important premise of the radical feminist critique, but it did not adequately represent the range of women's experience and the variance in their oppression. Minority and working-class women resented the white middle-class feminist who took on the oppression of all women as if her suburban home was the equivalent of a ghetto tenement.[55] Black women in particular responded to their intellectual and political exclusion from the movement with their own critique of the patriarchy, combined with an attack on the racism of white feminists. A 1979 article in *Feminist Studies* analyzed the ethnocentricity of four major theorists: Robin Morgan, Kate Millett, Mary Daly, and Simone de Beauvoir, each of whom generalized from her own cultural perspective and showed an insensitivity to the experiences of women in other cultures. Their tendency to deemphasize the differences in women's situations came out of a desire to focus on the shared experiences of sexism. But the result was a neglect of minority women and a failure to understand their disinterest in feminism.[56]

Many black women, for instance, had difficulty relating to the feminist concept of sisterhood because they had their own group identity as part of a collective liberation movement struggling against racism.

They also had their own sisterhood, but it was a source of emotional support rather than of political identity, which for them had always been linked to issues of race.[57]

Politically, black women of the seventies felt that the feminist movement failed to recognize both their presence and their needs. Culturally, they expressed anger at the lack of recognition for their accomplishments and experiences among both feminists and the cultural and academic world of men and women. Alice Walker, speaking at a convocation at Sarah Lawrence College in 1972, expressed her sense of frustration with the "ignorance, arrogance, and racism" that passed as "superior knowledge" in many universities.[58]

Black intellectuals who were also feminists struggled to make the connection between racism and sexism for blacks who rejected feminism. For instance, Barbara Smith, a writer and activist who had been involved in black feminist organizing throughout most of the seventies, noted the invisibility of black women writers among all segments of the literary world. Whether establishment, progressive, black, female, or lesbian—all segments of the literary world acted as if they did not know that black women writers and black lesbian writers existed. Yet she felt that black women needed feminism, and the feminist movement needed black women:

A viable, autonomous Black feminist movement in this country would open up the space needed for the exploration of Black women's lives and the creation of consciously Black woman–identified art. At the same time a redefinition of the goals and strategies of the white feminist movement would lead to much-needed change in the focus and content of what is now generally accepted as women's culture.[59]

In particular, Smith was trying to establish the fact that black women writers constitute an identifiable literary tradition. She pointed, for example, to the incorporation of language and folk tradition in the writings of Zora Neal Hurston, Margaret Walker, Toni Morrison, and Alice Walker.[60]

Black women's literature flourished in the seventies as a genre, and although the writers themselves may have felt slighted, several of them in fact received considerable attention from feminists and from the broader reading public. Toni Morrison's novels which were critically acclaimed, gave an intimate and realistic sense of growing up black and female in America. Racism and sexism were undercurrents, but like several other black women writers of the period, Morrison was more concerned with relations between blacks, especially black women, than between blacks and whites. Racism defined the framework of black experience, but whites were not a constant part of everyday life. As in the novels of Zora Neal Hurston, racism was a shadow, and blacks sought to move into the sunlight. Sexism was a *product* of poverty, illiteracy, frustration,—or, in other words, racism.

Yet the novels of Toni Morrison did not let the black man off the hook. Neither did Michele Wallace's controversial book, *Black Macho and the Myth of Superwoman* (1979). Wallace traced the patterns of interaction between black men and women from slavery to the present. Essentially, she wrote two essays—one that examined specific ideas about black men and their search for manhood, and one that analyzed myths about the strengths of black women. She argued that although the white man was originally responsible for the griefs of black women, more recently the black man played a larger role by rejecting the black woman in favor of white women in order to assert his new manhood. And the strength of black women was made the villain: "You crippled the black man. *You* worked against him. *You* betrayed him. *You* laughed at him. *You* scorned him. *You* and the white man.[61]

Wallace's book set off a wave of controversy in the black community. The feelings that she expressed touched a source of suffering and pain in the lives of black women. The seventies was a time of tension between black men and women, and this was clearly reflected in the writings of the decade. And yet the deeper theme seemed to be a search for identity within the black female culture, and perhaps no writer exemplified that particular effort more than Alice Walker.

Alice Walker, poet and prose writer, combines the sensitivity of race consciousness with an even greater awareness of what it is to be black and female—not simply in terms of oppression but in terms of strength, energy, and creativity. Her collection of prose *In Search of Our Mothers' Gardens* (1983) expressed the need for role models in the lives of black women writers, a revolutionary consciousness in relation to the black civil rights movement, and a finely attuned sense of herself as a woman. Walker prefaces the book with a definition of *womanish*—the term she used to describe her prose.

To be womanish was to be like a woman: "Usually referring to outrageous, audacious, courageous or *willful* behavior. Wanting to know more and in greater depth than is considered 'good' for one." To be womanish was to be responsible, in charge, *serious*. It was to love other women, sexually and/or nonsexually, to appreciate women's culture, women's emotion, and women's strength. But it also was to be committed to the survival and wholeness of an entire people—male and female. And it was to love: to love music, dance, struggle, the folk, herself—*regardless*. "Womanish is to feminist as purple is to lavender."[62] Thus, Walker's highly acclaimed novel *The Color Purple* was womanish. It was about courageous women, willful behavior, women's emotions and strengths. It was also about loving other women, and the survival and wholeness of all people.

Black women writers of the seventies, in spite of their relegation by whites and men to the margins of the literary world, in fact wrote about universal themes, but from within their own perspective, which was both black and womanish. They treated lesbianism, a subject that was as much or more taboo in the black community as it was among whites. And they began to come to terms with the reality of their relationship with black men. The writings of Audre Lorde—poetry and essays, as well as her autobiography, *Zami*—offer another example of universal themes from a black feminist perspective. Lorde dealt openly with the issue of lesbianism in the black community, but she also wrote about Malcolm X, growing up in Harlem in the 1950s, and feminist motherhood. Lorde did not have the same visibility that Walker and Morrison enjoyed, but she was widely read within the feminist community.[63]

The emergence of black women writers was representative of one of the central achievements of radical feminism: that is, the focusing of attention on women artists and literary figures who in another time and place might have gone unnoticed. The women-centered values of the seventies brought into prominence several gifted poets and prose writers who experienced the support of other women as they struggled with issues that had been referred to only obliquely in earlier decades. These included representatives of several generations of women—writers such as May Sarton, Adrienne Rich, and Susan Griffin.

May Sarton (1912–), like Alice Walker, exemplifies universalism in both her themes and her literary forms. Although Sarton views herself as a poet first, it is through her novels that most readers have come to her work. In addition, her journals have given the reader a sensitive view of the inner life of a writer, a woman, and a poet at various stages of her career.[64] Sarton's novels also focus on her characters' seeking personal fulfillment through self-knowledge and connection with others. The tension or balance between solitude and connectedness is her major theme, but Sarton also deals with other universal themes—death and dying, family relations, marriage, friendship (especially between women), and homosexuality.

Although Sarton's career as a writer began nearly twenty-five years before the advent of the women's movement, and although she seldom uses the term *feminist*, there is a symbiotic relationship between her work and a women-centered analysis. During the decades of the sixties and seventies, Sarton wrote increasingly about intense friendships between women—that is, different "kinds of love." Many of her characters, male and female, experience same-sex love affairs. In *A Reckoning* (1978), Sarton confronts the issue of homosexuality directly through the main character, Laura Spelman, but also through the experiences of her sisters, her mother, her son, Ben, her friend, Ella, and a young lesbian writer who comes to Laura, seeking advice about the publication of her novel. *As We Are Now* (1973) deals with love between an elderly woman and her nurse; *The Small Room* (1961) has a long-time lesbian couple as two central characters; *Kinds of Love* (1970) is a story of love between women who are deeply committed to each other in spite of their marriages and family life; and *Mrs. Stevens Hears the Mermaid* (1965) deals with homosexuality, as well as an intense friendship between a young man and an elderly woman.

Sarton in her writing goes beyond the boundaries of age and gender that constrain relationships between men and women in order to recognize the possibility, indeed, the probability, that most human beings have the capacity to transcend those boundaries and to experience many kinds of love. The term *lesbianism*, as the public perceives it, is much too narrow to encompass the kinds of love and friendship that Sarton envisions. Sarton, through her writing, subtly redefines the meaning of these concepts, while exploring the inner lives of women in relation to themselves and other women, as well as men.[65]

Adrienne Rich (1929–), as a poet and prose writer of a later generation, also addresses the issue of love and friendship between women, but she does so even more directly and self-consciously than does Sarton, and indeed, by the end of the seventies, she had placed herself at the center of the debate over women's sexuality in the context of the women's movement, not only as a writer, but as an activist. Rich's stance on lesbianism was more open, more political, and considerably more confrontational than was that of Sarton's.

Adrienne Rich began her literary career under the guidance and authority of her father who taught her to work hard and strive for excellence. She learned to write poetry that was elegantly crafted and tightly rhymed. By the time she was in her mid-twenties she had published two volumes of poetry, *A Change of World* (1951) and *Diamond Cutters* (1955), both of which received critical acclaim. Rich married at twenty-four and had three children by the time she was thirty. These years brought her frustration and anger as she struggled with the duties of motherhood and marriage to the neglect of her real work. "About the time my third child was born, I felt that I had either to consider myself a failed woman and a failed poet, or try to find some synthesis by which to understand what was happening to me."[66]

During this period, Rich experienced a tremendous conflict between her need for love and her desire to write, but by the 1960s and 1970s, she was moving toward a resolution of that conflict through her writing. In seven volumes of poetry published between 1963 and 1981, Rich explored the pain and anger of a creative woman in a culture that denies her creativity. Her poetry reflected her attempt to define her own experience as well as help other women to "re-vision" their lives.[67]

Rich's poetry was intensely political. Feminism has guided the development of her work and the direction of her life for the past twenty years. Her belief that women must fight to preserve their past culture in order to affirm their power is well exemplified in *A Wild Patience Has Taken Me This Far: Poems, 1978–81* (1981), which celebrates the accomplishments of women in an effort to create positive public images. It includes portraits of Willa Cather, Simone Weil, and Ethel Rosenberg, as well as of Rich's grandmothers—all of whom endured hardship or excelled in spite of adversity.[68] Rich's prose, particularly the essays in *On Lies, Secrets and Silences*, expressed her active attempt to move toward a women-centered community and life-style. Part of this vision included a redefinition of lesbianism that went beyond sexual preference and beyond the civil rights issue to lesbian feminism in the most radical sense. It was "that love for ourselves and other women, that commitment to the freedom of all of us, . . . to become a politics of *asking women's questions*, demanding a world in which the integrity of all women—not a chosen few—shall be honored and validated in every aspect of the culture.[69]

In 1980, in her article "Compulsory Heterosexuality and Lesbian Existence," Rich addressed the issue of heterosexuality as a political institution, the enforcement of which assured men the right to have physical, economical, and emotional access to women.[70] Rich redefined lesbianism, broadening its scope and meaning, as she had already done to some extent in earlier essays. To her, the "lesbian existence" meant the fact of the historical presence of lesbians, as well as the creation of the meaning of that existence. The term *lesbian continuum* included a range of woman-identified experiences—not simply a sexual experience between two women.[71]

Rich argued that the unearthing of the lesbian existence was potentially liberating for all women, and certainly other cultural feminists agreed with this basic premise. Prose writer and poet Susan Griffin, a product of the upheavals of the sixties and seventies, described her acceptance of lesbian feminism as a life-style and political commitment in the introduction to her anthology *Made from this Earth* (1982). She was at first reluctant to use the word *lesbian* with reference to herself— "To become a lesbian was to become a social outcast." But as she grew in her feminism, she gained the courage and the insight to reach within and find a deeper and more radical self. "I felt everything more intensely, including desire, and the wish to love and be loved. I could no longer pretend that I did not love women."[72]

The meaning of the term *lesbianism* was as subject to varied interpretations as was *feminism*. The responses to Rich's essay on "Compulsory Heterosexuality" indicated the range and intensity of the debate, as several feminist scholars attempted to define *lesbianism* in terms of its political significance and its meaning for women's lives. Did the term refer to deviance or normality, to universality or to a time-space continuum? Was its meaning political, cultural, sexual, or all three? Was sexual intimacy a necessary component? Was resistance to the patriarchy essential.[73]

The search for the answers to the questions raised by a women-centered analysis contributed to the ongoing vibrancy of radical feminism, as the women's movement entered the 1980s. Although the politics of feminism may have been in retreat, the theoretical debate continued, albeit with its own conservative faction—the profamily and sociobiological approach of Alice Rossi, Jean Bethke Ehlstain, and others, which added a new dimension to the meaning of feminism.

Also, the metaphysical feminism of radicals like Robin Morgan and Mary Daly came under attack from critics who argued with the basic premises of metaphysical feminism—that one woman's experience is all women's experience, and that biology and oppression are ties that bind all women who have ever lived. Rather than challenging the status quo, the radical feminists seemed to be embarking on an inner psychological voyage that few women could afford to risk: "Without a grounding in the realities of race, class, and history, the radical feminist voyage became a metaphysical or spiritual journey, rather than a political one."[74]

It is perhaps true that the radical feminists were in danger of marginalizing themselves on the outer boundaries of most women's experiences, but the movement made a major contribution to mainstream culture, not only in terms of the kinds of work that women were doing, but also in terms of stimulating the debate on the extent to which there was such a thing as "women's literature," or for that matter, women's culture.[75]

By the end of the seventies women had entered the mainstream literary culture and were in the process of redefining their role and their work in ways that assured their importance and permanency in the mainstream as well as on the margins. Women were asking the "nonquestions" of patriarchal society and turning them into central issues that could not be ignored. Finally, radical feminism made a concrete contribution that went beyond the intellectual debate to the grass-roots organizing efforts of women in their communities—efforts to create new spaces out of new concepts. The women-centered analysis often led directly to the women's center.

CHAPTER FIVE

Out of the Mainstream, into the Women's Center: The Practical Application of Radical Feminism

When Norma Swenson, Judy Norsigan, and ten of their friends founded the Boston Women's Health Book Collective in November 1971, they were reaffirming a commitment to feminism and women's health issues that went back several years.[1] The women's health movement, like other one-issue approaches to feminism, reflected the interrelationship between activism and theory, between social consciousness and feminist awareness. Many of the issues that became part of the women's movement of the seventies might have emerged without theoretical feminism, but the women-centered analysis provided a significance that went beyond single-issue, interest group politics to a broader critique of the male-dominated society. It lent a theoretical context that led women to see the connections between different issues and the meaning of these connections within the political community as a whole.

The cultural feminist-turned-activist was putting theoretical feminism to work on a very practical, everyday level, and the possibilities for application were unlimited, ranging from bookstores and printing presses to battered women's centers, rape crisis centers, and health collectives. Women established construction companies, day-care centers, theater and art centers, and alternative approaches to education. The proliferation of groups, collectives, and centers—what Jo Freeman has called the "small groups"—gave women a focus for their energies at the local level, but it also contributed to a nationwide network of activists on a particular issue.[2]

The small group branch of the movement had no formal national organization. Rather, it consisted of a decentralized network in which the basic unit was a group of five to thirty women held together by personal contacts and feminist publications. These groups varied in function, but they had a common style, emphasizing participation by everyone, a sharing of tasks, and the exclusion of men. The thousands of sister chapters around the country were virtually independent of one another, but they were nonetheless linked by numerous publications, personal correspondence and phone calls, and cross-country travel. They formed and dissolved at a rapid rate, especially in the early seventies, so that it was an impossible task to keep track of their rise and demise.

The women's centers that were established in many cities provided an important centralizing function, along with space for meetings, classes, informal gatherings, and emergency assistance to individual women. But the centers had no power over group activities, and most small groups were not associated with them. Thus, although the small groups shared a common culture, they were politically autonomous. The same conscious lack of hierarchy defined their inner structure. The lines of authority and process of decision making was not always clear. There was usually a power structure of some kind, but it was determined indirectly rather than through the overt methods of elections and designation of authority. This structureless form of organization was based on the belief in the ability of all women to share, criticize, and participate equally in decision making.[3]

Since the way in which things were done was as important to the cultural feminists as what was accomplished, personal commitment was probably the most important variable in the longevity and success of a group. And although participatory democracy was the practice within the group, exclusiveness was sometimes the stance toward others. The Boston Women's Health Book Collective is an example of an organization that began as an informal discussion group and then evolved into a core group of twelve members, who after working closely together for several years, had developed strong personal ties. In November 1971, they formed a legal corporation and decided not to take in any more new members. They have been a closed group ever since and have sometimes been accused of being clannish and ingrown. One of the members of the collective justified this stance on the grounds that it contributed to the permanence and longevity of the group:[4] "We're in it for the long haul. . . . It's not a training ground. We have continuity. I think the outside world values and appreciates it very much."[5]

Reference to the "outside world" underlines another characteristic of the small groups, which occasionally led to internal conflict. Although operating from a women-centered analysis, they had to come to terms with their stance toward nonfeminist women and organizations, or even establishment figures, who were either in sympathy with their particular issue, were necessary allies, or perhaps were the focus of that issue; for example, a battered-women's center had to work with non-feminist women, as well as law enforcement officers, lawyers, perhaps doctors or hospital personnel, and so on. Thus, the purity of the women-centered approach varied, depending upon the practicality of the situation.

For instance, the feminists of the peace movement were not usually separatists. Instead they tried to bring feminist qualities and ways of operating to the movement. The antiwar movement took on a new dimension when women activists began to develop a feminist interpretation of war, nonviolence, and disarmament. Many women had been involved in the peace movement before the Vietnam Antiwar Movement, but it was their experience in the New Left that awakened them to the feminist qualities inherent in nonviolent protest and to the need to move from "antiwar" to a broad sense of "living peace," much in the way one lived "feminism." This caused a great deal of tension between the sexes in the late sixties, but those who remained committed in to the seventies were able to bring about a restructuring of tasks and a raising of consciousness.

The social movements of the sixties, with their emphasis on sexual liberation, had led women to a greater awareness of their bodies and their need to control their own health, sexuality, and reproduction. The health reform movement actually preceded the emergence of a feminist consciousness: it was in the health movement that a women-centered analysis made the most sense because in practical terms it meant women were to take responsibility for their own health, their own bodies, their own lives. There was a kind of symbiotic relationship between the health movement and the women's movement since each brought recruits to the other.

The women's health movement of the 1970s was one of the most successful branches of the overall movement in that the issues it addressed hit a responsive chord in millions of American women. Furthermore, it provided services, involved women at a grass-roots level, raised consciousness on a wide range of health-care issues for which it created a national constituency, and provided a critique of the modern medical profession and the health-care industry. The emergence of the health-care movement indicated that many Americans, especially women, were feeling alienated from traditional health-care methods and out of control of their own bodies. "Radical, anarchic, sometimes leaderless, sometimes not, the women's health movement cannot be defined as one set thing. . . . What unites these women is their common femaleness, their distrust of organized medicine, their belief that self-knowledge of anatomy and bodily functions can be liberating, their insistence that women control the means of reproduction—and thus their lives."[6]

The key issue of the women's health movement of the sixties and seventies was reproduction. The sexual revolution of the 1960s not only increased women's sexual activity; it increased their awareness of the need to control reproduction and brought about an important shift in attitude on the part of the American people as a whole toward birth control and even abortion. The abortion reform movement originated among professionals, particularly those in the medical and legal professions or those concerned with population control. These groups were primarily interested in reforming abortion laws in order to make it possible for doctors to exercise greater freedom in determining the need for abortion in certain cases. But abortion soon became a women's issue, as feminists declared that abortion was not a privilege granted by the medical profession under certain circumstances but a right—and a decision that belonged only to the pregnant woman. By the late 1960s, abortion had become a feminist issue, and women demanded not abortion *reform* but repeal of all laws that inhibited their reproductive freedom.[7]

The abortion issue provided feminists with an activist arena at two levels—that of a political pressure group trying to influence public policy, and that of abortion referral services for women. Much of the activity at this second level, at least before *Roe v. Wade*, was illegal.

In 1969, for example, a University of Chicago student was operating an illegal abortion referral system from her dormitory, but she wanted a group to take over. Several women in the Hyde Park community near the university who were engaged in other kinds of activism took over both the service and the student's pseudonym "Jane." At the time, they did not intend to perform abortions themselves. Since the group had access to a steady supply of customers, they were able to negotiate with the abortionists and lower their fees. They could also help women who were unable to pay the full amount. But the real breakthrough came when these women realized that the abortionists were not M.D.'s, that lay persons could perform abortions, and that this was a service they could provide to women directly. One abortionist taught one of the women how to perform abortions, she taught the rest, and "Jane" fired the professional abortionists.[8]

Once the women actually began to perform abortions, the group adopted a nonhierarchical operating procedure. A number of tasks had to be accomplished, and ideally every woman was expected to try to perform every task, from administration to counseling to transportation to the abortion itself. "The ideology was that everyone *could* do everything, rather than an ideology supporting a division of labor and specialization. It was thought that the women with whom they were doing the procedures would benefit by seeing the Jane women change jobs, since it demonstrated that the skills where easily transferrable and not mystical."[9]

But in point of fact, not all the women were interested in assisting with abortions, and even fewer wanted the responsibility of doing them. As in most collectives, the participants varied in their commitment, interest, and skill. Nonetheless, equality of status was an important priority, and the women in Jane learned to see their work roles as holistic. When interviewed a few years later, the women reported a positive impact upon them in the areas of personal growth and increased competency, as well as political growth and a feminist orientation. A few of the women (five out of thirty-four), reported some negative experiences, but on the whole, the direction of change was positive.[10]

Many women felt a change in their relationships with other women—a kind of female bonding, characteristic of an environment in which both the coworkers and the clients are women. They also reported a general orientation toward women's issues. The Jane collective was an example, then, of a group of women who came together around an issue and evolved in their feminism from that activity. Some of the participants had already begun to develop a feminist consciousness, and some had participated in other kinds of activism, but still others had been political novices. The abortion service was a politicalizing expe-

rience. "[Before the service] abortion interested me as an issue particularly. Feminism didn't interest me at all. . . . I discovered I could get
them an abortion but there were all these other things wrong with their
lives. . . . I got more into thinking that what's wrong with a woman's
situation is that she is a woman."[11]

Thus, the Jane collective provided a service for women and gradually
developed a full-blown women-centered analysis of the political context
in which they operated. To some extent, this was true of other women's
groups as well. Hundreds of local organizations were working to make
changes in a health system that did not adequately serve women's
needs. Their work fell into three main categories: changing consciousness, providing health-related services, and struggling to change established institutions. Most of these groups began informally and either
grew out of or came to identify with the women's movement.[12]

For instance, the organization that eventually became Healthright
started out as a women's health forum in New York City around 1969–
70, before the legalization of abortion. Then, in the spring of 1971, the
New York legislature repealed its abortion law, and suddenly New
York had the most liberal abortion law in the country. Hundreds of
women flooded the city seeking abortions. Clinics sprang up overnight
to take advantage of their needs, but they did not always provide ade-
quate counseling or follow-up care. This situation was of concern to a
group of feminists in and around New York City. They began meeting
women at the plane, providing them with counseling and follow-up
care, and working to bring down the prices of the clinics. Out of this
direct action emerged the Healthright collective.[13]

The Boston Women's Health Book Collective mentioned earlier
started when a group of ten women gathered to discuss the "hottest
health issues" at one of the first women's liberation conferences, held
in Boston in 1969. The discussion, which included abortion and childbirth, was primarily experiential, and the women became aware that
they did not even know enough about their bodies to evaluate the
health care they were receiving. They agreed to continue meeting
through the summer, with each woman researching and writing on a
topic that was especially important to her personal experience. The
sharing of factual information and personal perspectives enabled these
women to develop a critique of the material they read and the health
care they were receiving.[14]

The next winter the women gave an informal evening course in Cambridge called Women and Their Bodies for about fifty friends and *their*

friends. The course was repeated two more times during the next year for other women, some of whom remained to help research and write up more information. Some of them went elsewhere to run similar pro- grams. Thus the course spread and the group gained in diversity and strength. By November 1971, the core group of twelve was ready to incorporate itself as the Boston Women's Health Book Collective.[15]

The collective took its name from its publication, a book that soon became the classic of the feminist health movement. In the summer of 1970, a few people in the group had pulled together the many papers that had been written and assembled a newsprint book that was later published by a local non-profit press. More that 200,000 copies were sold during the next two years, mostly through women's centers and by word-of-mouth. The title was changed from *Women and Their Bodies* to *Our Bodies, Ourselves*. In 1973, after much soul-searching, the group signed with a commercial press and brought out a revised edition. A second edition came out in 1976, and a third edition in 1979; *The New Our Bodies, Ourselves* was published in 1984.[16]

The book provided a focus for the collective and, in many ways, for the health movement as a whole. The collective did not offer health services; rather, it became a center of information for other women's health groups, government agencies, individuals, and organizations in- volved in activism touching on women's health issues. The collective also took an advocacy position of many issues, especially with respect to the health concerns of minority women or lower-class women who were not as well represented in mainstream feminist organizations like NOW or WEAL. But the key to their political activism was the centrality of information that had to be continually updated and revised. "It's all very well to take an ideological position, but you have to have some data, and we have the data," said one participant.[17]

The women's health movement is a clear-cut example of the inter- action between woman-centered analysis and a concrete issue of prac- tical concern to all women. The seventies saw a rapid growth of women's health centers and activist organizations, as well as the pub- lication of several journals and newsletters dealing with women and health. The groups varied somewhat in their focus, but they all held several basic values in common that defined them as feminists. First of all, the most important belief was that women, not professionals, are the best experts on themselves and their feelings—thus their emphasis on education and self-help. Second, there was a strong belief in an open, democratic, nonhierarchical approach, both among the members of a collective and between the members and the people they serviced. This approach was not easily achieved, and it was not always the most efficient mode of operation, but feminists who were reacting against the unequal distribution of power in the traditional doctor-patient, doctor-nurse relationships saw this as essential to the basic values of feminism—and indeed, in many ways it was the point of the feminist health movement. Judy Norsigian, a founder of the Boston group, noted: "The bottom line is to move people to take action, to encourage women not to let professional interest groups make decisions about their health and well-being."[18]

The number of groups in the movement and the range of their activities and services can only be suggested here: the Somerville Women's Health Project in Massachusetts and the Fremont Women's Clinic in Seattle were both located in poor neighborhoods, where medical services were unavailable. The Women's Clinic at Evergreen State College in Washington got started when establishment services were cut off. Groups such as the Beach Area Women's Clinic in San Diego and the S. E. Portland Women's Health Clinic provided check-ups and tests, counseling on nutrition and all aspects of reproductive health, and referrals where necessary, as well as exercise classes. The Feminist Women's Health Centers, influenced by the Los Angeles group and established in 1971, developed techniques of self-examination and in-depth counseling.[19]

Although the actual work of the health movement was grounded in local communities, by the mid-seventies there was nationwide coordination and activity. In 1975, thirteen hundred women attended the first National Women's Health Conference in Boston. In 1976, a National Women's Health Network, based in Washington, was established to provide a nationwide clearinghouse on health policy and legislation. Regional organizations evolved as well. In October 1978, a "founding weekend" for a northeast alliance of women health activists was held in the Monadnock region of New Hampshire, bringing together thirty-five participants from Philadelphia, New York City, Rhode Island, Connecticut, Massachusetts, and New Hampshire. This group formed "the Rising Sun Feminist Health Alliance—a regional group for women health activists sharing the common dream of woman-controlled health care for us all."[20]

The regional and national organizing efforts reflected an activist strain in the women's health movement that was committed to moving beyond the women's center in an attempt to influence public policy. This activism evolved from the 1960s and the beginnings of the abortion reform movement, the interest in natural childbirth, and attempts to hold the medical profession accountable for issues like sterilization, safety of the birth control pill, abuse of drugs, and unnecessary surgery.

The women's health movement had always combined the personal and the political, even before it developed a feminist perspective. In large part this was due to the centrality of the abortion issue. Throughout the seventies demonstrations, lobbying efforts, and petition campaigns were directed at influencing public policy on other issues as well. Some of these efforts were supported by groups that were not necessarily part of the feminist health movement. For example, during the Democratic National Convention in New York City on 13 July 1976, the Women's Health Action Movement (WHAM), a coalition of women's health groups, health workers, educators, and consumers, demonstrated with a march and a rally, hoping to influence the Democratic national platform on numerous health issues.[21]

Feminists involved in the health movement often had to make common cause with groups that had a different perspective on an issue of mutual concern, such as population control or sterilization. The feminist emphasis was on the right to *choice* on the part of the woman, and they tended to be more sensitive to the needs and values of minorities than were mainstream reformist organizations.[22]

Other aspects of the feminist health movement prevented it from simply merging with reform currents. The women involved wanted more than medical care: they wanted a sense of pride and strength in their bodies; they wanted to develop their own standard of what was "normal" in a woman's body. The medicalization of the female life cycle and the use of medical arguments to justify discrimination against women led to a feminist strategy to subvert the ideology of sexism at its base: in the sociological interpretation of biological sex differences.[23]

The activities and organizations that characterized the women's health movement reflected the ideals of cultural feminism. Self-help and know-your-body courses, and abortion, gynecological, and childbirth care presented not only an alternative to the mainstream health industry but also a feminist critique that redefined the patient and provider roles. For example, in 1971, the first Feminist Women's Health Center (FWHC) was established in Los Angeles by Carol

Downer and Lorraine Rothman. It offered a range of services, but the patient also encountered other women—lay women, like herself—who had learned their skills in self-help courses.[24]

Downer and Rothman were actively involved in helping other women establish self-help groups. In November 1971, they began giving demonstrations in communities across the country. By the mid-seventies there were at least fifty women-run clinics in the United States. There were fourteen FWHCs, modeled on the Los Angeles example, where women assisted in their pregnancy test and interpreted results, and participated in other forms of self-examination. Los Angeles and Oakland had a totally participatory clinic, in which the role of the provider became that of a facilitator, and significant healing relationships were formed between patients. "Instead of being a totally private and individual matter, health maintenance becomes a collective endeavor," it was explained.[25]

The FWHC provided a number of significant services, including women-owned, women-controlled abortion clinics, self-health clinics; paramedic training programs, free well-women clinics, which offered counseling, information, and gynecological and pregnancy testing, abortion health care and advocacy services, speakers' bureaus, and advanced research projects. Its philosophy stressed women's strengths rather than crises and oppression. It generated capital to be reinvested in similar programs, and it was political in the sense that it recognized that real change could occur only through organization, direction, and power: "Unlike most Free Clinics, our goal is *not* to provide an alternative health delivery system; we want to take it over."[26]

The inclination of the FWHC was to avoid a hierarchical organization, but a group engaging in such complex activities needed some kind of formal structure and means of defining leadership. Nonetheless, the structure was open to any woman who wanted to achieve a leadership position through her activism. A system evolved whereby a staff member could earn points depending upon her involvement, or she could disengage by simply backing off from center activities. The extent of her involvement determined her power and influence in the group.[27]

Other problem-centered groups emerged in the early seventies. Not all of them were feminist, but the problems they addressed assured a primarily female clientele, and feminist values of self-help were emphasized. These groups went beyond basic health needs to provide counseling, psychotherapy, or emotional support in a time of crisis or for a particular problem or family situation. Although they were responding to human service needs that could not be met through traditional professional resources, their services often entailed cooperation with professionals. Feminist self-help groups generally tried to resist that kind of cooperation, but sometimes professionals who were also feminists provided much needed expertise.[28]

A group that combined professional expertise with a women-centered perspective was the Feminist Counseling Collective (FCC), founded in March 1972 by the Washington, D.C., Area Women's Center. The collective comprised twenty women, ten full members and ten trainees (both professionals and paraprofessionals), who volunteered their time and skills to provide low-cost feminist group counseling. Its members saw the FCC as a model of an attempt to achieve a feminist ego ideal—a woman who was both strong and vulnerable. Their structure was nonhierarchical, with an emphasis upon an open and sharing relationship between therapist and client.[29]

Feminist self-help was particularly applicable to reproductive concerns. Birth control was a major feminist issue of the 1960s and 1970s which became politicized by concern about the birth control pill, as well as the controversy over abortion. In the mid-seventies, a self-help group was established in the Boston area to deal with the problem of fertility control. Its membership was composed of the facilitators of Fertility Consciousness/Women-Controlled Natural Birth Control Groups (FC/WCNBC). In these groups women were taught to detect fertility and to use this information for contraception, conception, and general body awareness. The women were taught technical information and were also encouraged to discuss conception and contraception within a political context that would increase their feminist awareness. Moreover, they were learning about each other through a group process that became an affirmation of sisterhood.[30]

The interest in controlling reproduction led naturally to an interest in controlling childbirth by removing it from traditional medical procedures and placing it into the hands of women. The 1970s saw the emergence of a movement toward out-of-hospital birth, and between 1974 and 1984, more than one hundred free-standing birth centers (FSBC) became operational. Conservative critics argued that the FSBC placed the mother and child in a situation of undue risk, and some feminists were critical because the movement tended to coopt activists who became appendages to the medical establishment. The FSBC was certainly not the answer for large numbers of women. Still in the experimental stage by the early 1980s, it provided an alternative for a narrowly circumscribed risk-classified socioeconomic group. Nonetheless, it reflected a new desire among women to control their reproductive process and to escape the oppressive features of the mainstream health industry.[31]

The feminist self-help movement, with all of its diversity, was an indication of women's coming of age in terms of consciousness and self-empowerment. The ideal of strong women and a collective sisterhood had strong appeal, but it also had its drawbacks. Not all self-help programs operated smoothly and successfully to achieve their objectives. Women in Transition, Inc., offers an example of a collective's early success and its eventual demise because of lack of funding, conflicting personal objectives, and disillusionment. Women in Transition originated as an outgrowth of the Philadelphia Women's Liberation Center. The program was established in September 1971 to provide a variety of services—in particular, emotional and legal support—to women who were separated or divorced, victims of wife abuse, or raising children alone. In addition, the staff members shared information and expertise with other organizations, engaged in public speaking, and offered consultation to social service agencies. They also wrote *Women in Transition: A Feminist Handbook on Separation and Divorce* (1975). Their goals were to provide direct services to women in need and to engage in activities related to social change.[32]

In spite of this impressive list of accomplishments, however, the staff of Women in Transition often differed among themselves about goals, strategies and tactics. Since they operated as a collective, everyone shared in the decision-making process, and there was no formal hierarchy in terms of salary or power. The group made a major effort to speak to the needs of low-income and minority women, as well as middle-class women, and there was a diversity of background represented on the staff itself. Finally, the women's close meshing of personal, political, and professional concerns contributed to a high degree of self-integration.[33]

The demise of the organization occurred primarily because of inadequate funding—a problem that plagued almost all women's centers of the seventies and eighties. Funding women's programs was not a high priority for either private foundations or government agencies. The staff members of Women in Transition were not enterprising about seeking out grant support, and at the same time, they provided all their services free of charge. Such idealism took its toll. The lack of funds and the uncertainty of long-range prospects contributed to personal tensions within the collective, as the women became discouraged and disillusioned with the reality of living on unemployment, stagnating in their professional careers, and struggling with the problems of operating in a collective mode. Said one women, "We all became experts in exhibiting the martyr syndrome from time to time: anger, frustration, feeling that you and you alone were working hard and keeping the agency going single-handedly."[34]

The internal problems of Women in Transition were probably replicated in other women's centers and collectives across the country. They were the normal difficulties of idealistic and well-intentioned human beings who were trying something new and exciting that was also very complicated. As one participant pointed out, "The marriage may be over, but it wasn't necessarily a failure." Although the services ended, the accomplishments had been considerable, and both participants and staff members grew personally and politically.[35]

The women's movement brought two other issues before the public in the early seventies—rape and wife beating. Although always a feature of domestic and street life, violence was placed into a political context by feminists early in the decade. Susan Griffin made an important early statement on rape in her essay, "The Politics of Rape," which was written in 1970. Griffin's essay, first published in *Ramparts* magazine in 1971, became part of her book *Rape: The Power of Consciousness* (1979).[36]

Griffin argued that rape was not the act of a madman or of a man suddenly overcome by sexual lust. Rather, it was a political act that underwrote the system of male dominance and was beneficial to all classes of men, whether they raped or not. "For rape is a kind of terrorism which severely limits the freedom of women and makes women dependent on men."[37]

The emergence of feminist consciousness with respect to male violence was a natural consequence of the women's liberation movement, its emphasis on women's right to control their bodies and lives, and on the connection between the personal and the political. When Susan Brownmiller's history of rape, *Against Our Will: Men, Women, and Rape*, appeared in 1975, there was not only a large feminist audience to receive it, but an attentive American public. Brownmiller placed rape in a political context that was cross-cultural and cross-racial, having nothing to do with national origins or racial or class background. Rape was simply an expression of man's physical dominance over women from prehistoric times to the present: "It is nothing more or less than a conscious process of intimidation by which *all men* keep *all women* in a state of fear."[38]

But not all women accepted Brownmiller's universal explanation for an act that had such a long and diverse history. Black women, in particular, were critical of her interpretation of interracial rape, claiming that she understated the significance of the sexual exploitation of black women during slavery. Black feminist Bell Hooks argued that although Brownmiller acknowledged the fact of brutal assault upon black women, she treated it as a historical incident relegated to a particular institution, slavery. According to Hooks, Brownmiller failed to see that the rape of black women "led to a devaluation of black womanhood that permeated the psyches of all Americans and shaped the social status of all black women once slavery ended."[39]

Black women were sensitive to the racial implications of the rape issue. Not only did they have their own honor to protect, but they knew that accusations of rape had historically been used against black men. In short, black feminists, although they were aware that rape was a feminist issue and a black woman's issue, were leery of the double standard that operated to the disadvantage of both male and female blacks.[40]

In 1975 a dramatic case of rape and alleged murder became a cause célèbre for feminists across the country, and gave black and white women an opportunity to come together in a common cause. Joanne Little, a young black woman, was raped by a white guard in a North Carolina jail where she was the only woman inmate. In the summer of 1975, while standing trial for murder, she described how she had killed her assailant in self-defense with the ice pick he had used to threaten her. Little was passionately supported within the black community as well as within the women's movement, and largely as a result of this mass campaign, she was acquitted.[41]

The antirape movement aroused women's consciousness on the rape issue, worked actively to change public opinion concerning the causes of rape, and redefined the parameters of what women would tolerate, individually and collectively. The antirape movement operated on many levels, but essentially it grew out of the attempts to assist women who had experienced rape. In 1971–72, Bay Area Women Against Rape was formed, and in June 1972, the first emergency rape crisis line opened in Washington, D.C. Rape crisis centers began to appear all over the country, usually started by former rape victims and feminist activists. The rape crisis centers, like other women's centers of the 1970s, tested the organizational and political skills of many women for the first time. Boards of directors, by-laws, work procedures, funding proposals, the coordination of hotlines, and negotiations with bureaucracies were all part of a practical effort to deal with this concrete issue so long ignored or mishandled by public officials.[42]

By 1976 there were approximately fifteen hundred projects—task forces, study groups, crisis centers—that were dealing with the issue of rape. Of these, about four hundred were autonomous feminist rape crisis centers. That is, they were not connected to any public agency and relied on their own resources for funding and expertise. The rape crisis centers offered self-defense courses, rape prevention seminars, support groups, and training sessions for professionals on how to provide emotional and practical support to victims. The centers also developed and distributed educational materials.

The Feminist Alliance Against Rape (FAAR) newsletter was started in 1974 to act as a political sounding board. The antirape movement began to demand legal and institutional reforms with respect to courtroom procedures, attitudes of police, methods of gathering evidence, and unsympathetic or arbitrary hospital policies. One of the most dramatic events calling attention to the problem of rape was the institution of "Take Back the Night" in 1977, when thousands of women across the country marched to show their solidarity and their right to walk the streets at night.[43]

Although the basic organizing principle behind the rape crisis center was a feminist interpretation of rape, often the women who volunteered to work in a center wanted to counsel victims, but had not really thought about rape in political terms. Thus, political education and consciousness-raising was an important part of the feminist center, not only for the victims of rape, but for volunteer workers as well. The atmosphere in the rape crisis center was that of a *feminist workplace*—a place where women could be involved in the decision-making process, could relate to one another as equals, and could feel themselves part of the women's movement in a positive way: "It's a place where a lot of women have come who would not consider themselves feminists, but through their work with the Center, they come in contact with the political ideas of the women's movement. They see these ideas in relation to a concrete problem. This experience breaks down barriers that exist between many women and the women's movement."[44]

There were other positive aspects to working in a feminist rape crisis

center: the possibility for self-education and development, the opportunity to place things into a political context and to understand the
contradictions of racism and classism, and the change to come into contact with women who were organizers and leaders in the community.
But there were also disadvantages, including fragmentation of work,
effort, and concentration, lack of funding, and the frustrations of seeing
the same problems over and over again.[45]

Perhaps the most frustrating experience for feminists in the movement was to see the rape issue coopted by government agencies and
professionals. Many centers found that they had to affiliate with traditional institutions in order to survive, but sometimes the agency that
provided funding or expertise did not acknowledge a feminist analysis
of rape or uphold individual and collective rights to self-determination.
As one woman put it, "A key difference between us and them was our
accountability to a movement, our deep involvement with women victims, our politics, our vision, and our simultaneous belief in and skep-
ticism about making institutions work better for women."[46]

The antirape movement, then, struggled with a characteristic feminist dilemma. In order to gain legitimacy and funding, antirape work
had to focus on the plight of the victim. Although this focus was justified, it sometimes meant a deemphasis on political analysis and organizing for social change. Women could more easily receive sympathy
or funding for rape victims if they played down the issue of male dominance. A similar dynamic characterized the battered women's movement that was closely connected to the antirape movement in
philosophy, structure, and political resources.[47]

The politics of the battered women's movement were complex and
diverse. Although feminist ideology played a role in the early movement, it was not always primary or articulated. The sense of belonging
to a movement, rather than ideology, motivated most women who became involved. The goals of the movement and the leadership in most
locales were feminist, but many women who did not consider themselves feminists played a significant role. More important, battered
women themselves were not usually feminists. The one belief that was
shared by all programs was that battered women faced brutality from
their husbands and an indifference from social institutions that made it
difficult, if not impossible, to obtain redress.[48]

Wife battering had first come to public attention in London, Eng-
land, where in 1971 Erin Prizzey founded Chiswick Women's Aid, an
advice center for women. Most of the women who came to discuss their

problems were battered women. In 1974, Prizzey published *Scream Quietly or the Neighbors Will Hear,* the first contemporary book about wife abuse. Meanwhile, in the United States, awareness of the problem was also growing, especially among feminists. The first shelter, Women's Advocates, was founded in St. Paul, Minnesota, in 1974. Additional shelters were established in urban areas around the country, so that by 1979 there were about 250. By this time domestic violence had become a public issue, and was considered to be suitable for state and potential federal legislative intervention.[49]

The battered women's movement faced problems similar to that of the women's health movement and the antirape movement with respect to the need for funding and the pressures to compromise political ideals to obtain it. The role of professionals within the movement also presented problems. Although a professional staff made it easier to obtain funding, professionals and feminists often differed over the acceptance of funding, the role of politics, and the importance of self-help. Also, the goals of the two groups sometimes differed, with professionals more concerned with providing a service, and feminists wanting to go beyond that to more significant social change.[50]

Although the divisions over issues of organization, politics, and ideology were not unique to the battered women's movement, the immediacy and the intensity of the issue of domestic violence perhaps made them seem more critical. But radical feminism was continually struggling with these issues. Those feminists who adopted a life-style focusing on intellectual and cultural pursuits were perhaps the *most* self-conscious about the decision as to whether they should adapt themselves to the mainstream culture and try to make a feminist contribution, or whether they should develop a feminist separatist alternative culture.

In the summer of 1974 a new feminist journal appeared, devoted to the "quest" for change within individuals, within the women's movement, and on a broad societal level. "*Quest* recognizes total change as a necessity for survival for the majority of people—not as an individual choice for those securing personal comfort," wrote Karen Kollias in the first issue.[51]

Founded by a women's liberation group in Washington, D.C., *Quest* reflected the tensions within the movement between theory and action. It was an attempt to bring these two together in a feminist institution based on principles of cooperation and sharing, with an independent economic base controlled by women. The articles published between 1975 and 1979 were perhaps the best representation of the cultural and political views of the radical wing of the women's movement in the United States. "*Quest* was envisioned as a tool for the already committed, not as a mass-audience magazine."[52]

One of the central debates of radical feminism pursued by *Quest* and other feminist journals was the option of a lesbian-separatist alternative with respect to work and life-styles. The philosophical cornerstone of lesbian feminism was that the institution and ideology of heterosexuality upheld male supremacy, and unless women could turn away from this unequal relationship, feminism was doomed to be reformist rather than revolutionary. Heterosexuality was not simply a private matter between a man and woman; it was the force that divided women one against the other.[53]

Yet, like the activists of the women's center, the lesbian feminists were caught in a dilemma. In order to move beyond the oppressive features of a marginal existence cut off from mainstream power, politics, and economics, women had to inevitably deal with male authority in a way that compromised lesbian feminist politics. The logical response to this dilemma was to create lesbian feminist living and working collectives. "Ultimately our ability to overcome male supremacy rests upon building an alternative to it."[54]

The concept and practice of the lesbian community offered a haven in a hostile world. Originally the focus for such a community was the gay bar, but it tended to assign and reinforce traditional sex roles under the labels "fem" and "butch." The awareness of alternative life-styles led to, among other approaches, the formation of collectives around a particular institution—a bookstore, coffeehouse, newspaper, or journal. But there was also the possibility of a loosely structured community life revolving around these and other institutions reflecting a general sense of shared values. For instance, San Francisco, with its large gay population, had an active lesbian community that was linked through a national network into other communities across the nation. Women who came from other parts of the country could expect to be put up with friends and could make contacts through the "Women's Switchboard." Newspapers, magazines, and books written by and for lesbians were easily available in the city, and the lesbian feminist point of view was presented on television and local radio. In addition, musical groups and artistic performances were often geared to a lesbian audience. Roughly two to five thousand women were active in the community at any one time during the seventies, out of an estimated thirty-five thousand lesbians in the city.[55]

San Francisco presents a special case because of its large lesbian population, but other large cities developed similar forms of community during the 1970s. By the late seventies and early eighties lesbian feminists were well-established in terms of their ideology and institution building, but like many feminists, they were facing the realities of a postfeminist conservatism in which the early enthusiasm turned to a less ebullient realism, and political activism gave way to an emphasis on individual advancement and financial security. (An exception was a march for gay and lesbian rights in Washington, D.C., on 14 October 1979, which attracted 150,000 to 200,000 participants.) But support for the basic tenets of feminism, although still present, had lost the sense of excitement and discovery that had characterized the early seventies.[56]

In the meantime, the women-centered perspective brought about important changes in the way women perceived art, literature, the media, and other cultural forms. Very early in the women's movement an independent communications network began to issue mimeographed newsletters and position papers clarifying what feminists stood for. By the mid-seventies there were more than 150 feminist presses or journals in more than thirty states. Including women's bookstores, the effect was a network of media control—women writing, typesetting, illustrating, printing, reviewing, selling, and reading other women's books, articles, and ideas. For radical feminists this development had revolutionary significance.[57]

The feminist press, like other aspects of the movement, unleashed considerable controversy about the role of feminist journalism within the women's movement. Although most feminists agreed that the standards of excellence had to be different from those of, say, the *New York Times* or any other large commercial newspaper, there was disagreement over what those standards should be. For instance, Donna Allen, who published *Media Report for Women*, emphasized fact over opinion: "we see our function as supplying factual information that is not easily available elsewhere, and we leave the formation of opinions about it to each individual." But other feminists questioned whether it was possible to distinguish between fact and opinion and felt that one of the chief characteristics of feminist journalism was that it was "advocacy journalism which champions the assumption of sisterhood."[58]

Feminist awareness also led to a sense of women's art as a political and personal statement distinctly different from the dominant male culture. Judy Chicago was the best-known representative of the women-centered art of the 1970s. Chicago pioneered the first women's art program in the country at Fresco State, California, in 1970–71, and was cofounder, with Miriam Schapiro, of the Feminist Art Program (FAP) and the Woman's Building in Los Angeles. From 1974 to 1980 she worked on *The Dinner Party*, a highly acclaimed work of collaborative art using female imagery symbolic of women's history, achievements, and struggles in Western civilization. In 1980 she began work on *The Birth Project*, a participatory art form with birth as the subject matter and using various needlework techniques.[59]

In her autobiography, *Through the Flower*, Chicago articulated the highly developed sense of women's experience that began to pervade her work by 1970. At that time there was no frame of reference within which to understand and value these insights. She was trying to compete within the male-dominated world of the artist, while struggling to overcome the social conditioning that restricted her artistic expression, until she finally realized her dilemma: "I had, in trying to make myself into an artist who was taken seriously in a male-dominated art community, submerged the very aspects of myself that could make my work intelligible. How could I make my voice heard, have access to the channels of the society that allows one's work to be visible, and be myself as a women?"[60]

Chicago's answer was to leave the structure of the male-dominated art community and commit herself to developing an alternative. In October 1971, she and Miriam Schapiro established the Feminist Art Program at the California Institute of the Arts in Valencia. Twenty-one young women entered this program, which was based on feminists principles of creativity and culture. Both Chicago and Schapiro felt that women's potential had not been given enough encouragement, and their achievements had not been given recognition. With the right kind of supportive environment, women's creativity could flower. They both placed a high priority on developing strong female egos in the students.[61]

The students were encouraged to accept their own life experiences and preoccupations as worthy subjects for their art. This meant that subjects such as makeup or shoes, usually dismissed as artistically trivial, were examined as a link to the long and complex tradition of human experience into which women had a particular insight. As Schapiro later recalled, "The real substance of the feminist contribution to the art of the seventies was that, for the first time in the history of art, women's life became the content of her art."[62]

The method used to elicit new subject matter and build strong female egos was a combination of consciousness-raising and involvement in a communal project—the creation of "Womanhouse." The group took over an abandoned seventeen-room house in downtown Los Angeles, forty miles from Cal Arts. The students spent a month of eight-hour days repairing and painting the dilapidated mansion. Many of them resented the hard physical work and were unable to see its relevance to art, but Chicago felt that this labor in common was indispensable to the building of a strong community. The house was created as an art form in itself, each room representing some aspect of women's experience. Womanhouse was open to the public as an art exhibit from 30 January to 28 February 1972.[63]

The Feminist Art Program and the creation of Womanhouse was an exciting experience for the participants, but not all the goals of the program were achieved, and the experiment lasted only a few years. Theoretically, the program was to be run democratically, with an emphasis on consensus and a near-egalitarian relationship between teacher and student. But the strong personalities and leadership of Chicago and Schapiro dominated the program, and many of the former students later indicated that they saw Chicago to be an authoritarian figure who imposed her goals upon the group.[64]

The most troublesome aspect of the FAP, according to its former students, was its separatism. Although they acknowledged that the program was most successful when the separatism was most complete, some of them resented what they saw as the program's hostility to men. Those who were in relationships with men felt continually pressured by conflicts of loyalty. Schapiro, as a married woman, ultimately had to forsake the separatist women's community: "One of the disadvantages with such a program is that you fall so in love with the community that you don't realize that in order to survive in the real world you have to play a different kind of role."[65]

Schapiro and Chicago diverged in their later careers. Schapiro reentered the wider art world, emphasizing traditional categories of art, but Chicago pushed in new directions with feminist art. Her two cooperative projects, *The Dinner Party* and *Birth Project*, reflected her strong commitment to art as an educational medium, performance art, collaborative projects, and art by nonprofessionals. The differences between the two women illustrate a schism in feminist art in the later 1970s, as well as the broader debate over the nature of women's contribution to culture.

The FAP demonstrated, however, that a community of women could effect change in their own creativity. The art that resulted from the interaction of the group was different from anything that was being done by male artists—either those working traditionally or those who were part of a conscious vanguard. It stimulated the debate as to whether a specifically female art existed, and if so, what its nature was. The debate itself encouraged the creation of women's art, and the art magazines and exhibits of the seventies carried examples of this art dealing explicitly with the female experiences of sexuality, domesticity, and social situations.[66]

Although women artists debated their relationship to the dominant male culture and the value of a women's community, the impact of feminism had to be acknowledged. An upstate New York artist, Judith Bush, confessed that she "did art" for years, but it was feminism that brought her in touch with her art as a personal expression of herself. She went from the traditional art forms—portraits and landscapes—to more abstract expressions of herself and her experiences as a woman: "My art has changed dramatically. . . . My work in the last several years has been very free-flowing. I never know where I'm going when I start. The imagery is incredible, based on where I am in time. I'm not worried about other people. I'm doing my art for myself."[67]

And yet Bush combined this personal approach to her art with an awareness of her indebtedness to the women's movement. To her the most important thing to come out of the movement was women taking each other seriously—seeing each other as people. By the 1980s she had adopted a holistic approach to feminism that allowed her to see the connections among life, art, and feminism. She organized the Women's Caucus for the Arts of Central New York, a group of about thirty women artists who met regularly to talk about their work and share experiences.

The impact of cultural feminism on women's individual and collective experience was revolutionary in that it created new issues, redefined old ones, and recognized women as central to an understanding of the total human experience. The debates over the nature of women's art, women's literature, and other cultural forms are not likely to be soon revolved, but they reveal an alternative that had never before existed. The women-centered analysis presented an appealing approach to resolving the dilemmas of women and creativity. As Judith Bush argued: "Why not listen to our own voice? We have something to say—our voices need to be heard. If we're going to speak on someone else's agenda then we're going to adapt ourselves to that agenda. We've got to allow ourselves to be truly authentic."[68]

The activists of the women's centers would have probably agreed. The purity, drama, and creativity of cultural feminism had considerable appeal to activists, intellectuals, and artists, but for some women, also committed to feminism, activism, and a creative life, the less dramatic but more tangible gains of academia provided another kind of alternative.

CHAPTER SIX

Scholars and Activists:
The Gender Factor in Education

The women's movement had a major impact on the field of education in several ways. It galvanized women into action to overcome discrimination, it stimulated research, and it opened a whole new field of inquiry—the field of women's studies—to scholars and students. Thus, the movement had two separate and yet overlapping objectives. One was to end discrimination and thereby improve women's access to educational opportunity and to power within the institution. The other was to add to the knowledge of women through research and writing, and through the creation of new courses and programs.[1]

Underlying both sets of objectives was a sense of mission that was characteristic of the movement as a whole, and that gave it a moral thrust and fervor that went beyond mere careerism or opportunism. At its most basic level it involved the liberal sense of justice that did not necessarily require a feminist perspective, but simply a recognition that women deserved equal opportunity within the system. At another level was the need felt by some feminists to reinterpret their disciplines through research and writing, to revise the curriculum through the creation of new courses and the integration of feminist scholarship into traditional courses, and to move toward a transformation of the university, or what Sonia Johnson has called the semiversity.[2]

The women's movement in education, like the movement in general, has to be understood in the context of other reform movements of the

1960s and seventies, and it was characterized by a similar diversity and complexity.

The black revolution was one aspect of the social dissension of the late 1960s that combined a critique of the schools with a critique of society. A new progressivism in education emerged in response to racial unrest, antiwar sentiment, and student activism. The result was a substantial body of educational protest literature, as well as a number of experimental developments, such as the open education movement, the free school movement, the alternative schools movement, and the de-schooling movement. All these movements shared certain assumptions about the shortcomings of the existing public schools, the corruptness in American society, and the need for radical change in both.[3]

The demand for reform that characterized the politics of education in the decade after 1965 undermined the authority of schools and universities to control their own affairs. Educational administrators found themselves embroiled in power struggles with students, the courts and civil rights agencies, faculty and teachers' unions, and political action and special interest groups. Increased federal intervention in educational institutions was based on Title VI of the Civil Rights Act of 1964, which gave federal officials the power to withdraw funds from any program violating antidiscrimination laws and regulations. Since federal funding for education at all levels expanded rapidly after 1965, the threatened cutoff of these funds was an impressive weapon. "With Title VI as the stick and federal funds as the carrot, the federal government became a significant factor in setting rules for the nation's schools, colleges, and universities.[4]

In the midst of this reform ferment, the women's movement began to make its own claims upon society, and the schools became prime targets, as feminists pointed to their negative role in socializing female students to accept an inferior status. The reformers at the elementary and secondary levels were often parents who were concerned about discrimination and sex-role stereotyping in school textbooks, the classroom, guidance counseling, extracurricular activities, and personnel policies. At issue was the restrictive nature of sex roles on the natural development of young people, and the integral role played by the schools in the process of socialization.[5]

There was another explanation for directing special attention to education. Most feminist leaders were well-educated middle-class and upper-middle-class white women. According to one survey, nearly 90 percent of them had at least a B.A., and a third held graduate degrees.

They knew from their own experience that the university was a male domain, and as educated women, they placed a high value on education both as a means of advancement and as the best lever with which to reconstruct society.[6]

It was the liberal branch of the movement that tended to see educational reform as necessary to the advancement of women as individuals. Thus they picked up the issue of equal rights and used it to hammer an opening wedge, focusing especially upon the male-dominated universities. Not all these women considered themselves feminists—at least not at first. Bernice Sandler, an early activist in Women's Equity Action League (WEAL), expressed her initial position on women's issues as very conservative, but when she experienced discrimination three times within a few weeks in 1969, she was forced to reevaluate that position.[7]

Sandler's experiences were not unique, but they served as a catalyst, propelling her into a career of commitment to women's issues in education. At the time there was no law that prohibited discrimination on the basis of sex in educational institutions. Title VI of the Civil Rights Act of 1964 prohibited discrimination against beneficiaries of federally assisted programs, but only on the basis of race, color, and national origin. Title VII of the Civil Rights Act forbade sex discrimination in employment, but until 24 March 1972, when the act was amended, colleges and universities were exempt from coverage.

Sandler fell back on Executive Order 11375, issued by President Lyndon Johnson and effective 13 October 1968. This executive order forbade discrimination by all federal contractors, but unlike the former Title VII, it did not exempt educational institutions, and unlike Title VI, it did not leave out sex discrimination. Sandler used the order to devise a historic class action suit under the auspices of WEAL. On 31 January 1970, WEAL filed a complaint with the U.S. Department of Labor against all the colleges and universities in the country. Nancy E. Dowd, WEAL president, asked that the Department of Labor investigate admission quotas and discrimination in financial assistance, hiring practices, promotions, and salary differentials. More than eighty pages of materials documenting these charges were submitted.[8]

The group was requesting an immediate class action and compliance review of all institutions holding federal contracts. But at the same time, the organization filed specific charges against 250 institutions, including the University of Maryland, the University of Wisconsin, the University of Minnesota, Columbia University, the University of Chicago, and the entire state university and college systems of California, Florida, and New Jersey. In October 1970, WEAL filed a class action suit against all the medical schools in the country, the Professional Women's Caucus filed a similar suit against the nation's law schools in April 1971, and NOW filed charges against Harvard University and the entire state university system of New York. Additional complaints by individual women and women's campus associations brought the number of formal charges to more than 360.[9]

Bernice Sandler was probably the single individual most responsible for the class action suits. As chair of WEAL's Action Committee for Federal Control Compliance in Education, she was described by a Washington reporter as "the scourge of the universities." Sandler was the one who realized the potential, at least on a temporary basis, of the executive order, and she was the one who devised the class action campaign. A contemporary, Joan Roberts, at the University of Wisconsin, acknowledges her central role: "What *really* was the bombshell on most campuses was Bunny Sandler's filing of complaint actions, and that was the trigger. . . . it is the political action and legal action taken by Sandler that forced the issue of women's status wide open on every campus."[10]

The act of filing charges legitimized the issue of sex discrimination and confirmed that it really did exist. It made it easier for women to band together, and it caused campus administrators to take a new look at women. Campus committees on the status of women were established, and women took it upon themselves to examine their status and push for reforms. Before WEAL took action, there were only two known reports on sex discrimination—these were at the University of Chicago and Columbia University. But within two years of the filing of the first class action suits, there were reports on more than one hundred institutions.[11]

In 1970 Congresswoman Edith Green, a member of WEAL's advisory board, held congressional hearings on discrimination in education as a step toward amending Title VII of the Civil Rights Act. Sandler provided Green with names of appropriate people to appear at the hearings, and she was then hired by Green to put together the written record of the hearings: two volumes of over a thousand pages. Green had six thousand copies printed and one was sent to every member of Congress, to women's groups, and to university libraries. This important document established once and for all the concrete facts of sex discrimination in education.[12]

The Green hearings were a landmark in women's history because for the first time feminists were able to make their case in a prestigious forum that established the legitimacy of the issue. The hearings also contributed to the climate of opinion that made possible Title IX of the Higher Education Act of 1972, which specifically prohibits discrimination on the basis of sex in elementary and secondary schools, colleges, and universities. The interpretation and enforcement of Title IX remained an area of policy conflict. The compliance regulations did not come out for another three years, and women spent much of the seventies attempting to have them implemented.[13]

The struggle for equal rights in education was both a collective and an individual effort that involved some traditional organizational strategies as well as unprecedented acts of personal courage and sacrifice. As an example of the organizational strategy, the National Coalition for Research in Women's Education and Development (NCRWED) was formed to capitalize on the knowledge and expertise that had been accumulated through women's continuing education programs—nearly four hundred of which had been established on college and university campuses during the 1960s.[14]

The purpose of the NCRWED was research directed toward the recommendation of future national policy in women's education. The activities of the group, which included the publication of a quarterly journal, *Comment*, research activities, and the organization of a conference, were supported by the Johnson Foundation of Racine, Wisconsin, the Exxon Education Foundation, the College Entrance Examination Board, and the Carnegie Corporation.[15]

This kind of support was reflective of the role of foundations in assisting most of the mainstream feminist organizations of the 1970's. Historian Susan Hartmann has noted that foundation funds not only inaugurated programs to benefit middle-class and professional women but also supported various projects benefiting blue- and pink-collar workers, minority women, welfare mothers, and women abroad. The Ford Foundation, in particular, was a major contributor to women's causes and programs. By the mid-seventies, Ford accounted for half of all private philanthropy in the area of women's equity.[16]

The National Organization for Women, through its Legal Defense and Education Fund, established the Project on Equal Education Rights (PEER). This privately financed advocacy group played a watch-

dog role on education issues, monitoring the government and pressuring it to do more for women in the field of education. In 1974, PEER
drew together a group of feminists from several national organizations
to form the National Coalition for Women and Girls in Education. It
also tried to organize community groups and parents to look at their
own school districts and identify problems and published information
for parents, teachers, and school administrators who were concerned
about equity issues in education.[17]

In 1971, the Association of American Colleges (AAC) established the
Project on the Education and Status of Women, and hired Bernice Sandler as director, a position she held throughout the seventies and into
the eighties. The project was based upon the rather optimistic assumption that there were many people of goodwill in the field of education
who would make the right decisions if they had the best information
available. Thus, the primary function of the project was to develop and
distribute materials that identified issues and provided recommendations for overcoming barriers to equity for women in higher education.[18]

The project published a newsletter, *On Campus*, which contained information about women's status in educational institutions. Sandler's
office became the center of an informational network on every possible
issue relating to women and education, including sexual harassment on
campus, the classroom climate for women, and the integration of all-
male colleges, along with more traditional equity issues. Sandler's intent was to stay on the leading edge by identifying an issue and then
dropping it, letting someone else pick it up and carry it. The project
provided research and information to college administrators, faculty
members, and women's organizations, emphasizing positive perspectives of women that encouraged the potential for policy change.[19]

Sandler felt that being part of a nonwoman's organization—the
AAC—gave the project and the information it distributed more credibility than if it had been part of a women's group, such as NOW or
WEAL. Credibility was, indeed, a major problem for women seeking to
combat discrimination. Joan Abramson, a victim of discrimination at
the University of Hawaii, wrote an account based on her own personal
experience, which enumerated the barriers to women's equity in education. Credibility was always the first barrier to be hurdled: "Complaints of discrimination are met almost inevitably with challenges to
the academic credentials of the complainer. As far as the academic es-

tablishment is concerned, everyone is rewarded on the basis of merit, and therefore any woman complaining of discrimination is only publicizing her own mediocrity."[20]

Organizational efforts were important in establishing sex discrimination as a legitimate issue, but it was the personal struggles of hundreds of individual women who had the courage to initiate suits against their colleges and universities that told the story in human terms. And it was these individual cases that drew attention to the movement and convinced even the most powerful and prestigious of universities that women were serious about obtaining their rights.

In 1971–72, Harvard University became the target of a complaint filed by NOW with the office of Health, Education and Welfare (HEW), which charged that Harvard's employment policies toward women and minorities were inadequate and illegal. At the same time, Franziska Hosken, a college teacher, architect, journalist, and architectural critic, brought a suit against Harvard stemming from two applications for faculty appointments at the Harvard Graduate School of Design (GSD), which she made in 1970–71. Hosken claimed that her applications were either refused or ignored. Her purpose in pursuing the case was to initiate change toward more equitable faculty appointment practices throughout the university.[21]

The GSD was a classic example of the haphazard method of faculty appointment that characterized Harvard and indeed most universities before the reforms of the 1960s and 1970s. Familiarly known as the "buddy system" or "the old boy's network," this procedure was essentially based upon personal recommendations of faculty members to their dean or chairman. Quite naturally, it tended to be self-perpetuating, effectively excluding women and minorities. In 1971–72, the GSD had only two women faculty, neither of whom was tenured. In the spring of 1972, five more were hired, although the first two lost their jobs. Also, the new appointments were primarily due to pressure from President Derek C. Bok and the GSD's special committee on the status of women. Even then, the appointments were not made under defined criteria, but through the traditional buddy system.[22]

Hosken's case highlighted the fact that Harvard had been slow in developing an affirmative action plan, and even slower in making it public. In 1970, HEW had requested Harvard to file an affirmative action program to correct deficiencies in both minority hiring policies and in the method used in faculty appointments, or else face the loss of over

$60 million in federal money. Harvard continued to be embroiled with HEW in its attempts to develop an affirmative action program through the spring of 1973. The university submitted its third proposal—which took over one year to complete, at a cost of nearly $250,000—to the federal government in early May 1973. The extent to which Harvard was serious about complying, at least on paper, was due to pressure from individuals like Hosken, from women's groups, and especially from the federal government. In the previous year, federal contracts had accounted for about one-third of Harvard's income. Yet, even with this kind of leverage, the government would not have forced the issue if it had not been pressured by women's activism.[23]

Harvard was also subject to criticism on the basis of its admission and financial aid policies, particularly as other Ivy League schools began to respond to the reformist climate. In December 1972, Yale instituted a sex-blind admissions policy to begin in the fall of 1973. The school resolved to recruit more women in order to achieve a ratio of three men to two women in the class of 1978. Also, unlike Harvard's stiff quota admissions policy, Yale's ratio was intended to bend to the qualifications of the applicants in each year. According to Yale president Kingman Brewster, "To continue to impose a quota on the selection process would require us to admit a less talented class than we could have."[24]

President Bok confessed that Harvard was just beginning to investigate the possibilities of changing the admission ratio. He noted that Radcliffe's status as a semiseparate institution complicated the matter.[25] In the spring of 1973, the Standing Committee on Women, a watchdog committee without enforcement power, revealed that the Harvard Graduate School of Arts and Sciences was accepting women and offering them scholarships at a "startling lower rate" than men. A few departments had decreased the differences between men and women since 1967–69, but at least eleven departments *increased* the gap. Six departments were singled out as demonstrating a clear and continuing pattern of inequality.[26]

The attention directed to Harvard was replicated at colleges and universities across the country, but the prestige of Harvard, its reliance on federal funding, and its public image made it an example to other institutions and gave the issue of sexual equality a certain legitimacy. But activism on the part of women's groups and individuals also created greater resistance. As Joan Abramson has pointed out: "Avoidance, denial, wrath—all the defense mechanisms of injured pride seem to be triggered by a charge of sex discrimination. The result is that fighting to support one's charge or even to obtain a hearing on it is like wading through a huge vat of oatmeal mush: one just never manages to leave much of a footprint."[27]

"Wading through oatmeal" is perhaps an accurate metaphor for the affirmative action efforts and the litigation suits of the 1970s. The process was physically exhausting, emotionally and financially debilitating, and seldom rewarding in terms of professional gain. But it was something that had to be done, and the price was paid again and again by courageous women who for whatever reason—anger, pride, a sense of justice, professional commitment, or a feminist consciousness—chose to take a stand.

In July 1973, the Equal Employment Opportunity Commission (EEOC) charged Tufts University with bias in hiring, recruiting, and other employment policies. This was a precedent-setting case because it was the first suit brought by EEOC against a university. The agency had received vastly increased powers in June 1972, which allowed it to go into court on behalf of complainants. The complainants in the Tufts case were Christiane L. Joost and Barbara E. White, assistant professors in the university's Department of Fine Arts. Both claimed discriminatory practices in connection with their failure to be rehired.[28]

The case of Professor Joost was particularly controversial, combining elements of sexism, political discrimination, and a personality confrontation between Joost and her department chairman, Ivan Galantic. Joost received overwhelming support from her students, who organized a campaign to have her rehired. More than 750 of them signed a petition in her behalf. Joost also received support from a male colleague who concurred with her accusations of unfair treatment from Galantic, which he had experienced as well. Galantic resigned as chair of the department, although he remained in a teaching capacity. His successor, classics professor John Zarker, wrote a letter in support of Joost to EEOC, but he refused to make the letter public and declined to comment on the case.[29]

The Joost case exemplified the frustrations that women experienced in dealing with the politics of discrimination. The Tufts administration, using what a group of Joost supporters called "nontactics," refused to address the issues or give reasons for the dismissal of Joost. This group contacted other women in the Boston area who had experienced discrimination and discovered a similar pattern of administrative silence, vague innuendos, personality attacks, and the use of arbitrary criteria for tenure, hiring, and firing. Also, governmental agencies, such as HEW or EEOC, were notably ineffective. Women academics had to act independently in their own behalf while simultaneously pressur ing the government to help. Pressure from students and concerned faculty was sometimes a factor forcing an administration to act.[30]

The chance of success was greater and the significance of the action was enhanced if faculty women were able to recognize the commonality of their interests and wage their protest collectively. But the collective strategy was not easily accepted by all women. It undermined the meritocratic ideal, according to which rewards are distributed on the basis of individual ability and hard work. Also, complainants often found it necessary to articulate their cases in individualistic terms, focusing on their personal and professional qualities rather than on systemic patterns of discrimination[31]

And yet a feminist perspective became an almost inevitable part of the process. Coming to terms with the experience of discrimination was extremely painful at several levels. It meant that the women who had been denied tenure had to sever their connections with the institutions they had served devotedly and from which they received their professional identity. But the obvious pain of separation and loss was intensified by the tendency of many women to blame their own deficiencies. Filing a sex discrimination charge meant overcoming this psychological component and recognizing that an injustice had been done to them because they belonged to a particular group. In other words, they had to move beyond seeing themselves as individuals able to make it on their own merit. This was difficult for women who were accustomed to success. As Emily Abel described them, "They take pride in being 'special' and 'exceptionally deserving,' and focus on elements that separate them from other women on campus, whether students, secretaries, research assistants, librarians, or teachers. The discovery that they share problems with other women threatens their sense of uniqueness."[32]

The thrust of the women's movement was to overcome this individualistic tendency and to encourage women to recognize their commonality and act within a collective support system. Women varied in their ability and willingness to do this, and the amount of support they received from other women also varied.[33] But many of them claimed they were motivated by idealistic concerns, ranging from "working for other women," to transforming the university and redistributing power. If they were active feminists, and especially if they were connected to a women's studies program, they were naturally more likely to see their case within a broad political context and to draw on support from other women.

Although the women's studies connection provided a base of support, participants were often subjected to special harassment because of that connection. The very fact that they were involved in activism, or that their research reflected a feminist perspective, made them less valued and greatly feared by their departments and universities. Thus, discrimination resulted not because they were women per se but because of the political implications of their work as feminists.

Joan Roberts, a founder of the women's studies program at the University of Wisconsin–Madison, personified the collective consciousness of the women's movement on campus in her activism, her teaching and scholarship, and her devotion to the principle of cooperation among women. She saw her negative tenure decision as an issue of sexual politics: "It was clear that they had to get rid of me. You can't have an assistant professor who is going to the newspaper every day, and taking on the institution, and organizing women, and all that kind of stuff. Certainly not someone who is saying these 'wildly crazy things' in women's studies classes."[34]

Roberts was denied tenure in February 1974 on the grounds of an unsatisfactory research and publication record. Yet she had come to Wisconsin in 1968 with one book published and a second forthcoming. At the time of her tenure review she had several publications and almost a dozen items under submission to journals or in the process of revision. She had contracts for two new books and was negotiating a third. She was also an active member of the department, the university, and the community.[35] Robert's work in the field of women's studies was innovative, but it did not fit into conventional academic categories. Furthermore, her activities within the university were also in women's studies; she was a leader in developing the women's studies program. She had helped organize a feminist support group—the Association of Faculty Women (AFW)—and was its cochair during its first year, 1971–72. Beyond the university, Roberts was one of the founders of the state Coordinating Council for Women in Higher Education (CCWHE), and was cochair during CCWHE's first year, 1972–73.[36]

Given her commitment to feminism, and her intellectualization of that commitment, it is not surprising that Roberts saw her experience as part of a general purge of feminist activism on university campuses. "It's not hard to prove a purge. I could go through and name them. It was pretty standard." Roberts's decision to fight her tenure decision was based on her leadership role and her interpretation of the politics of her case. If she did not put up a fight, other women leaders would suffer the same fate, but if she went down fighting, the administration would know that they could expect a similar fight from other women. It was necessary to "break silence"—to raise the issue of women's oppression in the public arena.[37]

Roberts carried on a five-year suit against the University of Wisconsin, which was eventually settled out of court on 13 December 1978. She had, by this time, established herself as an associate professor with tenure at Syracuse University, where she served as chair of the Department of Child and Family Studies. But the period of transition, which included two years of unemployment and serious health problems, had extracted a high price personally and professionally. Roberts's strong convictions and her steadfast commitment to the women's movement was the underlying source of her strength during this ordeal.[38]

In some cases, expectations of sisterhood led to disillusionment. In December 1975, Judith Long Laws, an assistant professor of sociology at Cornell University, received a negative tenure review. Laws was a pioneer in the study of sex roles and women's legal issues. She was a productive scholar and an active consultant in equity cases, the most famous of which was the AT&T case of the early 1970s. But an impressive publishing record, professional activism, and service to the university, especially in the area of women's studies, were not enough for the Cornell Department of Sociology. Laws was denied tenure in February 1976. When she wrote a statement supporting her scholarship and alleging irregularities in the tenure procedure, she was granted a second vote and once again was denied tenure in December 1976.[39]

The ostensible reason for Laws's tenure denial was her publishing record, which was deemed to be of not very high quality. The chairman of her department wrote that "her research has declined to zero while her writing is shifting toward the polemic and away from the major forms of theoretical work. If I have to make a fallible guess as to where her work is taking her, it would have to be away still further from the traditional academic role."[40] Thus, it was the *quality* of her publications, not the quantity, that was under question, for in fact, Laws was one of the most prolific people in the department. At the time of her tenure review she had two books projected to be published in 1976, as well as ten published articles and numerous reviews and papers.[41]

Two interrelated factors operating in the tenure decision of Judy Long Laws characterized the problem for women at Cornell University. One was sex discrimination and the other was the unwillingness of the academic establishment to grant the legitimacy of research in women's studies. Cornell University was slow to respond to the pressures of affirmative action during the 1970s. By the end of the decade there had been little progress for female faculty. From 1971 to 1979 their representation went from 7.6 percent to 8.3 percent, an increase of less than 1 percent. Of the tenured faculty, only 6.1 percent were female, as compared to a national average of 16.5 percent. Women were vastly underrepresented among the higher administrative posts: of the seventy-six academic heads, only one was a woman; of fourteen deans, one was a woman; and of six vice presidents, not one was a woman.[42]

This pattern of discrimination was dramatically revealed to the public in October 1980, when five Cornell faculty women filed a class action suit. Their intent was to represent all women faculty at Cornell since 1972—about two hundred women. Designated "the Cornell 11," because originally there were eleven women involved, the five women included Judy Long Laws; Donna Zahorik, an assistant professor in psychology who initiated the suit; Antonia Glasse, an assistant professor of Russian literature; Jacqueline Livingston, a photographer in the arts department; and Charlotte Ferris in extension education.[43]

The "Cornell 11" case was an example of women acting collectively to redress their grievances from a system that had failed to respond to a decade of activism. But, as in the Joan Roberts case, the price was high, and the returns very low. In March 1983, U.S. district judge Howard G. Munson ruled that the women were not the victim of sex discrimination. He claimed that the university had treated them "fairly and neutrally" in denying their requests for tenure. By this time, the "Cornell 11" had spent fifty thousand dollars on the case.[44]

The emotional, financial and professional costs varied for the women as individuals. Judy Long Laws received a cash settlement out of court in 1985, but it was a mere token in comparison to the money and time she had spent on the case, as well as the personal anguish she had experienced. She felt isolated during 1976 when she went through her two negative tenure decisions. Also, in spite of her apparent connection to the "Cornell 11," she never felt a part of that group. Her expertise in issues of sex discrimination was never really utilized, and to Laws, the group seemed ineffective and concerned mostly with their "victimization," rather than with winning that case. Laws emerged from her experience at Cornell feeling bitter toward the university, the sociology department, and women on campus who, she felt, did not value her contribution to women's studies and equity issues.[45]

Although feminists reacted differently to their attempts at sister-hood, disillusionment with affirmative action had set in as early as the mid-seventies. In the early years of the decade, the WEAL class action suits had raised hopes that perhaps women and minorities actually *would* achieve fair representation on the nation's campuses. But the lack-adaisical performance of HEW, and the reluctance of civil rights chief J. Stanley Pottinger to enforce the rules of compliance, led to frustra-tion on the part of feminists. The department's sluggish performance was caused by a lack of staff, an unwillingness to apply sanctions, and difficulty in obtaining vital employment data from universities. The critical weapon in HEW's arsenal was "contract compliance." But to ac-tually cut off or terminate ongoing contracts with universities proved to be extremely difficult, even though noncompliance was widespread. By the end of 1980, no institution had lost any federal monies because of lack of compliance with Title IX regulations.[46]

As a policy, affirmative action reflected the optimistic reform values of the 1960s—societal justice was to be achieved through governmental intervention and the cooperation of an enlightened educational com-munity. But it was implemented in the 1970s—a decade of retreat from equality and government intervention to a kind of neo-Darwinism that was to characterize the Reagan administrations of the 1980s. In part the retreat from affirmative action was due to a well-organized opposi-tion, the Committee for a Rational Alternative, which managed to cre-ate the illusion that a dangerously successful program of "reverse discrimination" was in operation, undermining the intellectual and professional credibility of the nation's colleges and universities:

The campaign mounted by established faculty groups against the concept of affirmative action hinged on a defense of the special status of the university and its commitment to academic excellence. . . . This self-proclaimed merito-cracy in the university was to be preserved at all costs, and only those who created and operated the system were considered capable of judging its perfor-mance.[47]

Government enforcement of affirmative action undoubtedly posed a real and potential threat to the autonomy of a university and the distribution of power within it—and in fact, that was the intent, at least as far as many feminists were concerned. Affirmative action required more than neutrality; it required the employer to make additional efforts to recruit, employ, and promote qualified members of groups formerly excluded, even if that exclusion could not be traced to discriminatory actions on the part of the employer. It was based upon a simple premise: that "a benign neutrality in employment practices will tend to perpetuate the status quo indefinitely."[48]

In 1971, EEOC announced its guidelines for colleges and universities, which included establishing a policy and assigning responsibility for its fulfillment, setting specific, attainable hiring goals, and finding minority or women candidates who would qualify. Also, the focus was to be upon getting women and minorities into upwardly mobile positions.[49]

Affirmative action had a modest impact on the employment of women faculty members. Throughout most of the decade, the proportion of college and university faculty positions held by women, according to AAUP annual surveys, held steady at roughly one-fifth: in 1973–74, it was 22.5 percent, and in 1977–78, 22.1 percent. Women made some gains in the lower ranks. For instance, in 1974–75, 27.9 percent of all assistant professors were female, and by 1977–78, the figure had risen to 30.1 percent, which perhaps was promising for the future. But for associate professors, the figures were 17.3 percent in 1974–75, and 16.6 percent in 1977–78; for full professors, 10.1 percent in 1974–75, and 8.2 percent in 1977–78.[50]

Lack of progress was even more apparent in the areas of tenure and salary. In 1974–75, only 46 percent of women faculty members had permanent academic tenure, whereas 64 percent of the men were tenured. By 1977–78, the figure was 45 percent for women and 66 percent for men. Salary differentials similarly reflected overall inequities. At each level, women earned about 90 to 95 percent of the earnings of male faculty members. But women faculty were much more likely to be in the lower ranks—so that in 1974–75, they earned an average of 82.6 percent of the earnings of men. By 1977–78, the gap had widened: women were earning an average of 80.1 percent the earnings of men.[51]

Black women experienced even less progress than women as a whole. The civil rights movement of the 1960s and the women's movement of the 1970s seemed to be primarily directed at black men and white women. Black professional women were concentrated in the field of education, but they seldom reached the top. When they did, they found themselves an isolated subgroup that had neither race nor sex in common with the white males who dominated academe.

Constance M. Carroll, an assistant dean in the College of Arts and Sciences at the University of Maine, reflected on the psychological impact of this isolation. Although she was in touch with most academic departments of the university, she never, except in the case of black studies and minority programs, came in contact with another black woman professor or administrator. There was no one with whom to share experiences and gain support—no one with whom to identify. As she said, "It takes a great deal of psychological strength 'just to get through the day,' the endless lunches, and meetings in which one is always 'different.' The feeling is much like the exhaustion a foreigner speaking an alien tongue feels at the end of the day."[52]

The seventies was a decade of high expectations accompanied by a corresponding frustration for black women in academe. On the one hand, HEW investigations spotlighted the inequities of race and sex, and consequently, colleges and universities stepped up their hiring policies. Black women were recruited to fill secretarial positions, to staff black studies and minority programs, and occasionally, to fill junior administrative posts. But overall, their gains were insignificant—much less than those of white women or black men.[53] But the public perception of their progress during the 1970s was that they "had it made," primarily because of the public attention received by affirmative action and the high visibility of those few black women who did, in fact, "make it." The occasional appointment that went to a black woman was often seen as the consequence of affirmative action (or "reverse discrimination") rather than of the woman's merit. Wrote Ruth Fischer: "It's hardly a secret that a double-minority academic is a hot item in today's marketplace. Given the exigencies of affirmative action, many colleges and universities understandably jump at the opportunity to appoint a black woman, thus killing two birds with one carefully aimed stone."[54]

Mary Berry, who was named a provost at the University of Maryland in the fall of 1974, noted ruefully, "I'm not so naive that I'm not aware of two of the reasons why I got this job." Berry, nonetheless, also happened to be qualified. Her credentials included a B.A. and M.A. from Howard University, a Ph.D. from the University of Michigan, and a J.D. from the University of Michigan Law School. Yet she was still haunted by the vestiges of racism and sexism. Professionally, gender was the most important factor, but socially, it was race. Berry was a

strong supporter of the women's movement, but the race question remained her primary issue.[55]

Affirmative action, whether directed toward gender or race, generated more discussion and controversy than actual change—at least with
respect to employment in education. As federal agencies backed off
from strict enforcement, colleges and universities became bogged down
in clerical work and data gathering. The policy became, therefore, a
limited response to a series of individual complaints, followed by negotiated settlements that sidetracked the larger issue of correcting inequities. The concept of a broad plan for institutional change, if it had
ever existed at all, was lost. The university community simply failed
to respond to that possibility.[56] An administrator in a top post at a major
university expressed her frustration at women's status within the system: "Having spent my whole career in higher education, one of the
greatest disappointments is that higher education has not taken the lead
ever on issues of feminism, women's equality, fair play—in fact, higher
education has lagged behind other institutions of society. What I see at
this university is that there are a great many men who just do not want
women around as colleagues and professionals."[57]

Yet it would be a mistake to understate the amount of change that
did occur. Women's perceptions of themselves changed, and new opportunities were opened to them. Changing moral values, reflecting the
student movement and the counterculture of the 1960s, meant that
fewer restraints were placed on the private lives of women students.
Educational opportunities opened up in response to the WEAL class
action suits and to Title IX which outlawed sex discrimination in
elementary and secondary schools, as well as in postsecondary institutions. Feminists used Title IX to redefine issues of equal opportunity—both in sports and in other educational activities—as issues of
role equity, but Title IX also dealt with questions of privacy and potentially radical change in traditionally male-dominated areas of society. For instance, one scholar suggested that "the athletics issue may
well mask a growing concern over changing sex roles and not a concern
about the impact of Title IX on revenue-producing sports."[58]

In fact, the major opposition to Title IX was mounted by the men's
athletic establishment—in particular, the National Collegiate Athletic
Association (NCAA) and the leadership of some universities with major
commitments to men's intercollegiate sports. The NCAA, an organization of 726 member institutions, had the capacity to support lengthy

litigation. In 1978 its revenues totaled $13.9 million, with self-generated revenues deriving from championship games and televised football and other sports programs. The men's athletic establishment attempted to maintain the status quo, while insisting there was no need to provide equity because there was no real demand among women students.[59]

But women's groups organized in defense of Title IX. In 1974 some sixty groups, including WEAL, NOW, NWPC, and more traditional organizations, such as the LWV, AAUW, ACE, AAUP, and the Girl Scouts, joined to form the Education Task Force, which later changed its name to the National Coalition for Women and Girls in Education. In spite of this vigilance, women students did not gain equality in sports during the 1970s. In 1978 only 13 percent of what was spent on men's intercollegiate sports was spent on women's intercollegiate athletics, although this amount had risen from 2 percent in 1974.[60]

But even incremental change is a kind of success, and Title IX also affected other aspects of women's educational experience. Increasingly women's sports received additional funding, scholarships were made available to women athletes, and more options in sports were opened to women. Also, admissions, access to courses, counseling, housing and other facilities, scholarships, and employment practices all came under the purview of Title IX. Although federal enforcement was constrained, feminist activism, internal pressures, and public opinion necessarily forced colleges and universities to revise their traditional gender-bound policies.

In 1974, the Women's Educational Equity Act Program (WEEAP) was established to provide funding for action projects promoting equality of women's educational opportunities. The act recodified in 1978 as Title IX, Part C, to include a new emphasis on helping educational agencies and institutions meet the requirements of Title IX. The National Advisory Council on Women's Educational Programs was also established by the WEEAP. Title IX's influence on vocational education was strengthened by the Education Amendments of 1976. The amended act stated that overcoming sex discrimination and sex stereotyping in vocational education was a major purpose of federally assisted vocational education programs. Block grants were awarded to states willing to develop programs to meet that purpose.[61]

In the colleges and universities, women students became recognized as important clientele during a period when these institutions were facing declining enrollments and looking for customers. Women's enrollment increased to the point that they actually outnumbered male students nationwide. They, however, were overrepresented in two-year institutions and were more likely to be part-time students, and their degrees remained concentrated in female-intensive fields.

On the other hand, there was a significant movement of women into certain male-intensive fields. From 1970 to 1979 the percentage of women earning degrees in law grew from 5.4 to 28.5, and in medicine from 8.4 to 23.0. From 1974 to 1979 the percentage of women earning bachelor's degrees in business and management grew from 12.8 to 30.5. Bernice Sandler noted that by the early 1980s, the Cornell School of Veterinary Medicine was admitting 60 percent females. At one time they had admitted not more than two a year.[62]

These figures were indication of a new direction for educated women, but the long-range consequences remain to be determined. The great majority of college-educated women remained in female-intensive fields, held degrees from less prestigious institutions, and were less likely than men to take an advanced degree. In other words, there were opportunities for individual advancement, but significant structural change had not yet occurred.[63]

When Bernice Sandler was asked in the early 1980s to testify for the reintroduction of the ERA, she examined her files, expecting that with a little updating she could use her testimonies from the early seventies. But the old report was testimony to a decade of change. The quota systems of the premovement days were gone, and *overt* discrimination was no longer considered acceptable. There was an awareness of sex discrimination as a legitimate issue, although most male administrators and faculty still thought it happened on some other campus, not their own. Women's issues had become institutionalized through laws, through commissions on the status of women and professional caucuses, and through women's studies courses. Recognition of new issues, such as sexual harassment and "date rape" was widespread.[64]

Meanwhile, a feminist consciousness was nurtured by the thousands of women's centers and women's studies courses and programs that sprang up on nearly every campus across the country. The early seventies was characterized by an enthusiasm, an excitement, that was unlike anything that had gone before in the history of women. Anne Truax, director of the Women's Center at the University of Minnesota, recalled that the first women's course for college credit on the Minnesota campus, offered in the spring of 1970, had an enrollment of twenty-seven students. It was offered again the next year—twice in the daytime and once at night, and it filled every time. In the spring of 1971, a conference on women and equal rights held at the university attracted 475 people:

Anything anyone put forward was instantly snatched up. It seemed to me that every time I turned around, someone was having a national conference or a consultation. People were flying us all over the map. It was wonderful! It was almost more than any one person could stand. It was so exciting, and there was so much support, almost in the air, that you didn't mind doing it.[65]

Joan Roberts recalled an excitement that was a kind of joyous relief, as if everything were happening for the first time in history. "If we go into a decline again, there has got to be something that says what we literally, genuinely *did*, not what we wrote, because those of us most heavily involved had no time to write." Roberts located twenty-eight women at the University of Wisconsin who were willing to help her develop a women's studies course. It was interdisciplinary and involved women from the community as well as the campus. The university radio station broadcast it over the air, so that it touched the lives of countless women beyond the classroom. Other women faculty used it to develop their own courses. Thus, this first course, initiated in 1970, formed the core of what later became women's studies at the University of Wisconsin.[66]

Women's studies was taking shape in a similar form on other campuses across the nation. In fact, these courses and programs were probably the most rapidly growing and innovative addition to college curricula in the 1970s. They transmitted the excitement and self-discovery of the women's movement to the college campuses. In addition to the traditional academic goals of mastering subject matter, women's studies was dedicated to the less traditional goal of personal change, effected in a manner similar to consciousness-raising. The courses challenged basic self-concepts and sex-role beliefs and encouraged women to adopt more positive attitudes toward themselves and other women.[67]

The long-range objective of women's studies was to transform the academy. Florence Howe, a professor of American studies, first at Goucher College and later at the State University of New York–College of Old Westbury, best articulated the basic intellectual and political impulses behind women's studies in her many articles, essays, and lectures. Howe was active in the Modern Language Association, serving for a time as president, and she became president and publisher of the Feminist Press. She argued that no other program in recent history was so clearly committed to change in the curriculum and, to some extent, in the structures of colleges and universities.[68]

Women's studies owed its initial existence to the women's liberation movement of the late 1960s, which gave it a revolutionary thrust and defined it as a necessary part of women's struggle for self-determination—a tool for radical change that combined the personal and the political with the intellectual. Although women's studies had a grass-roots, localized history on individual campuses, it very early developed a national network. On each campus there were people who initiated courses and made the intracampus connections, but there were also people who reached out and established a sense of movement nationwide. Sometimes it was the same people.[69] At Cornell University, Sheila Tobias called for a new program of female studies in 1970, following a successful conference on women in the winter of 1969, and a team-taught, multidisciplinary course on "female personality" which attracted some four hundred students in the spring of 1970. At the same time, Tobias became involved in compiling a collection of syllabi, reading lists, and shared experiences that came out of courses on other campuses. *Female Studies I* was published in the fall of 1970, the first in a series of ten. In December 1970, *Female Studies II* was published, an anthology of sixty-six course outlines and bibliographies collected by the Commission on the Status of Women of the Modern Language Association and edited by Florence Howe.[70]

The rapid growth of women's studies reflected the shared perceptions of students and scholars who sought to redefine themselves and the world through their academic life. Between 1970 and 1975, 150 new women's studies programs were founded, and as many more were added between 1975 and 1980. The number of courses totaled some 30,000 by the end of the decade, taught at most of the colleges and universities in the United States. This growth was documented in the *Female Studies* series, and in other publications of Know Press, established in Pittsburgh in 1969, and of the Feminist Press, established by Howe and Paul Lauter in 1970. In 1972, two multidisciplinary journals, *Women's Studies* and *Feminist Studies*, began to publish scholarly articles in the field, and the *Women's Studies Newsletter* became a forum for the movement.[71]

Signs: A Journal of Women in Culture and Society began publication in the fall of 1975, under the editorial leadership of Catharine Stimpson and associate editors, Joan Burstyn and Domna Stanton. It soon became the most successful women's studies journal of the decade, receiving an enormous number of articles each year—sometimes as many as five hundred. It had a circulation of eight thousand at the end of the first year, and eventually settled at about sixty-five hundred—the fifth largest journal of the University of Chicago Press. During the early years of the movement, very few books were published, and much of the really innovative work was being done in article form. Thus, some early articles in *Signs* were crucial to the development of the field and became classics of the movement.[72]

The tremendous outpouring of research and scholarly writing completely reshaped many disciplines—history, literature, and sociology, in particular. But feminist research, from its early inception, was committed to crossing the barriers of disciplines in order to address the complex reality of women's situation. Feminist scholarship challenged the traditional disciplines at the same time that it was shaped by them, and since many feminist scholars were active in the women's movement, they viewed their scholarship as part of that activity. This naturally led to antagonism from male colleagues and administrators who were suspicious of scholarship that seemed to openly serve political or social ends. This was a problem many feminist scholars faced in the 1970s in having their work accepted by the male academics who were determining their fate.[73]

Even by the end of the decade, male scholars were reluctant to accept the new literature of women's studies and acknowledge its impact on their discipline. Joan Burstyn, looking back from the mid-eighties, felt that the real breakthrough for the women's movement of the seventies was in the conceptualization of ideas—this is what *Signs* and other women's studies journals were about. Women were in effect saying "let's break into the arena where the concepts are developing, because *that's* where the source of power is in this society." And that's what women have done, according to Burstyn, but the men still refused to read it and acknowledge it.[74]

During the first five or six years, the women's studies movement had no center or national organization. It was primarily a network of individual courses, campuswide programs, and regional conferences and organizations that sometimes represented a particular discipline and sometimes focused upon women's studies in its multidisciplinary complexity. For instance, Gretchen Kreuter was a historian who lived in St. Paul and taught in occasional one-year positions while raising her children. For the first decade of her academic life, Kreuter played the role of "faculty wife," in spite of the fact that she completed her Ph.D. before her husband and did most of the research and writing on their several publications.

In the early seventies, Kreuter decided to assemble some of her women friends at the Minnesota Historical Society. They met regularly through the academic year, 1972–73, and then formed Women Historians of the Midwest (WHOM), a scholarly support group that included public historians, schoolteachers, graduate students, and established faculty members, although the latter were in a clear minority. The group successfully negotiated the grantsmanship procedures of the 1970s and obtained funding to produce three films on women in Minnesota history for the 1976 Bicentennial. They also held several professional conferences during the 1970s and 1980s that attracted scholars of national repute.[75]

Women historians were particularly successful in organizing themselves both regionally and nationally. Probably the most exciting academic conferences of the decade were held by the Berkshire Conference on the History of Women, on a triennial basis. The 1975 conference held at Radcliffe College still lives on in the memory of its many participants. Several thousand women attended—many more than expected—and everyone present experienced an emotional high that is still shared retrospectively.

I had been going to historical conferences for years—they were the *dullest* things. There were very few women and the women who *were* there . . . didn't speak to each other. We were kind of the appendages of the male department chair, or our advisors, or our husbands, or something. The contrast between that kind of a professional meeting and what we experienced at Radcliffe was just immense.[76]

Thus women's studies was not only a new area of study, a consciousness-raising device, and a challenge to the male-dominated universities; it was an intellectual and emotional outpouring of energy and excitement that crossed all the major disciplines and laid the foundation for a major shift.

By the late 1970s, when the academic world was in the doldrums, faculty positions were in short supply, and the sense of expansion that had characterized the sixties was all but dead, there was an enormous excitement among women's studies scholars. The traditional aspects of professional meetings—the job hunt, the sessions and meetings—were often depressing, but there was almost always a "women's group" where a remarkable enthusiasm prevailed. In spite of male resistance, indifference, and sometimes downright hostility, women had entered the academic establishment on their own terms.

In 1977 the National Women's Studies Association (NWSA) was founded for the purpose of facilitating communications and encouraging the development of teaching and research. It was designed to express both professional and feminist values through a complicated structure that allowed equitable representation to every possible constituency. The idea was to counter the tendency toward exclusiveness that was characteristic of many other professional organizations. The success of the first convention and subsequent annual conferences suggests a promising future in terms of organizational strength and professional credibility.[77]

But an inclusive national structure did not necessarily guarantee unity and harmony within the movement. Women's studies is an intellectual microcosm of the women's movement outside of the academy. The very fact of its diversity and its intensity and moral fervor made it susceptible to dissent and conflict. The same issues that divided the women's movement beyond the campus were operating within women's studies, including the possibility of co-optation, the integration of theory and practice, the tensions between academics and activists, the division between cultural feminists and socialist feminists, and the position of blacks and lesbians within the movement.[78]

These problems were particularly critical during the early and middle years of the decade when the movement at times seemed ready to split wide open because of the internal strife. Catharine Stimpson, fearful that the movement would be destroyed from within, wrote an essay in 1973 that analyzed the sources of these quarrels relative to women's acceptance of cultural stereotypes about femininity which made it difficult for them to trust other women in power situations. Adrienne Rich addressed the issue of women's studies' possible co-optation in two important essays that envisioned a university transformed by feminist principles. Women had to learn to use their power constructively to change the male academy.[79]

While the struggle went on in journals and at conferences, it was also a reality on individual campuses where personalities, politics, and sexual preferences created tensions within women's studies programs that already had plenty to contend with in terms of external opposition. The real issue was often simply defining who was a "real feminist." Token women who did not identify with a women's group were sometimes the victims of trashing by militant feminists.[80]

Essentially the same issues, the same complexity and ambiguity, characterized trashing on campuses as it did within the broader movement. By the end of the decade many of the early tensions between academics and activists had eased somewhat, although lesbians and minority women continued to push for their inclusion in the scholarship of women's studies. The thrust of the movement in its second decade appears to be in the direction of mainstreaming. One of the frustrations of feminist scholarship is that, in spite of a decade of research and writing, women's studies has not been accepted by the established male-biased curriculum. Feminist scholarship and course work is available on many campuses, but only on an elective basis. The failure of affirmative action to appreciably increase the number of women on college faculties means that the field of women's studies will see only limited growth in the next decade, unless women scholars' now in graduate school are more fortunate in cracking the male preserves of academia.[81]

Affirmative action and women's studies may have been slow to change men's attitudes, but they *did* have the power to change women's lives, whether as faculty members, administrators, scholars, or students. For the women who were participants in these events, the experience had a permanent impact on their lives, their values, and their stance toward the world.

CHAPTER SEVEN

Making Choices:
The Liberal Dilemma of Work and Family

The debate over women's role that erupted in the 1970s focused in particular on the change in women's employment patterns and its impact on family life. This was a debate with a long history, for as a recent scholar has pointed out, "the presence of women in the labor force has continually inspired controversy, investigation, and reform." Other historians have noted either the tension between women's work and family life or the tendency of these two spheres to overlap and complement each other.[1] Whichever interpretation is emphasized, it is clear that the connection between work and family has been historically more complicated for women than for men. That basic fact remained the reality throughout the decade of the 1970s.

The 1970s witnessed a "subtle revolution" in the work and family patterns of American women. The percentage of women at work rose from 43.3 percent in 1970 to an unprecedented high of 51.2 percent in 1980. For the first time in American history there were more women in the labor force than out of it, and the predictions for the future suggested that by 1990 about 70 percent of all women of working age would be employed or looking for a job. A dramatic drop in women's fertility accompanied this trend. During the baby boom years of 1955–59, the fertility rate had risen to 3.7 births per woman; in the years of 1975–80, it dropped to 1.8 births per woman. These trends underscored the interactive quality of the relationship between women's work and family decisions.[2]

Women of the seventies were faced with more options in their personal and family life than any previous generation of American women. Feminism was only one of a whole range of stimuli that encouraged both women and men to rethink their roles, their relationships with each other, and their work and family life. The 1960s critique of the family and traditional sex roles permitted life-style experimentation among young people coming into adulthood.[3] The symbiotic relationship between the mass media and public opinion created a consumer-oriented environment that exploited the commercial potential of the two-paycheck family and professional upward mobility for both males and females. Finally, public policy during the period from the late 1960s through the mid-seventies tended to encourage women to enter the labor force.

Throughout the 1960s women were already working in larger numbers. Also, by the end of the decade, they were in a state of heightened awareness with respect to the new social significance given to employment outside of the home. Betty Friedan's *Feminine Mystique* had argued convincingly (for well-educated middle-class women, at least) that they could find more than a paycheck in the labor market; they could find fulfillment in the form of a career, and at no significant personal sacrifice. Thus, work was not so much a bread-and-butter issue as a means to self-definition beyond the family.

The majority of American women who were moving into the labor force in the 1970s sought individual solutions to the inevitable tensions in both the private and public spheres of their lives. If their job was indeed a career that paid well and offered a certain psychic satisfaction, then perhaps it was worth it. But given the double burden of home and work that most married women workers bore, it is not surprising that few of them found their jobs to be an attractive alternative to family life. Most of them saw work as only a temporary or occasional source of family income.[4]

The actual facts about women's employment in the early 1970s belied the possibility of economic liberation. In 1973, only 14.5 percent of all employed women were in professional occupations, and over half of those were either teachers or nurses. Clerical workers represented 34.3 percent of the female labor force; blue-collar workers, 16.2 percent; and service workers, 21.6 percent. More than two-fifths of all women workers were concentrated in ten occupations, which included such traditionally female jobs as elementary schoolteacher, secretary, nurse, waitress, domestic service worker, and typist.[5]

Also, most women worked because they had to work. In 1974, 42 percent of the women in the work force were single, widowed, divorced, or separated. Another 16 percent were married to men earning under $7,000 a year. (Median income for four-person families in 1973 was estimated at $13,710). About 29 percent of all working women were married to men earning over $10,000 a year, but even these women were usually working for economic reasons—to attain a higher standard of living for their families, to provide for children's education, or to help support aged parents.[6]

And yet it is clear that an increasing number of middle-income married women were moving into the work force. By 1972, the typical middle-class family had multiple earners, largely because of the wife's employment. This trend can be seen as a step in the direction of the "good life," but like other manifestations of modernization, it had both advantages and disadvantages. The 1970s was a transition period in which both men and women felt the disruptive effects of role change which occurred in the context of a changing socioeconomic climate. The last years of the Vietnam War brought an economic crisis which included two recessions—1969–70 and 1973–75—and the onset of the highest inflation in decades. Concomitantly, an energy crisis had become evident by mid-decade, and this contributed to a sense of "limits to growth" and general economic insecurity.[7]

A changing social climate was reflected in several value-laden demographic shifts, such as the postponement of childbearing by young married couples, fewer children born, and smaller family units. Also, more single, never-married women were choosing to keep and raise their own children, the divorce rate was rising dramatically leaving women on their own, and unmarried couples were living together in arrangements that provided for the long-range security of neither.[8]

Under these conditions of social and economic uncertainty, it was logical and, indeed, necessary to accept the presence of wives and mothers in the work force. This accommodation was affirmed by the state through a number of legislative initiatives, including the Equal Employment Opportunity Act of 1972; the 1972 Amendments to the Equal Pay Act of 1963, to extend occupational coverage; the Women's Educational Equity Act of 1974; Public Law 95–555, 1978, which banned discrimination based on pregnancy; the Tax Reform Act of 1976 and Revenue Act of 1978, which established tax credits for child

care; and Amendments to the Comprehensive Employment and Training Act of 1973, which targeted jobs and training for disadvantaged
women, single parents, and displaced homemakers, and provided funds
for research on flextime and part-time work.[9]

The legal climate of the seventies was also more accommodating to
women. Between 1971 and 1976, the Supreme Court, under Chief Justice Warren Burger, struck down a number of laws that discriminated
against women in the areas of unemployment insurance, maternity
leaves, dependency benefits for military personnel, and Social Security
benefits. In addition, the landmark decision of *Roe* v. *Wade* had a profound impact on women's control over their reproductive lives.[10]

Although the court had an overall positive record, it did not have a
real commitment to sexual equality, nor did it fully understand the
nature of sex discrimination. For instance, some of the decisions that
went against women were based on an uncritical acceptance of weak
rationales and an inability to perceive subtle discrimination. So, although some real gains were made for women that gave them more
control over their lives, in fact, they witnessed only *partial* sexual
equality during this decade. Women were still the victims of a sex class
system in which they were at the bottom and in which many of the
social and economic changes that were occurring placed the greatest
burdens upon those least able to bear them.[11]

Women and children were the ones who were most affected by the
family instability of the 1970s, which included divorce, family violence, teenage pregnancy, and the feminization of poverty. There were
some positive aspects to family life as well—for instance, a genuine
attempt by many couples to attain an egalitarian marriage, a new emphasis on fathering, and more flexibility in family form and structure.
These positive developments were intangible, yet hopeful signs of the
positive impact of feminism on people's personal lives. The negative
signs were more concrete and therefore easier to measure. The evidence
indicates that women were more often the losers when family life went
awry.

The rising divorce rate is a case in point. Throughout the 1950s, the
divorce rate stayed around fifteen per thousand married women aged
fourteen to forty-four. By 1977 the rate had climbed to an unprecedented high of thirty-seven. The number of separations was much
higher, since some couples separate but never divorce, and many other
couples live together out of wedlock and eventually separate. The rise
in the rate of separation and divorce and the increase in the number of

people choosing to postpone or reject marriage altogether combined to leave an increasing percentage of women and men outside the structure of marriage. In 1950, almost 80 percent of American households contained husband wife couples; this figure had dropped to a little more than 60 percent by 1980.[12]

The sharp rise in the divorce rates began around 1960 and rose dramatically during that decade. By 1975 there was almost one divorce for every two marriages: the actual number was over a million, twice as many as in 1966 and three times the number registered in 1950. Most of the marriages that dissolved in the 1970s were not the consequence of "women's liberation," but were, in fact, based upon a traditional understanding of the sex roles, which means that the man was the primary breadwinner and the woman the primary parent. But although roles and earning power were still sex-related, the basis for ending a marriage was changing to the disadvantage of the dependent partner.[13]

A NOW report of September 1970 pointed to the importance of the economic aspects of marriage and divorce, especially in terms of their impact on dependent housewives, who were often ignorant of their lack of economic rights and their precarious financial situation. Under the prevailing system, a housewife could lose her livelihood, her capital, her credit rating, her health and medical benefits, her old age insurance, and her Social Security. She could also suddenly became the sole support of her children.

The property rights laws were crucial to the problem. In forty-two states a woman had the right to receive and acquire property and own it separately from her husband. But the husband had the same right, plus he had much more opportunity to acquire property. Since the married woman had no defined legal interest in her husband's earnings or property, naturally she had none at the time of divorce. Only eight states had community property laws that regarded marriage as a partnership.[14]

Thus, divorce was financially more attractive to men than to women, but another important factor was the liberalization of divorce laws. During the 1960s a person had to have fault-based grounds for divorce, but in January 1970, California became the first state to institute a no-fault divorce law that permitted either party to divorce when "irreconcilable differences caused the breakdown of their marriage." This sweeping reform quickly spread to other states, and by 1981 every state but South Dakota and Illinois had adopted some form of no-fault divorce.[15]

The "California experiment" was intended as a progressive reform that would eliminate sham testimony, restore dignity to the courts, and reduce hostility. In addition, the law was based upon a concept of legal equality that would recognize wives as full equals in the marital partnership. Unfortunately, it overlooked the fact that marriage, as it has been traditionally structured, does not have an equal impact on men and women.[16]

In other words, the liberal reforms that tried to achieve sexual equality in the legal sense of the word failed to anticipate the inequitable impact of a sex-class system that had systematically subordinated women within marriage and provided them with no means of support or security beyond marriage. Barbara Ehrenreich has observed that Americans have arranged their lives around an "informal and highly imperfect pact called the family wage system." The system operated like a vast private welfare system in which men were paid a "family wage" on the expectation that they would share it with their wife and children. The corollary to the idea of a family wage was the idea that women should not earn enough to support anyone, not even themselves. This corollary remained in place during the 1970s, while the rest of the family-wage pact unraveled, leaving women and their children facing a new economic reality.[17]

Basically, liberal feminists were on record in favor of divorce reform, and, indeed, feminism was often seen as the *cause* of the high divorce rate. But most politically involved feminists recognized the dangers of a narrowly defined legal equality within an inequitable socioeconomic system. Although NOW was active in attempting to reform the property, marriage, and divorce laws, the organization opposed the unilateral no-fault divorce statutes, which made it easy for men to legally abandon their families. The tendency of some of the more militant feminists to describe marriage as "legal prostitutions" was in part a reflection of their outrage at women's apparent dispensability—by their husbands and by the courts: "It is this situation which has led to the resentment intelligent, competent and proud women have for being regarded as sex objects to be kept or kept well only so long as they please their husbands."[18]

The availability of divorce in the 1970s certainly made it easier for women to leave bad marriages, but it did not improve their economic relationship vis-à-vis their husband, and, in fact, it was more often men who were initiating divorce. As one scholar has observed, men had been in flight from commitment to marriage and family since the 1950s.

The Practical Application of Radical Feminism: Anti-rape demonstration.

The Gender Factor in Education: Day care center, New York City.

The Liberal Dilemma of Work and Family: Fifth Avenue march.

The Media and Women's Liberation: Image makers Barbara Walters, Jane Fonda (below), Gloria Steinem and Billie Jean King (facing page).

Reformers, Radicals, and Reactionaries: Anti-ERA demonstration at
NOW conference, Houston.

The social climate of the 1970s gave them the permission to do that. "Male self-interest could now be presented as healthy and uplifting; the break from the breadwinner role could be seen as a program of liberal middle-class reform."[19]

American attitudes became increasingly tolerant of the nonmarried state during the 1970s. Whereas in the 1950s, over half of the American public believed that unmarried people were "sick," "immoral," or "neurotic," by 1976, only 33 percent held that view, 51 percent viewed them neutrally, and 15 percent were favorably disposed toward people who remained single. An entire singles industry grew up—bars, spas, vacation clubs, therapy, condominiums—to serve this clientele.[20]

Thus, one of the most striking characteristics of the decade of "women's liberation" was the rise in the number of men living alone—from 3.5 million at the beginning of the decade of 6.8 million at the end. Almost two-thirds of these men were in the never-married category, and 70 percent of them viewed marriage negatively. The number of women living alone also increased, but only half as fast because single women were more likely to be living with children.[21]

It was this combination of factors that contributed to the process that by the late seventies had a name—"feminization of poverty."[22] By March 1977, the number of families headed by women reached 7.7 million, the highest level ever recorded. These families were more likely than husband-wife families to have children under age eighteen and to have very low incomes. In 1976, one out of every three families headed by women was living below the officially defined poverty level, compared with only one of eighteen husband-wife families. They were also more likely to live in central cities, to rent rather than own their own homes, and to reside in public housing.[23]

The popular perception is that the rise in the number of female-headed families in the United States has been due to the high rate of illegitimacy, especially among young black women. But, in fact, marital dissolution is a much more important factor. Only 18 percent of the nearly 10 million female-headed families in the country are headed by an unwed mother: over 50 percent are headed by divorced mothers and the remaining 31 percent by separated mothers. Between 1970 and 1977, divorced women accounted for three-fifths of the total increase in families headed by women.[24]

The connection between divorce and poverty has been made by several recent studies, the most thorough being Lenore Weitzman's *The Divorce Revolution* (1985). Weitzman claims that when income is compared to needs, divorced men experience an average 42 percent rise in their standard of living in the first year after divorce, while divorced women and their children experience a 73 percent decline. The reduction in income often meant residential moves and inferior housing, diminished or nonexistent funds for recreation and leisure, and intense pressures owing to inadequate time and money. Financial hardship caused social dislocation and psychological stress. On a societal level, divorce increased female and child poverty and created a large gap between the well-being of divorced men and that of their former families.[25]

The explanation for this disparity lies primarily in a court system that reflects the values of the broader society and therefore devalues women's contribution to family life. The "equal division" of property sometimes requires that the family home be sold in order to divide the proceeds, which forces the women and her children into an expensive housing market. In addition, the unequal earning capacity of men and women and the unequal focus on the man's career during the years of marriage mean that the divorced woman usually cannot hope to command a comparable wage. Finally, the financial demands placed on the woman's household and the failure of many divorced men to meet their financial obligations contribute further to the disparity in their standards of living.[26]

Divorced women and their children were representative of women's social and economic downward mobility into poverty, often from a seemingly secure position within the middle class. But another factor contributing to the feminization of poverty was the increasing tendency of young unmarried women to conceive and bear children out of wedlock and to keep their babies rather than give them up for adoption. About one-fifth of the increase between 1970 and 1977 in the number of women who were heads of families was among women who had never been married.[27]

This tendency reflected the changing social climate and sexual values that created a much more tolerant attitude toward illegitimacy within society as a whole. It was also due to long-term demographic changes within the black community. One was the movement of blacks from the rural South to the ghettos of the North. The second was the outmigration of the black middle class and working class during the 1960s and 1970s. These two facts, combined with the institutional racism that bore heavily upon those blacks trapped in the ghetto, contributed to a ghetto culture which included a high rate of illegitimacy among very young black women and a lack of familial responsibility on the part of black men.[28]

The ghetto had been the focus of liberal reform during the 1960s. There were several important studies of the black family and black culture, all of them underscoring the impact of racism on blacks as a social group and the need for whites to take collective responsibility. "Liberal intellectuals began to focus on how blacks differed from other immigrant groups—the much greater degree of oppression they had suffered, as this country's only non-voluntary immigrants and only slaves, and the deep psychological scars left by the black experience."[29]

The reformers of the sixties emphasized the concept of community, along with a tolerance and, indeed, encouragement of diverse values. Thus, the ghetto as a valid community was an important theme underlying the War on Poverty and the Community Action Programs of the late 1960s. At the same time that these programs were being initiated, the ghettos were already declining in population. For instance, Woodlawn, Chicago, had a population of about 81,000 residents in the early 1960s; by 1970 it was down to 54,000, and by 1980, 36,000. In the space of a decade, 38 percent of its black residents had moved away. The solution to ghetto poverty, according to early 1980s political wisdom, was *not* to rebuild the ghetto, but rather, to escape from it.[30]

For black women, the intersection of race, gender, and class made such a solution virtually impossible to achieve, apart form the occasional exceptional case. The decade of the seventies, at least in the *collective* experience of black women, was one of entrapment in an environment of poverty that belied the public perception of economic opportunity and affirmative action for black men and all women.

The black women's economic situation in the seventies can be viewed in two ways. One is to see the experience of poverty as quantitatively and qualitatively different for black women than for white women, emphasizing race and class rather than gender. This interpretation is valid in that all the social trends affecting the white female population were greatly intensified for black women. Their divorce rate was higher than that of whites and their remarriage rate was lower. In 1970, 30 percent of black families with children present were headed by women; by 1981 that figure was up to 47.5 percent. The comparable figures for white women were 7.8 percent in 1970 and 14.7 percent in 1981. According to 1980 data more than half of all births to black women were to women who were unmarried—55 percent, up from 38 percent in 1970.[31]

   Black female heads of household were much more likely to be living in poverty than their white counterparts—52.9 percent in 1981, as compared to 27.4 percent for white women who were heads of household. By 1982, two-thirds of all poor black families were headed by women. The impact on young children was devastating: in 1981, 67.7 percent of black children in female-headed households were poor. The comparable rate for white children in female-headed households was 42.8 percent, but these white children were a much smaller proportion of white children as a whole. Nearly one-half of all black children—44.9 percent—were living in poverty, in comparison to only 14.7 percent of white children.[32]

   It is obvious that black women and their families experienced poverty more intensely and more frequently than white women. Race and class were the important factors contributing to this culture of poverty. On the other hand, black women's occupational pattern more nearly corresponded to that of white women than it did to that of black men. Apparently in the area of employment, gender was more important than race. Also, recent studies indicate that wage discrimination is more extensive and costly when based on sex than when based on race. In both of these areas, black women lagged behind white women, but not nearly as far as they were behind black men.[33]

   From 1960 through the 1970s black women workers made significant gains in upgrading their occupational status. Between 1965 and 1978 the percentage of black women in white-collar jobs nearly doubled, from 23.5 percent to 45.5 percent. The percentage in service occupations, including private household jobs, declined by nearly 40 percent, from 54.1 percent to 33.4 percent. (The proportion of white women in service work during those years remained about the same: 19.8 percent to 19.1 percent.)[34]

   This occupational shift was due to the difference between generations entering and leaving the labor force. By 1970, three-fifths of the black women who were household workers were over forty-five years of age, and 72 percent of all household workers resided in the South. Meanwhile, 25 percent of the black women entering the labor force were clerical workers compared with only 3 percent of the retiring black women in that occupation; and 53 percent of the retiring black female workers were private household workers while only 8 percent of the entering black women were moving into that occupation. The percentage of black women who were professional and technical workers went from 7.5 percent in 1960 to 11 percent in 1970.[35]

The decade of the seventies saw further occupational progress for black women. The gain in professional and managerial positions was moderate—from 11.4 percent in 1970 to 15.7 percent in 1979. But there was a substantial increase in clerical and sales work, from 21.4 percent to 31.7 percent; and a sharp decrease in private household workers, from 19.5 percent in 1970 to 8.0 percent in 1979. In nearly every category, black women continued to earn less than white or black men, but by 1977, black women who were employed full time had higher earnings than white women in several important categories—professional and technical workers, and managers and administrators. (Some researchers have attributed this anomaly to the more interrupted work histories of white professional women.) Black clerical workers earned almost exactly the same as white clerical workers, but black women in the work force as a whole in 1977 earned less than white women.[36]

It is clear that the experience of black women in the seventies differed qualitatively and quantitatively from that of white women. Race, gender, and class came together to intensify the impact of family instability and economic disruption. Other more positive trends, such as the civil rights movement and affirmative action, had a positive effect on individual black women, and the changing structure of the economy and black migration to the North affected their overall occupational status. Also, by 1979, on the average, black women had completed nearly as much schooling as white men and women. For black women the median number of years of schooling was 12.0; for black men, 11.7; for white men, 12.5; and for white women, 12.4.[37]

The unique experience of black women, historically as well as in the seventies, led to a profound distrust of feminism, as noted in chapter 4. Black women were more likely than white women to value family more than work and were more likely to view racial oppression as a more serious problem than sexual oppression. This attitude, along with the tendency of white feminists to marginalize the black women's experience or to generalize and universalize the experience of all women, created a divisiveness between black and white women in the seventies. White feminists emphasized the similarities in women's experience, whereas black women emphasized the uniqueness of their own experience.

During the early 1970s, when the reform initiated by the civil rights movement seemed to promise a new tomorrow and the concept of community was in its heyday, there were several studies done on black communities that stressed the strength of the black family, particularly its women, and the uniqueness and adaptability of black culture.[38] Although this has remained a constant theme in the writings of black women throughout the 1970s and 1980s, by the end of the decade black feminists were beginning to take issue among themselves with the idea that racism was the primary oppression that black women had to confront. Barbara Smith, scholar, activist, and feminist, became involved in building a black feminist movement in 1973, and in 1974 she was a founding member of the Combahee River Collective, a black feminist organization in Boston. A political statement drafted in 1977 articulated the collective's commitment to the multiissue approach to analyzing oppression. "As black women we see black feminism as the logical political movement to combat the manifold and simultaneous oppressions that all women of color face."[39]

Black male–black female relationships had been the topic of several black writers for a number of decades, but by the late seventies, it had become the focus of books, magazine articles, academic journal articles, public forums, radio programs, television shows, and everyday conversation. Black women were beginning to analyze openly their relations with black men, and the connections between racism and sexism in their own lives. Then, during the 1976–77 theater season, a brilliant work by a black woman playwright made its debut on Broadway. Ntozake Shange's *For Colored Girls Who Have Considered Suicide/When the Rainbow Is Enuf*, set out to "sing a black girl's song" through the use of twenty-odd poems, or playlets, which form a single statement, a choreopoem. Shange's work is an ironic, bitter, humorous, and brutal look at the black woman's experience. It dwells on the sexism of black men as well as on the racism of whites.[40]

Shange's play, along with Michelle Wallace's *Black Macho and the Myth of the Superwoman* (1979), exposed a crack in the concept of racial solidarity, and led to public recognition on the part of black feminists that sexism was an issue. Wallace's book stirred up a tremendous negative reaction from many black women (see chapter 4), but there were those who acknowledged the brutality of their existence within black communities, and their reluctance or inability to rely upon the black men in their lives. Although the instability of lower-class black family life could still be attributed to racism, some black feminists were willing to see the similarities between their own lives and those of white women on certain issues.[41]

Both black and white women were victims of family violence during the 1970s. Like many other issues that were raised by the women's movement, the question of domestic violence against women could be interpreted as an individual problem or a social construct. In either case, the first barrier to be surmounted in confronting the problem was "the trap of silence," which was perhaps even more stultifying for minority women than for white women. A black woman working in a community social agency revealed her feelings of confusion as she began to understand the extent of the violence directed against women within the community: "Fear of being cast out of the community silenced me in the beginning. Loyalty and devotion are enormous barriers to overcome. . . . Disclosure is so easily confused with treason."[42]

Black women, like whites, began to break the silence with respect to domestic violence. One group, calling itself Battered Minority Women (BMW), defined battering as the "systematic deprivation inflicted upon third world men by society which, in turn, is inflicted upon third world women." That is, women were beaten because black men were deprived, and the solution was for women to involve themselves in the struggle for racial justice. Responsibility lay with white society, then, not black men. Members of BMW did not consider themselves feminists, and they did not see the need to be part of the larger women's movement. Although they provided temporary refuge for battered women, they were proud of their high rate of return to the home.[43]

Not all black women agreed with this analysis. To one writer, it seemed to reinforce the theory of the black matriarch—"the strong black women willing and able to accept beating in support of her man." Also, although black men undoubtedly had to endure deprivation because of racism, were they any more oppressed than black women? And who was responsible for this oppression—the "black matriarch" who could find a job when her man could not? The debate over relative oppression was senseless, according to this writer, and it was time for black women to confront the issue of violence against women and work within the system to find justice. Freedom from racism could not be accomplished at the physical and psychological expense of black women. "We have paid our dues, and black men must be held responsible for every injury they cause."[44]

There was another weakness with the analysis of BMW: it overlooked the fact that white men also engaged in wife battering, and that domestic violence was an issue that cut across class and racial lines. One of the important contributions of the women's movement of the seventies was that it made this fact public and offered an interpretation within a political context.[45]

The issue of domestic violence undercut the ideal view of family life as the source of comfort and nurturance for its members. Although a certain amount of violence within the family has always been considered acceptable, the point at which it crosses the line and becomes pathological has never been defined. In its attempt to deal with the dilemma presented by tension between private family life and the public good, society has tended to deny the very existence of violence or to see it as a matter of personal deviancy. Sometimes the woman is defined as the deviant one—perhaps she was "asking for it" by not being appropriately submissive. Since wife abuse has always been viewed as a private matter, women who were victims had little support from the police, the social service agencies, or even their families until the decade of the seventies. Even in the seventies, although there was a growing awareness of the problem, many women could find no escape from the brutality of their daily lives except through extreme measures of retaliation.

On the evening of 9 March 1977, Francine Hughes set fire to the gasoline-soaked bedroom where her husband slept. She then drove to the police station with her three young children and screamed, "I did it! I did it!" A week later the case of *The People* v. *Francine Hughes* began to move through the legal process that would culminate in her trial. Hughes was arraigned on a first degree murder charge. When her lawyer requested bail, circuit judge Michael Harrison denied the request: "After all, what kind of woman would burn up her husband?" This was the question her lawyer, Aryon Greydanus, had to answer through the course of the trial—"and show that it might be any woman trapped in the situation Francine Hughes had described when he talked to her at the jail."[46]

Francine Hughes's story, told first to her lawyer and later to writer Faith McNulty, and eventually made into a television movie, recounted a history of senseless brutality that she suffered for more than a decade from November 1963 when she married Mickey Hughes until she killed him in 1977. Perhaps the most shocking part of her experience was not the behavior of her husband but the inability or unwillingness of anyone to help her, including her family, her in-laws, and the civil and social service agencies where she sought help. She went to law enforcement agencies, to social workers, to lawyers, to a judge, to Al-

Anon. Everywhere she was turned away and told to go home or to leave her husband. But no one could offer her help or protection. She tried to run away several times, but Mickey always found her. She finally divorced him, but he refused to leave the house.

Francine Hughes's experience was a classic example of chronic marital violence. A decade earlier it would have received little attention, but the climate of the seventies provided an attentive and even sympathetic audience. By the time that Francine came to trial her case had become a cause célèbre. On 4 November 1977, she was acquitted of the murder charge: not guilty, by reason of temporary insanity.[47]

The brutality suffered by Francine at the hands of her husband was not particularly unusual. Rather, it reflected the values of a culture in which male violence was not only accepted, but admired. The only thing new about wife-beating in the 1970s was that it was finally recognized as a social problem. Suddenly feminist lawyers, therapists, and women's crisis and antirape workers were reporting hundreds of calls and visits from abused women in need of housing and legal assistance. Certainly the feminist movement itself gave a political context and permission for battered women to speak out and ask for help. By the mid-seventies the formation of shelters and larger informal feminist networks provided the setting for a national battered women's movement.[48]

At first there was no reliable data on the extent of wife abuse, not even within police departments, where it was trivialized and viewed as a nuisance or primarily as a danger to police officers. In 1974 Richard J. Gelles published *The Violent Home*, a study based on research among families in which social workers suspected violence. Not surprisingly in that particular sample 55 percent of the husbands admitted hitting their wives. In a more representative group with no known history of violence, one in eight wives had been beaten. Gelles estimated that there were about 6 million abused wives in the United States.[49]

Other studies, reports and estimates began to surface speculating on the extent and severity of this social issue. A study published at the end of the decade estimated that one-third to one-half of all women who lived with male companions experienced degradation in the form of brutality or threatened brutality, and about 41 percent of all women killed in the United States were killed by their husbands. Wife abuse had reached the stage of a national epidemic.[50]

In 1978 the National Coalition Against Domestic Violence (NCADV) was set up to encourage communities to accept responsibility for the problems of women abuse, and to help women to empower themselves. The coalition had a national office in Washington, D.C., where it supported the work of its voting members—approximately 150 independent, community-based organizations serving battered women in a variety of ways. The basic philosophy underlying NCADV was that woman abuse was a social problem rather than an individual problem, and that it could be eradicated only through widespread social change.[51]

The abuse sustained by women and children was often sexual, and throughout the seventies, feminists made the connection between wife battering, child abuse, incest, and rape as well as the more public forms of exploitation, such as sexual harassment and pornography. In 1970, Susan Griffin's essay "The Politics of Rape" defined rape as a political issue and linked it to man's power within the family as well as in the broader society. Adrienne Rich, in an essay written in 1977, argued that familial relations are patriarchally controlled, and the mother-child relationship is the first to be violated by patriarchy.[52]

Even those who did not write from a feminist perspective were apt to see powerful societal forces putting pressure on family members and destroying inner security. One study argued that the glorification of violence in film, television, and books contributed to a "cult of violence." There is an acceptance of violence in our everyday life in the news stories and on the television screens to the point of desensitization. It has become harder and harder to shock people with stories of violence and horror. And yet this "cult of violence" does not cause violence within the family, according to the authors. It only feeds it. Family violence is a symptom of people's unsuccessful struggle with the pressures of a technologically complex society: "Ironically, coping with such pressures by rechanneling them through violence in the home may ultimately squelch our chances for survival at all, for no society of any consequence can survive if its family institution crumbles from within."[53]

This dire prediction of the future of the family was mirrored in the apocalyptic messages of the New Right and the Moral Majority that began to contribute to the debate over the family by the late seventies. But most of the popular and semischolarly literature of the decade offered a wider range of possibilities with respect to both diagnosis and cure. There was even a recognition of new strengths in the family life, such as flexibility, diversity, and openness between the sexes and between parents and children. Some of these interpretations, especially those written by feminists, called for far-reaching changes. Others already saw the changes taking placed.[54]

Radical feminists like Susan Griffin or Adrienne Rich predicted or called for changes that involved a cultural revolution, which appeared possible because of a new consciousness.[55] But few American women of the seventies saw the changes in sexual relationships in such radical terms. Yet there was certainly a heightened sense of consciousness about personal relationships, as well as the changing nature of power within the family and on the job. Bookstores abounded with the latest advice on a fascinating range of possibilities—relationships with parents, siblings, lovers, spouse, children, or friends. Everything and everyone was in flux, but not necessarily for the worse. The emphasis was on adaptability and taking control of one's life.

The classic book to open the seventies and focus on this element of change and adaptability was Alvin Toffler's *Future Shock* (1970). Toffler's book was attention grabbing, indeed, shocking to some; his timing was superb, for his message spoke to the remnants of the sixties counterculture who were moving into the "me generation" fast-track lifestyle of the seventies. Essentially, his point was that "unless man quickly learns to control the rate of change in his personal affairs as well as in society at large, we are doomed to a massive adaptational breakdown."[56]

Toffler was apparently unaware of the women's movement. But some of his insights about family life seemed to reflect women's changing roles. For instance, he predicted the end of the mystique of motherhood under the influence of new birth technology. He projected a whole series of interesting possibilities for the future family—streamlined families, parenthood after retirement, professional parenting, communes, and "homosexual daddies." (He was reticent about the possibility of "homosexual mommies.") Toffler was suggesting diversity, choices, options—words that forecast accurately the tone of personal life in the seventies. He explained that the "odds against love" in a rapidly changing society where people were constantly being forced to adapt and grow separately and at a different pace than their spouse were overwhelming. The sensible strategy to adopt was that of "temporary marriage": "Rather than opting for some offbeat variety of the family, they marry conventionally, they attempt to make it "work" and then, when the paths of the partners diverge beyond an acceptable point, they divorce or depart."[57]

Toffler pointed out matter-of-factly that most participants in temporary marriages go on to search for a partner who more nearly matches their own developmental stage. He had no awareness of the inequitable impact of marriage on the respective partners. But he had the perfect formula for the "flight from commitment" described by Barbara Ehrenreich, and for what was to become the singles culture of the seventies.

Another widely-discussed early-seventies advice book—one for couples who wanted the conventionality of marriage and the freedom of being single—was the O'Neills' *Open Marriage* (1972). Nena and George O'Neill, themselves partners in such a marriage, argued persuasively for a marriage based upon a new openness to oneself, to another, and to the world. Open marriage was "expanded monogamy." It would retain the fulfilling aspects of an intimate in-depth relationship but eliminate the restrictions of monogamy. The O'Neills' description of open marriage, although it involved commitment and a certain togetherness, once again seemed well suited to the upwardly mobile professional couple each of whom received an identity and purpose outside the home as more-or-less economic equals, and who shared a comfortable, even luxurious, life-style.[58]

The problems with these modern solutions to the confinements and restriction of family life was that on the individual level, they deemphasized personal responsibility, and on the societal level, they did not take into account important elements of the population—small children, middle-aged dependent housewives, black women and children in the ghetto, and most of the working class and lower middle class, regardless of race, age, or gender. Open marriage was the glamorous side of the seventies. Ironically, it was picked up by neoconservatives as representative of women's liberation.

But the concept of an open marriage was symbolic of a new freedom in defining relationships that did have a positive effect for many people. The tolerance for nonmarital liaisons, greater sexual openness, and new family forms, meant that many individuals who either by choice or necessity could not be part of a traditional family setting had other options. The 1980 census revealed that more than 3 million U.S. households were composed of unrelated people living together. According to the *New York Times*, what these unmarried couples, same-sex roommates, and elderly companions sought was not just cost sharing but a semblance of family and a sense of coming home.[59]

Families were changing not only with respect to form and permanency but also with respect to family roles. Housework and parenting, two areas of domestic life traditionally given over to women, became arenas of contention during the seventies, as more women struggled with the dual roles of work and family, and feminist ideas began to seep into the public consciousness. Feminists attacked the inequities of women's domestic role very early in the women's movement, but it was not until the mid-seventies that it became an important issue for certain liberated couples and the media. By the end of the decade, although a lot of light had been cast on the subject, the illumination was still very dim. Most women, even those working full time, were still responsible for the household and were still the primary parent.

Pat Mainardi's essay "The Politics of Housework," published in 1970, was the first political analysis of what many men and women saw as a trivial issue but what feminists were beginning to recognize as part of women's oppression. Letty Cottin Pogrebin has commented on the trivialization of housework, which is supposed to come naturally to women but is a joke when men clumsily perform it. But while housework was trivialized, polls and studies of the 1970s showed that it was a major source of conflict between parents and children, and the primary cause of domestic violence: "Conflicts related to cooking, cleaning, and home repairs more often lead to physical abuse between spouses then do conflicts about sex, social activities, money, or children."[60]

Time budget studies done in the 1970s indicated that for the first time in fifty years the average number of hours spent doing housework had declined. This was true not only for employed women but for full-time housewives as well. Most contemporary household hints in women's magazines and household manuals were meant to save time, whereas in earlier decades they tended to enlarge the job. Between the mid-sixties and the mid-seventies, the amount of time spent on housework declined from forty-four hours to thirty hours a week for full-time housewives, and from twenty-six hours to twenty-one hours a week for employed women.[61]

Explanations for this decline are several: a shift in priorities, a lowering of standards, and a more efficient use of household time. To some extent, the emerging philosophy that housework is everyone's responsibility made a difference, but the difference was small. The survey mentioned above reported that men increased the time they spent on domestic chores from nine hours a week in 1965 to ten hours in 1975. Women had done 80 percent of the housework in 1965, and were still doing 75 percent of it in 1975.[62]

And yet there were indications of a shift of attitude among men—even if it did not exactly result in the creation of happy little house-husbands. A mid-eighties study concluded that the majority of men were far more psychologically involved in their families than their jobs, even though men performed relatively little housework and child care compared to women. Only a small percentage of men had greater work than family involvement, and they were overrepresented among the more educated and occupationally successful. Also, a number of studies in the late seventies indicated that both parents were spending more time with children than they had earlier in the century, and that men were taking on an increasing share of the total family work—from about 20 percent in the 1960s to 30 percent by the early 1980s.[63]

But the question remained: why did husbands continue to do much less than their wives within the family, even when the wife was employed? A number of factors might be cited, including involvement in the work role, modeling after one's father, social attitudes, lack of support from wives or peers, and lack of specific skills. But even if the variance in men's family work time could be explained through a combination of social factors, a deeper question remained—was it that men simply did not want to participate? In other words, were the explanatory factors simply used by men to reinforce their aversion to family work? As one observer put it, "At a deeper level, the question really being asked is whether men are or are not morally responsible for their low family participation. Does this low participation occur because of factors which men are really not responsible for, or do men bear an ultimate responsibility for it?"[64]

The question was never satisfactorily resolved during the 1970s, but the men's liberation movement has as its underlying theme the need to reassess masculine prerogatives that were victimizing men as well as women. Theoretically, it promoted a kind of psychological transformation in which men would shed their burdensome masculine traits and find their authentic self. Part of this transformation encouraged the "flight from commitment" as well as the openness about male homosexuality.[65]

Another part of the transformation was a new emphasis on fathering. In 1974, *Ms.* magazine ran a special issue in which articles on working fathers, the father's role in childbirth, and the "fathering instinct" predominated. Actor Donald Sutherland was the subject of an article accompanied by photos of himself and his wife (particularly himself) during the birth of his child. Other less illustrious fathers testified to the importance of their fathering role.[66] The romance of fathering was perhaps most sympathetically portrayed in the Academy Award–winning film at the end of the decade *Kramer vs. Kramer*, starring Dustin Hoffman. The popularity of this film underscored the belief that fathers are unfairly denied custody in favor of irresponsible mothers by traditional judges. In fact, during the seventies it became apparent that if men actually *wanted* child custody, they had a very good chance of getting it. A California study done in 1977 found that 63 percent of all fathers who requested custody were successful. This figure compared to 35 percent in 1968 and 37 percent in 1972. "The power to decide child custody often lies with the father, not the mother. If he wishes to exercise that power, he is likely to win."[67]

Nonetheless, very few men actually took advantage of this possibility during the 1970s, and in fact, the number of men raising children on their own actually declined during the decade. Although men often expressed interest in custody, very few followed through and requested it during the divorce proceedings. Yet the new standard of the "best interests of the child," which began to prevail in the courtroom, meant that the mother could no longer assume automatic custody. Moreover, "beneath the surface of the statistically infrequent paternal custody awards is a bargaining climate in which women who are scared or threatened may feel compelled to give up or compromise their financial interests in order to retain custody."[68]

The self-consciousness about fathering naturally extended to mothering as well. Several notable feminists took a serious look at motherhood and its impact on women and children, and on gender relations. Dorothy Dinnerstein, in the *The Mermaid and the Minotaur* (1976), spelled out the consequences of the predominant female presence in infancy and early childhood and argued strongly for shared early parenthood. According to Dinnerstein, the current "sexual arrangements"—the division of responsibility between males and females, and the psychological interdependence implicit in that division—maintained a "human malaise" that badly needed to be changed. Although society's male-female arrangements provided some pleasure and comfort, they also were a major source of human pain, fear, and hate, and a sense of deep strain between women and men.[69]

Dinnerstein defined the problem in psychological rather than social terms. Similarly, Nancy Chodorow, in *The Reproduction of Mothering* (1978), argued that biology and role socialization were insufficient explanations for women's mothering role. Rather, she used a psychoanalytic object-relations theory to explain the reproduction of sex, gender, and family organization. "The structure of the family and family practices create certain differential relational needs and capacities in men and women that contribute to the reproduction of women as mothers."[70]

The complexity of these feminist interpretations of mothering belied the ease with which the mass media transformed women's work and family roles. Letty Pogrebin pointed out in a 1978 *Ms.* article that every woman was supposed to want Everything, and Everything meant the three-ball juggling act: job, marriage, children:

> First, personal success. Become established in a career. Maybe 10 years later when you are self-confident and accomplished (these instructions rarely admit women's real problems in the job market), then get married. Add children to the scenario after there's enough money for live-in help, and before the biological clock strikes midnight.
> Voila! You've got it *all*.[71]

It was the "superwoman" image that reigned in the seventies, and ironically, it was attributed to the feminist movement, perhaps because of the pervasive influence of Friedan's cure for the "problem that has no name." In fact, the liberal feminist solution—the balancing of career and family—was not the answer to the women's question, except in a very few individual cases. It was certainly not an answer to the basic inequities in the labor market and in family life that continued to affect marriage, divorce, child support and custody, housework, parenting, and interpersonal relations during the 1970s. The semblance of equality that was struggling to emerge did not address the need for a major restructuring of values and attitudes of both men and women. Instead, the juggling act remained gender-specific, and the burden of change was almost entirely upon women.

The feminist critique of the 1970s went far beyond the superwoman image, in spite of the limited perception of the public and the media. It was the media and its focus on liberal feminism, equating liberation with the combination of motherhood and career, that gave feminism its antifamily image. In fact, the second wave of feminism, unlike the first, which had focused on suffrage, was very much concerned with the family. By making the connection between the political and the personal, the home and broader structure of society, it politicized the family issues of child care, housework, wife abuse, divorce, and abortion, and sexuality.[72] In doing so, it provided grist for the emerging New Right, which attacked feminism of all kinds, but this attack was to some extent based on a false impression of feminism created by the media's focus on the sensational and, in particular, on those who had made it to the top.

CHAPTER EIGHT

"You've Come a Long Way, Baby": The Media and Women's Liberation

The seventies was the decade of Watergate, the energy crisis, and the jogging and health food craze. It was also the decade of women who made it—in sports, politics, television, and film. Whether it was feminism, individualism, or media hype, a lot of women became household words during the decade, and the Virginia Slims slogan reflected the perception of many Americans who watched, sometimes uneasily or with real hostility, but occasionally with pride and satisfaction, as women made headlines.

One of the headlines of the decade occurred on 20 September 1973, when Billie Jean King, the most sensational player in women's tennis, stepped on the court of the Houston Astrodome to face Bobby Riggs in what was widely touted as the "match of the century" and the "battle of the sexes." Riggs was a fifty-five-year-old ball-control artist, a former tennis great who had won Wimbledon in 1939 and Forest Hills in 1939 and 1941. He was also a hustler and a compulsive gambler who usually had a gimmick. In 1973 his gimmick was women's liberation. King was a hard-working, dedicated tennis star who had determinedly fought her way to the top of the women's circuit and was one of the first women players to go pro. She had just come off of two successive $100,000 seasons—in 1971 and 1972—and had been named *Sports Illustrated* first-ever Sportswoman of the Year. King was also in the forefront of women's fight for equality in the world of tennis.[1]

Both of these personalities had great public appeal which lent itself well to the kind of media buildup that followed the announcement of their match on 11 July. The match itself, as well as all the hoopla that accompanied it, reflected the impact of the media on American society and its ability to create and foster eccentric and colorful personalities, as well as broader developments, such as the women's movement and the mass consumption of sporting events.

The relationship between sports and the media can be traced back to the 1920s when radio broadcasting played a major role in the development of the first Golden Age of sports. But the most spectacular rise of sports occurred during the post–World War II era. In particular, between 1960 and 1970 the impact of television revolutionized sports as a form of mass entertainment. Thus, on Super Sunday, 12 January 1969, more than 60 million Americans arranged themselves in front of their television screens. These "super spectators" were the product and, in part, the creators of the new culture of the mass spectator sport.[2]

Sports became big business in the 1960s and 1970s as it had never been in earlier decades, primarily because of the influence of television. It cost up to $135,000 a minute to advertise on television the day of the 1969 Superbowl. Network payments for major league baseball went from $3.25 million to $16.6 million in a decade; the combined AFL–NFL schedule was worth $7.6 million in 1963 and went up to $34.7 million in 1969.[3]

The close symbiotic relationship between the media and the world of sports had, by the 1970s, affected how, when, and where the game was played, who played, and how much they were paid. The media created an aura of excitement around athletic events that encouraged the proliferation of teams, leagues, and super stars. The events could not have occurred without the athletes themselves, but there would have been far fewer teams, fewer events, and fewer high-paid stars without the media to create the audience and to generate the capital to pay the higher salaries and pensions that modern athletes were beginning to demand.[4]

Tennis did not have the mass appeal of the big-money sports, but by the late sixties it was going through its own kind of revolution, moving from being an "all-white, country club sport, steeped in the traditions of affluent amateurs" into the professional arena of promoters, agents, and demands for higher compensation and professional status. In the fall of 1967, the British Lawn Tennis Association voted in favor of open tennis—that is, the acceptance of both professional and amateur players in tournaments. The 1968 Wimbledon championship was the first open Wimbledon in history. It was won by two newly turned professionals— Rod Laver and Billie Jean King, who took her third straight title that year.[5]

By 1970 professional tennis was established, the prize money was flowing, and fans and promoters were becoming an important part of the game. But Billie Jean King noticed very early that women were losing status, money, and playing time. The disparity in prize money was at ratios of 3:1, 4:1, 5:1—sometimes even more. For instance, when King won the Italian Nationals in 1970, the prize was $600. The men singles winner got $3,500. Also, the number of tournaments for women was being cut back on the assumption that the fans preferred to see the men.[6]

The situation came to a head at Forest Hills in September 1970, when several top women players started to talk about boycotting the last two tournaments of the season. Temporarily suspended from the USLTA, they participated instead in the first Virginia Slims circuit tournament, which was held in San Francisco the first week in January 1971. The Virginia Slims circuit was sponsored by Philip Morris through Virginia Slims cigarettes. It was originally intended to be an eight-tournament women's professional tennis circuit, but it grew to fourteen tournaments played over three and a half months in early 1971. As the tour expanded and the prize money increased, more and more women became interested. But it was risky taking a stand against the sanctioned tennis leagues. The real ringleaders were Billie Jean King, Frankie Durr, Ann Jones, and Rosie Casals. King recognized that if women's tennis was to survive, it needed publicity, and her strategy was to get as much media coverage as possible. "In every city we'd hit the media—hard. We'd go to every newspaper and radio and television station in town, and once we got to them, our press was fantastic.[7]

The tour exacted a high price from King and the other players, emotionally and physically. It combined a transient life-style and the pressure of public relations with a demanding playing schedule. Over the long run, the goal was the establishment of a permanent tour, better prize money for women players, and recognition of the importance of their contributions to the game. But problems remained. Women were not given equal prize money, nor did they receive equal coverage from the media, or equal endorsement opportunities. Billie Jean King became the leading spokeswoman on these issues. In 1973 she began a new magazine, *womenSports*, to close the communication gap and give women athletes some visibility. And she continued to be outspoken about women's lack of equality in tennis.[8]

It was at this point that Bobby Riggs, self-appointed male chauvinist, entered the picture and turned the demand for equal rights in the sporting world into a media circus. He challenged King to a match, goading her to prove that women's tennis was as good as men's, and that women deserved equal pay: "You insist that top women players provide a brand of tennis comparable to men's. I challenge you to prove it. I contend that you not only cannot beat a top male player, but that you can't beat me, a tired old man."[9]

Billie Jean refused the challenge the first time around, and Margaret Court, the powerful Australian ace, picked it up. The Court-Riggs match was held on Mother's Day, 1973, and Court went down to a humiliating defeat, 6–2, 6–1, after succumbing to Bobby's psychological warfare. King felt that she had no choice but to avenge the loss. That is why, on 20 September she happened to be playing in the "match of the century"—which she herself described as one of the most important matches of her career. In the first stage of that career she had struggled to become number 1 woman tennis player in the world. The match with Riggs was the culmination of the second stage—the fight for equality for women tennis players.[10]

King won the three-set match easily, 6–4, 6–3, 6–3, but it was a tough match for her, mentally and physically, primarily because she took it very seriously, trained very hard, and placed a great deal of significance on the outcome. Her view was that it proved two things: that a woman *can* beat a man and that tennis could be a big-time sport— and that it would be once it got into the hands of people who knew how to promote it. King and her husband, Larry King, were to move actively into this field over the next several years.[11]

The match with Riggs also underscored the power of the media to create a sensation and the ability of an individual, in this case, Bobby Riggs, to use the media to hustle the attention of the nation. The publicity surrounding Riggs and, to some extent, King in the weeks before the match equaled the anticipation of a championship fight or a Superbowl football game. The event itself resembled the excitement of a circus: balloons, bands, noise, and a near-capacity crowd at the Astrodome. Millions of Americans watched the spectacle on television, as

Riggs presented King with a giant Super Daddy and King presented Riggs with a genuine Male Chauvinist Piglet. The betting was heavy—the Las Vegas odds were 5 to 2, Riggs.[12]

King beat the odds—rather easily, in fact, when it came to playing the actual match. She won because she was an excellent tennis player and a dedicated and hard-working athlete. The kind of success that King was experiencing by the late sixties and early seventies was the culmination of years of concentrated hard work and determination. She was on top of her game and on top of the women's tennis circuit. She had financial success and national recognition. In effect, she became the actualization of the Virginia Slims slogan, "You've come a long way, baby."

Since King did not smoke and did not approve of smoking, she had been uncomfortable with the idea of a major cigarette company sponsoring a women's athletic event. But she was a pragmatist who was able to live with her misgivings: "Without Virginia Slims and the money and encouragement they've poured into the women's game, we'd be nowhere. We'd be at the mercy of the male officials as we always have been. . . . You give a little to accomplish something big."[13]

Another problem with the sponsor was that the "You've come a long way, baby" slogan trivialized the meaning and the impact of women's liberation. The ad played on the image of women's progress by turning the clock back to an earlier and apparently more amusing era when women's secretive attempts to indulge in smoking subjected them to the wrath of irate husbands. The freedom to smoke cigarettes in the seventies was clearly equated with the liberation of women. Furthermore, although the slogan made some sense relative to the life and accomplishments of a Billie Jean King, when applied to the women's movement as a whole and the economic and social position of many American women during the seventies, it missed the mark, overstated the extent of advance, and understated the goals of the movement.

In effect, the media as a whole, whether through television, mass-market magazines, movies, fiction, or advertising, picked up the new ideas of the women's movement, but trivialized and debased them. In commenting on a *Playboy* interview entitled "The Liberation of a Congressional Wife," one feminist critic pointed out that liberation had become a fast fix: "The fact that real change requires struggle, fortitude, moral courage, and time is overlooked. Instead, serious subjects are treated frivolously and frivolous subjects are presented as if they were serious. Words that describe change and struggle were applied to actions no more profound than the painting of a toenail."[14]

It was this trivialization of feminism that gave people a skewed vision of what was happening. The general public had no reliable way to evaluate the changes women were undergoing or the notion of success that was being promoted at any given time. The media could create superstars overnight and just as quickly destroy them through benign neglect. Whether it was the fault of a fickle public or the crass media, individuals found it hard to stay on top in a decade of superstardom.

One small, but significant group of women who made it to the top by virtue of their marriage to powerful men were the first ladies of the seventies—the women who were cast into a rigidly defined role that exemplified an American ideal of womanhood that remained surprisingly constant, even in this decade of change. The public treatment of first ladies revealed its expectations of women, but it also revealed what was really admired, even when expectations were disappointed. Beauty, glamour, wealth, and material possessions were attributes that attracted the most attention, and the woman who possessed all of these was actually a former first lady, Jacqueline Bouvier Kennedy Onassis.

Onassis owed her fame and high regard to the sixties—the era of "Camelot" when she and her husband, John F. Kennedy, had reigned as a unique American form of monarchy. After the assassination of her husband, Jacqueline Kennedy continued to represent what once had been. She lived a life of quiet dignity, devoted to her children and insisting on privacy. Then, on 18 October 1968, barely four months after the assassination of her brother-in-law, Robert Kennedy, she announced that she was going to marry Aristotle Onassis, the Greek shipowner and multimillionaire, a man twenty-nine years her senior. Onassis had an unsavory reputation, and his background and values gave him an image totally unlike the late John F. Kennedy. The marriage was widely regarded as an incredible disaster.[15]

The former first lady's image was badly tarnished by her marriage to Onassis, and her material extravagance over the next several years contributed to her fall from favor, although certainly not from public view. "Jackie watching" became a favorite pastime of the press, and Jackie Onassis received at least as much attention as the several incumbent first ladies throughout most of the decade. But press coverage and public reaction was no longer idolatrous. It was pervaded with cyni-

cism, and indeed negativism, about Jackie's life-style. At the same time
it reflected an envious admiration. Jackie Onassis was the perfect symbol of the seventies "me-generation" in contrast to the buoyancy and
idealism of the early sixties. She had changed with the times—in fact,
a step ahead of the times.

It is hard to imagine an American heroine who more directly negated
the feminist vision of the 1970s. The women's movement basically ignored Onassis, and she never showed any inclination to involve herself
in or take a stand on a feminist or political issue. After the death of her
second husband in 1975, she tried to establish a sense of autonomy by
taking a job with Viking Press for a $10,000-a-year salary. Her efforts
were not received too sympathetically by most feminists who felt that
her salary—which she obviously did not need anyway—had the effect
of holding down women's wages, and that she should use her great
public and political influence in support of women's issues.[16]

In 1977, Onassis left Viking Press for Doubleday in protest of a Kennedy exploitation book the press intended to publish. In October 1977,
Boston Globe columnist, Ellen Goodman, wrote a sympathetic portrayal
of Jackie's dilemma as a single, forty-eight-year-old women whose children were grown and whose limitations were almost as impressive as
her freedoms. She still had to answer that universal question: "What
do you do with the rest of your life."[17]

At some point each of the first ladies of the 1970s was faced with
that question. They all seemed to be products of the "Cinderella complex" of the mid-twentieth century, and they had all achieved power
and adulation in that role. But they also had to face a similarly abrupt
departure from the White House. Pat Nixon, Betty Ford, and Rosalynn Carter could not compete with Jacqueline Kennedy in terms of
glamor or fame, and yet, like her, they were the focus of media attention which portrayed them in superficial and often unfair ways.[18]

The Onassis legend provided a kind of counterpoint to the feminist
movement, but it was not high tragedy. Pat Nixon's story came closer
to claiming that dubious distinction. Perhaps no first lady has ever
matched the pathos of Pat Nixon's ordeal, but the press played to it,
even in the years before Watergate. This dutiful wife, devoted mother,
and ideal homemaker was more often an object of pity, or even contempt, than admiration. She was called Perfect Pat, Political Pat, and
Plastic Pat, but she was also "a good sport" and "unsinkable," especially
after Watergate. She always adjusted; she never complained; she never
criticized her husband (at least not in public); and above all, she exer-

cised self-control. But the public viewed her with neither warmth nor interest. She purposely kept a low profile while in the White House, and the press accordingly gave her less attention than her predecessors or successors, except during the election year of 1972, when she was active in the campaign.[19]

Pat Nixon played what was perhaps the hardest role of any woman (in the public eye, at least) of the 1970s. In the face of incredible adversity and general public contempt, she was destined to stand by her man and support him openly and uncritically. Pat Nixon could adjust, but she could not change. She remained constant to her rigid values of devotion and loyalty, and in that sense, it could be said that she remained true to herself. But she really had no choice. And in the tremendous outpouring of publicity surrounding Watergate—much of it encouraged or sustained by the main actors themselves—Pat Nixon was little more than a pathetic footnote to a drama of tragic and historical import.[20]

The public image and the consequential attention that Pat Nixon received came to her almost entirely through the office of her husband—much more so than was true of other recent first ladies, who at least created a distinct style of their own. But in the climate of the early women's movement, she served primarily as a negative or passive example of women's changing roles. The tragedy of Watergate intensified her reclusiveness in the last year of the presidency, as well as her resentment of the public role that had been thrust upon her.[21]

The trauma of Watergate was superseded by the entrance of the Ford administration—a breath of fresh air, for the White House staff, in particular, but also for the nation as a whole. Betty Ford, the wife of President Gerald Ford, became very quickly the darling of the public. Her down-to-earth, warm, and folksy style contrasted sharply with the chilly self-restraint of Pat Nixon, and the press and the people were immediately drawn to her. What speeded this process of acceptance was Betty Ford's own personal ordeal: in later September 1974, very soon after the first family had taken up residence at the White House, she went into the hospital for a mastectomy. Not only did this become front-page news, but Betty Ford clearly expressed a desire to make her operation public so that other women could profit by her experience. The image that was projected, and that the American people resonated to, was one of quiet courage and great inner strength. Ford reflected later that this experience helped her realize the nature of her power: "Lying in the hospital, thinking of all those women going for cancer checkups because of me, I'd come to recognize more clearly the power of the woman in the White House. Not *my* power, but the power of the position, a power which could be used to help."[22]

Ford was also known for speaking her own mind on controversial issues in a way that identified her as something of a free spirit. In July 1975, she taped an interview with Morley Safer for the "60 Minutes" show on CBS, in which several difficult subjects were discussed: premarital sex (she said it might lower the divorce rate); abortion (she favored the Supreme Court's decision to legalize it); and drugs (she didn't think her children were very interested in drugs). But in answer to a question that caught her off-guard—what would she do if her daughter told her she was having an affair?—Ford gave a very "modern" response. She wouldn't be surprised, she said, and she would want to counsel and advise and know something about the young man.[23]

There was a tremendous furor in reaction to this interview, particularly with respect to her comments on her daughter. At first Betty Ford was concerned that she had become a real political liability to her husband, but over the long run her openness had a favorable impact. Within a few months her popularity in opinion polls had climbed to around 75 percent, far outdistancing the president, who was struggling with the economy, the winding down of the Vietnam War, and the aftermath of the pardon he had given Nixon. In December 1975, Betty Ford was selected as Woman of the Year by *Newsweek* magazine, and a Republican campaign button read "Betty's Husband for President in '76."[24]

Betty Ford was the closest thing to a feminist, since Eleanor Roosevelt, who ever resided in the White House. When her press secretary asked her whether she considered herself a liberated woman, she had a carefully reasoned response: "Any woman who feels confident in herself and happy in what she is doing is a liberated woman. It's a general feeling of positiveness and really being able to live with yourself, I think. Yes, I feel liberated."[25]

Although Ford did not feel that a woman had to have a job or career to be liberated, basically she had a personal, individualistic definition of liberation that meshed well with the liberal feminism of the mainstream women's movement. She was, in fact, warmly embraced by the mainstream, and she supported most of its political goals. She was a strong backer of the ERA, and she tried to influence President Ford to appoint women to high office. Carla Hills came into the cabinet as secretary of housing and urban development (HUD), and Anne Armstrong was named ambassador to Great Britain. In January 1975, the president signed an executive order establishing a National Commission on the Observance of International Women's Year. Betty Ford was present at the ceremony. When her husband turned to her and asked if she had any words of wisdom, she returned, "I just want to congratulate you, Mr. President. I'm glad to see that you have come a long, long way."[26]

Betty Ford took a highly visible position on women's issues. She worked very hard on the ERA, phoning and writing to legislators and giving speeches. On the whole, she received a favorable response from the American people, but ERA opponents picketed the White House, and right to life people came carrying signs with pictures of fetuses on them. In 1977, when she attended the National Women's Conference in Houston, her presence on a platform, along with Lady Bird Johnson and Rosalynn Carter, led to a flood of critical letters. Many of them were addressed jointly to all three women: "How can you women be up there promoting a bunch of lesbians?" was the question most often posed.[27]

The final ordeal Betty Ford had to confront occurred after she left the White House, but while she was still in the public eye. That was her dependency on drugs and alcohol. In recent years there has been more awareness of the pressures of political life and the particular kinds of tensions to which political wives are subjected. Much of our present awareness has been gained through Betty Ford's willingness to face her own problems and make them public. Her dependency on drugs had arisen out of a long-time back disability. For fourteen years she had been on medication for arthritis, a pinched nerve, and muscle spasms. A single drink, on top of the pills, could cause blurred speech and drowsiness—in a word, the appearance of drunkenness, and along with it, a certain amount of speculation on the part of those who worked with her.[28]

The former first lady entered a treatment center for alcohol and drug rehabilitation in 1978. Her candidness with the public was, in effect, a repeat performance of her mastectomy operation in 1974. Although she was no longer first lady, she was still a public figure, and as such, her problems were subject to public scrutiny.

The last first lady of the 1970s, Rosalynn Carter, took an activist position even before she entered the White House, and from the very beginning, the Carter administration was a family affair. In fact, Rosalynn Carter stressed, both in her autobiography and in her interviews with the press, that her relationship with her husband did not change drastically when they entered the White House: "I often acted as a sounding board for him. While explaining a particular issue to me, he could think it through himself; and I and the rest of the family often argued with him more strenuously than his advisers or staff did. To us he was the same participant in our nightly dinner table discussions that he had always been."[29]

But Rosalynn Carter was a great deal more than a sounding board. She had some definite policy goals she enunciated early in the administration. She was interested in mental health, policies for the elderly, lowering the cost of health care, and acting as a goodwill ambassador for the administration. All of these were traditional "women's concerns," and none of them really appealed to the imagination of the public.[30]

Rosalynn Carter experienced very quickly the frustration of trying to educate the public on a substantive issue, when she held her first press conference and announced the President's Commission on Mental Health. She had invited professionals, scientists, parents of the mentally afflicted, and volunteers to the ceremony. The president appeared briefly and signed an executive order setting up the commission, and the first lady talked about her plans and answered questions. But the next day when she picked up the *Washington Post*, she found not one word on the commission or the press conference. The paper instead carried the "wine story"—the Carters had decided not to serve hard liquor in the White House on the state floor but rather wine, as a way of saving money and returning to a pre-Kennedy days tradition. The wine story created a major flap. "Our mental health commission was not news—I was told by the press it was not a 'sexy' issue—but 'no booze in the White House' obviously was."[31]

What caught the attention of the press more than the issues themselves was the enormous influence that Rosalynn Carter had with her husband. In June 1977, when she visited Latin America, she was much more than a "goodwill ambassador." Her purpose was to impress on all the countries she visited the sincerity of the Carter administration's commitment to human rights and to social and economic progress. Her mild, but forceful style was very effective in getting her message across, and President Oduber of Costa Rica announced, "It is the first time since President Kennedy that a U.S. administration brings us a message that kindles hope, love, and attachment."[32]

Yet the contingent of American journalists traveling with the first lady were not foreign policy experts or Latin American specialists. They were primarily correspondents and reporters from the "style" sections of major metropolitan newspapers and news magazines, and they were more interested in the trivia of her daily routine than in the reaction of Latin Americans.[33] On the other hand, the trip did attract a great deal of press attention that seemed to indicate a growing awareness of the important role of this new first lady - a role that was to become more controversial as it became more visible.

Meg Greenfield, *Newsweek* columnist, noted that Rosalynn Carter's power was not an "uppity woman" issue but rather a question of the proper role in government of unelected family members of elected officials. By asking to be part of the political and governing process, Rosalynn Carter was, in a sense, making herself accountable for whatever influence she might exert. "I calculate that before it's over, Mrs. Carter—a remarkable woman—will have demonstrated whether or not a political wife who comes out of the kitchen can stand the heat."[34]

The first lady's special influence was picked up as a press item and remained her particular trademark for the rest of the Carter administration. She was known variously as the "second most powerful person," "Mrs. President," the "president's partner," and the "steel magnolia." But the attention she drew was a two-edged sword, and the criticism mounted in the second year when she began to attend cabinet meetings. On 7 August 1978, she entered a cabinet meeting forty minutes late and slipped quietly into one of the two empty chairs in the room. It just happened to be that of the vice president. Nobody is supposed to use the vice president's chair when he is not present, but Rosalynn Carter was seemingly unaware of this particular protocol. She remained there the rest of the meeting, and when she left she was very upbeat: it had been a good meeting with a brisk, lively discussion. That was the point, as far as the first lady was concerned, rather than the protocol of who sat where.[35]

Sometimes referred to as a "seventies' style Eleanor Roosevelt" because of her activism and her attempts to redefine and broaden the scope of her role, Rosalynn Carter nonetheless had a frustrating struggle to establish a clear-cut image that rang true, or was even of interest, to the American people. The popular press acknowledged her hard work and her skills—she had "the best mind for statecraft and politics" of any previous first lady, and she was the first presidential wife to keep regular working office hours—nonetheless, her image remained fuzzy. She seemed to spread herself a little too thin over too many areas. Certainly she never developed the public persona of an Eleanor Roosevelt, but as some suggested, she was really more like Harry Hopkins, Robert Kennedy, or even Henry Kissinger.[36] That is, rather than setting off in her own direction and concentrating on her own issues, she served primarily as an advocate for Jimmy Carter. This was the role she increasingly fulfilled, especially from mid-1978 through the 1980 election.

The source of her power was her absolute loyalty to the president. She was a true adviser to him on almost every issue: she read what he read, edited his speeches, met with his aides, sat in on his cabinet sessions, substituted for him on the road, and consulted on everything from political strategy to personal charges. Rosalynn was, in short, a one-woman kitchen cabinet. And in answer to those who were critical of her power, *Newsweek* pointed out that "the charge is easily refuted because Presidents have always been free to pick their closest advisers and many have relied on their wives in the past. And because no one questions the role played by other unelected advisers, such as Jody Powell or Hamilton Jordan, the real fear of Rosalynn's power may lie simply in the fact that she is an ambitious woman."[37]

Rosalynn took a forthright stand on the ERA and an active part in the 1977 National Women's Conference in Houston. But her position on abortion was shaky. She opposed it for herself, but did not feel she could decide for another woman. Jimmy Carter had a more conservative position, and of course, the Carter administration were years of retreat on the abortion issue.

A common experience of all the first ladies was the limitations placed on their freedom—the freedom to act or not to act, to be themselves, to strike a new pose, to move beyond the confinement of an exceedingly demanding, yet rigidly defined role. In becoming "political wives" they had implicitly accepted this burden, and by the time they became first ladies there was no going back, no real choice. Their lives were truly appendages to their husbands'. The public's satisfaction with their status offers an interesting insight into the underlying public sense of the correctness of traditional family roles and the necessity for maintaining them even in the most atypical family life-style imaginable.

Political *wives* were a category apart from political *women*, the latter being those women who made a reputation for themselves on the basis of their own achievements in public life rather than those of their husbands. The seventies provided a relatively favorable climate for a handful of women politicians who not only established names for themselves but also took on a particular recognizable image that was to a large extent self-defined.

Very few women political figures of the 1970s became household words, but certainly if anyone attained that level of notoriety, it was Bella Abzug, congresswoman from New York City. Abzug was representative of a new breed of politicians who came out of the sixties and focused on the concerns of new constituencies, including minorities, youth, and women. Abzug had been an activist throughout the 1960s, involved in Democratic reform politics and the women's peace movement. She was continually frustrated by what she saw as misrepresentation of the people, as government leaders and political parties operated in ways contrary to their wishes. "One of my abiding passions has been to break through the existing electoral bottlenecks that prevent grassroots Americans, men and women, from getting the leadership that really represents their best interests and desires."[38]

Abzug was interested in power: personal political power for herself, but more important, political power for women. She felt that it was essential to change the process—to open up the political parties by changing their structures and their nominating procedures; to open up government by electing more women, minorities, and other underrepresented groups. These were the major concerns of the political wing of the women's movement, and Abzug was its most outspoken and demanding advocate. Her disgust with male politicians who ignored women's social and economic needs was a major catalyst behind the organization of the National Women's Political Caucus (NWPC).[39]

Abzug made an impact on the politics of the seventies because she took a strong stand on controversial issues and because she had a highly visible and controversial image. Her tough talk, fighting spirit, feminist stance, and colorful profile—complete with big hat and loud, flashy style of dress and manners—were both assets and liabilities. As one commentator put it: "Abzug had been a hot media commodity for nearly a decade, and her years in Congress did nothing to overcome the 'Battling Bella' image which once she nurtured and which now has become a permanent fixture in the public's consciousness. A good part of every Bella campaign had to be devoted to overcoming that image."[40]

Abzug had a loyal core of supporters, but she was also a polarizing force. As many people were drawn to the voting booth to cast ballots against her as to support her. "Nobody in American politics can stimulate a backlash quite like Abzug, not on the merits of her message, but on her mode of delivery."[41] Strong feelings about Bella surfaced very early in her career, when she first ran for Congress in 1970. At that time she was the darling of the New Left, New York's flashiest candidate. As a civil rights activist, antiwar leader, feminist crusader, she was a symbol for every cause. And she stated her political stance unequivocally: I'm a woman. I'm strong. I have something to say. And I like the big fight."[42]

Her personal characteristics were unique but at the same time harmful to Abzug's long-range political career. By the late seventies she had become a stereotype and her star had begun its descent, but Bella herself was unwilling to accept that fact. She lost three races in less than eighteen months in which she had begun as the front runner and wound up the loser. In 1976, Daniel Patrick Moynihan beat her in the U.S. Senate primary; in 1977 she ran fourth in a mayoral primary; and in 1978 she was defeated by an unknown Republican, S. William Green, in a district in which Democrats had a three-to-one edge in registration and that Ed Koch had carried by 70 percent in a previous election.[43]

Ellen Goodman explained Abzug's loss to Green as a defeat for "personality politics." The late seventies were low-key; Bella was high-decibel. The times were cool; Bella was hot. The gray people were winning; Bella was Technicolor. "We've decided that personality polarizes, and charisma alienates. We think we're looking for peacemakers. Or is it just for peace and quiet?"[44]

Bella Abzug gained her notoriety from her personal style as much as her politics, but there were other women politicians of the seventies who made their mark by becoming identified with a particular constituency or political event. Shirley Chisholm became well known as a representative of blacks and women, and whereas she was never able to claim the fame or the political influence of Abzug, she was known as a fiesty, independent, straight-shooting congresswoman. In 1972, when she ran for the Democratic nomination for president, she had difficulty garnering support from the "realists" among the ranks of reformers. Gloria Steinem gave her only ambivalent support at best, yet she wrote a flattering portrayal of the "ticket that might have been" for *Ms.* magazine.[45]

Steinem pointed out that the Chisholm candidacy was rarely analyzed while it was going on and was given even less attention in the traditional postmortems. And yet a Harris poll taken in February 1972 found that Chisholm was getting 35 percent of the vote among black independents and black Democrats, and a support among women of all races that was three times greater than her support among men. Thus, Steinem argued, she was vying with Mayor John Lindsay of New York City, Senator George McGovern, and former senator Eugene Mc-Carthy for the liberal and left-of-center vote.[46]

What Steinem did not recognize was that the liberal and left-of-center vote was no longer the dominant force in American politics. When she proclaimed confidently "The Chisholm candidacy didn't forge a solid coalition of those people working for social change; that will take a long time. But it began one,"[47] she was reflecting an unwarranted optimism that was characteristic of early 1970s liberals. The hope of the liberal-left feminists like Abzug, Chisholm, and Steinem was that a social movement could be constructed from the several disparate elements in the American electorate—women, youth, minorities, and other underprivileged, nonestablishment groups. They even believed that there was a long-shot possibility that such a coalition could be formed within the Democratic party.

For one brief moment in 1972, anything seemed possible. This was the moment when Frances "Sissy" Farenthold, a forty-six-year-old Texas state legislator and reformer, made a bid for the vice presidency. Most of the convention delegates had never heard of Farenthold when she was placed into nomination, but she ended up receiving over 420 delegate votes, second only to that of Senator Thomas Eagleton, McGovern's ill-fated choice. Farenthold's support came from women delegates as well as black, Spanish-speaking, and youth delegates who saw her candidacy as a rallying point for excluded groups. The media, however, never gave her candidacy serious attention.[48]

The major media event of the mid-seventies, if not the entire decade, was clearly the televising of the Watergate hearings. The "women of Watergate"—Martha Mitchell, Pat Nixon, Pat Dean, and Rosemary Wood—received considerable publicity within their own well-defined roles. But two women politicians made a name for themselves based upon their membership on the House Judiciary Committee. Democratic congresswomen Barbara Jordan of Texas and Elizabeth Holtzman of New York were the only women on this thirty-eight-member committee. They both cast a vote in favor of the Articles of Impeachment—one of the most historic public acts of the century which led within two days to the resignation of President Richard M. Nixon.[49]

The process of reaching that decision had been long and involved, stretching over the spring and summer of 1974. It meant confronting a mass of evidence and, finally, the enormity of what had happened to the presidency. Both Jordan and Holtzman defined their decision in constitutional terms and articulated a deep commitment to the U.S. Constitution and the need to educate the American people as to its importance.

Both Holtzman and Jordan commanded the respect of their colleagues as well as that of the public and the press. Holtzman was viewed as "pretty strong on the pro-impeachment side." She was known for working very hard, studying the issues very carefully, and being better prepared than 90 percent of the committee members. "But she doesn't always know when to shut up," said one newspaper.[50]

Holtzman had come to Congress in 1972 after scoring a major upset victory in the Democratic primary over fifty-year House member and long-time Judiciary Committee chairman Emanuel Cellar. Her battle against Cellar was the stuff of legends. She had very little money and indeed ended up spending only $37,000 on the campaign. At the age of thirty, she had served just two years as Democratic state committee-woman from Brooklyn. Cellar, in his eighties, was a formidable national institution who referred to his opponent as "a toothpick trying to topple the Washington Monument." But Holtzman recognized his basic weakness: he had lost touch with the people—he wasn't a vital presence in the district and he wasn't paying any attention to his constituents. "When I first went out campaigning, I was in a supermarket handing out leaflets and someone said 'God, she's running against Cellar' and started screaming with joy and running around the supermarket shouting, 'Can you believe it? She's running against Cellar'"[51]

Holtzman won the primary by 526 votes—essentially by shaking hands at every subway stop and every supermarket in Brooklyn. She easily won the November election in the overwhelming Democratic district. Her performance during Watergate and her reputation as a lawyer on the Judiciary Committee prompted Eleanor Smeal, NOW president, to approach her in March 1977 with the idea of a congressional extension of the time limit for ratification of the ERA. Thus, during the ninety-fifth Congress, the now seasoned congresswoman acted as chief sponsor of the controversial ERA extension bill. Holtzman also helped organize the first Congresswomen's Caucus, which created a mechanism for bird-dogging women's concerns in Congress. Without the caucus, the extension victory might not have been possible. It was a way for women to support each other's legislation as well as to work with women's groups.[52]

Holtzman's image in the press and in her district was—in sharp contrast to that of Bella Abzug—low-profile, low-key, and very straight. In an age of *People* Magazine gossip, Holtzman maintained her privacy. Several of her constituents said "she reminded them of a secular, modern nun—clean-scrubbed, earnest, dedicated, straightforward and private." Yet her private life was important—"to regenerate one's spirit." Her style was reserved. To some people she appeared shy, and to others cold. Not all feminists felt comfortable in her presence. Like most women in the public eye, Holtzman's personality was often subject to attack.[53]

Her career, like that of other women politicians, inevitably raised the issue of the feminist movement in politics, and how women politicians react to women's issues. Holtzman was oriented to women's rights rather than to feminism, and she was more individual than movement identified. She had a good relationship with movement organizations and took a good stand on women's issues, yet feminists seemed to want more from her. In 1979, when Holtzman was serving, there were only 17 congresswomen and 514 men. This meant that women were highly visible and gained a great deal of recognition, but it also meant that they were burdened with high expectations. They were expected to lead on women's issues, and when this leadership was not forthcoming, feminists were disappointed. Holtzman clearly supported women's issues, but she was not a movement leader and did not claim to be one.[54] "There is an important distinction between the roles of feminist leaders and Congresswomen in effecting change through the political process. The women's movement is a political force that creates the conditions necessary for social change to occur. . . . The Congresswomen's role is responding to that pressure and implementing changes legislatively."[55]

Barbara Jordan, Holtzman's colleague, likewise played down the feminist issue, and in fact, throughout her short but spectacular career, she followed a strategy of moderation. Jordan was the first black woman to become a Texas state senator, the first black woman to represent a southern state in the House of Representatives, and the only black woman to sit on the House Judiciary Committee during the Watergate proceedings. Her style was low-key, and her initial success was due to her intelligence, hard work, and healthy respect for the practical politics of a legislative body. But those are the qualities of the ordinary successful politician, and Jordan went far beyond the ordinary. She also possessed a tremendous desire to serve, a strength and honesty that kept her true to her principles, a commanding physical presence, and an impressive oratorical style.[56]

All these qualities won her the respect of her white male colleagues, first in the Texas State Senate and later in the U.S. House of Representatives. But it was her role on the House Judiciary Committee that gained her a national reputation. On the evening of 25 July 1974, Jordan had her opportunity to explain to the American people her understanding of the broad constitutional issues underlying the impeachment process, and in particular, her feeling that the Constitution was being subverted by the president of the United States. "With that speech Barbara Jordan became a national figure. Through the medium of television millions had watched and heard her and had been overwhelmingly impressed. Blacks and women, in particular, were proud to claim her, but the appeal of her dignity, her articulateness, her concern, transcended racial and sexual lines."[57]

Jordan's photograph was featured in both *Time* and *Newsweek* that week. The *Washington Post* carried the complete text of her speech the next morning on its editorial page. It was the only Judiciary Committee member's speech to be carried in full. *U.S. News and World Report* called Jordan one of the Democratic party's "new luminaries" and quoted an unnamed observer as saying, "When the Democrats get around to nominating a black on their national ticket, they may well turn to Barbara Jordan."[58]

Barbara Jordan's superior intelligence, legislative skill, and a certain moral authority made her within a very few years one of the most influential members of Congress. In February 1975, she was featured in a front-page profile in the *Wall Street Journal*. In 1976 she was chosen as one of the two keynote speakers at the Democratic National Convention held in New York City. Her address, which followed that of the former astronaut and congressman from Ohio, John Glenn, was the highlight of the evening and one of the highlights of the convention. She was greeted by a standing ovation and interrupted again and again by wild applause and cheering. Her impressive speech, delivered in her sonorous, almost hypnotic voice, brought an overwhelming response of pride not only from convention delegates but from all segments of the population. "There were tears in the eyes of many of her listeners, both at the convention and at home, and for others the breathless, almost light-headed feeling that comes after a profoundly moving experience."[59]

Barbara Jordan was one of the few women political figures of the seventies to earn the respect of her colleagues and achieve a positive public image as well. Her sensitivity to the workings of the democratic political system—her understanding of its strengths and acceptance of its limitations—along with a formidable public presence were the keys to her success. These were skills she consciously cultivated during her youth and her early career. Jordan was one of the few women of the decade who projected a strong self-image that was not created or distorted by the media. Rather, she made use of the media to enhance her own objectives.

Political women like Abzug, Chisholm, Holtzman, and Jordan captured the imagination of only a select group of Americans—those who were politically aware or those who were directly affected by a particular candidate. The women who made their impression on the public overall did it through their impact on popular culture—film, television, or popular music. In these fields there was a wide range of diversity in image and style, and the heroines of popular culture played a large part in shaping their own images. And yet here, too, there was resistance to any real change in the public's perception of women's roles.

At the beginning of the decade the media were not only tightly controlled by men; they had not yet felt the challenge of the women's movement. Certainly the impact of the media, especially television, and their powerful influence on thought and opinion in America was generally recognized. The modern mass production and distribution of information, ideas, and art had become the principal agent in the creation and control of public opinion and popular culture.[60] That women played almost no role in this process was certainly a factor contributing to the trivialization of their issues and the generally negative treatment of the politics of the movement. The founding of *Ms.* magazine in 1972 was in large part a reaction to this imbalance. Throughout most of the decade the magazine acted as a barometer of the women's movement in its popular form, accessible to the casual woman reader as much as to the dedicated feminist. Gloria Steinem, its founder and editor, became a media celebrity in her own right as writer, editor, and political activist.[61]

By the end of the decade, *Ms.* had many imitators, or at least many publications that recognized the commercial importance of the emerging "new woman" market. Magazines such as *Working Woman*, *New Woman* and *Savvy* reflected this appeal to the new image of the liberated woman. The more established magazines such as *Vogue*, *Glamour*, and *Ladies' Home Journal* also picked up the theme. But the message of the women's magazines encouraged sexual and economic liberation in order to better pursue the rewards of upward mobility in a consumer society.

To most people of the seventies, the media meant television, and the number of women present in the major television programs was a good measure of their secondary status in popular culture in general. In 1973, during the prime-time evening hours on the three major networks, there were sixty-two shows with regularly appearing leading performers. Forty-eight of these programs had male protagonists, eight had men and women sharing the lead, and six shows had female protagonists. There were no women anchoring a news program, and none appeared on a regularly scheduled sports show or as a game show host or evening talk show host.[62]

And yet in the few cases when women did have the lead, their roles indicated the dawn of a new era. Throughout most of the 1950s and 1960s the Lucille Ball format of the "dumb broad" had dominated the television image of women. But by the early seventies, the "Mary Tyler Moore Show" had set a new standard. Mary was an over-thirty career woman, unmarried, and not particularly concerned about it. Her show was well-written, the humor evolved from good characterization, and Moore became the most realistic and identifiable "heroine" on television. She was not a feminist, and she certainly knew her place in the office hierarchy, but she was "the superb straight woman for a terrific bunch of second bananas."[63]

The many other female personas of the seventies—Valerie Harper's "Rhoda," Diana Rigg's "Diana," Bea Arthur's "Maude," and Jean Stapleton's evolving interpretation of Edith in "All in the Family"—seemed to indicate a growing acceptance among viewers of strength and diversity in their women stars. Several comediennes of the period also broke new ground and showed long-term staying power. Carol Burnett was star of one of the most popular and longest running comedy shows in television history, and Lily Tomlin, although she never acquired the long-term television success of Burnett, showed a similar creativity in her development of characters.[64]

Women also created distinct styles and images in film during the seventies. Although they did not experience the success of the big blockbusters of the decade—*Sting*, *The Godfather*, and *Jaws*—that featured male stars, a number of significant new talents appeared, including Diane Keaton, Bette Midler, Meryl Streep, Cicely Tyson, Sissy Spacek, and Sally Field. Barbra Striesand, Shirley MacLaine, and Anne Bancroft continued careers that had emerged in the 1960s. There were also some important films that confronted women's issues in a way that was reflective of new concerns and a certain courage.

Jane Fonda, movie actress, peace activist, feminist, and "fitness queen" perhaps represented as much as any single woman the various stages of femininity and feminism from the 1960s to the 1980s in celebrity form. Fonda was one of a family of actors—her father was Henry Fonda and her brother Peter Fonda—but she built her career on her own terms, and the films she made reflected her values and her personal growth during the 1960s and 1970s. In her early films, Fonda was basically a sex object: in *Barbarella* (1965), she starred as the ultimate sexual fantasy, and in *"Barefoot in the Park"* (1967) she played a perky "little girl" opposite Robert Redford. The first really important film that reflected her growing political consciousness was *They Shoot Horses, Don't They?*—a Depression Era story of dance marathoners and despair.

Fonda's emerging feminist perspective became first evident in her Oscar-winning role in the film *Klute* (1971), in which she played a high-class call girl. When a *Ms.* interviewer suggested that the role was "sexy," Fonda responded with an explanation that echoed the new feminist consciousness: "No, not really, because it asked questions about the nature of exploitation of women, and the reasons for it—it didn't exploit, it investigated."[65]

But it was her collaboration with Vanessa Redgrave in the film *Julia* (1977) that was most clearly representative of the mid-seventies feminist climate. Based on an episode in Lillian Hellman's memoir, *Pentimento, Julia* was one of the few films of all time to focus on a serious relationship between two women—both of them strong, forceful women with important political and intellectual concerns. In spite of impressive performances by the two leads, Redgrave and Fonda, however, the film did not reach its full feminist potential. It tended to flatten the friendship and miss the emotional subtleties that had characterized the memoir. The director seemed to become entrapped in the issue of sexuality rather than emotion and was apparently unable to accept the reality of an intense, yet platonic relationship between two women. "In his hands, the friendship is little more than an extended teenage crush," said *Ms.* magazine.[66]

The Turning Point (1978), costarring Anne Bancroft and Shirley MacLaine, capitalized skillfully and sensitively on women's issues, in particular, relationships between women. The film placed the emotional intensity of lifelong friendship into the context of career versus marriage, that specifically woman-oriented dilemma. But it also managed to confront universal problems—fear of aging, fear of loneliness, and the complications of parent-child relationships. As critic Marjorie Rosen observed, the film "focuses on women's choices and women's problems, and ultimately involves us thoroughly in their dynamics and emotional upheaval."[67]

A less spectacular effort, *Girl Friends* (1978), had a particular appeal to feminists because it dealt with the ordinary and avoided the media hype of films featuring the big stars. The story line showed the impact of marriage on a friendship between two women, and as one critic noted, it had "a fragmentary day-to-day style that registers smaller, less generalized—and less glamorized—shocks of recognition."[68]

Jane Fonda's career, more than any other film star of the seventies (with the possible exception of Vanessa Redgrave), showed a consistency and continuity of political consciousness. After *Julia* she continued to play roles that underscored her activist values, including *Coming Home* (1978), a critique of the Vietnam War, and *China Syndrome* (1979), a warning about the dangers of nuclear power and the ever-present possibility of human error. Fonda believed deeply in the educational value of films, and to that end, she formed a film company, IPC Films, Inc. (IPC stood for Indochina Peace Campaign). She was influenced by her political values and activism by her relationship and subsequent marriage to sixties activist Tom Hayden.[69]

Yet by the early 1980s, although Fonda was still doing interesting work in film, her career had taken a new twist with her highly successful venture into the "health industry." She published and performed for *The Jane Fonda Workout Book* (1981), which included tapes and a complete fitness program for individual home use. The enthusiasm with which Fonda's publications (there were several editions) were received by women of the eighties was an extension of the fitness boom that had emerged in the 1970s. The fitness and health craze had an impact on both sexes, but what was unique was the extent to which women were engaging in physical activities that they had never before ventured to try. These included long-distance running, weight-lifting, and body-building, as well as aerobics, tennis, and a variety of team sports. The sight of an adult woman jogging through a public park or along a thoroughfare in shorts and T-shirt would have been greeted with ridicule and astonishment at earlier periods in American history.

But by the mid-to-late seventies, it was a commonplace occurrence. Women were training for twenty-six-mile marathons as well as shorter road races. And most large cities had a "women's night" at their city park playing fields to provide for the growing number of women's softball teams.

Much of this was a positive reaction to women's liberation in the most literal sense of the term. Women were liberating themselves from the old conventional restraints on their physical capabilities and allowing themselves to participate in athletic endeavors on their own terms. But another part of the body consciousness of the seventies and eighties was less positive in its implications. Throughout the period women were obsessively concerned with body image, and this increasingly came to mean an obsession with slenderness—a physical characteristic that became practically a moral virtue in and of itself. Certainly the media—especially television and women's magazines—encouraged this obsession. The ideal of "thin is beautiful" was promoted by using abnormally thin models. The old adage "you can't be too rich or too thin" became the grounds for a new women's issue of the 1980s: the concern with eating disorders.[70]

By the end of the 1970s a new image of womanhood had emerged—one that reflected some aspect of women's liberation but too often defined the successful woman in terms characteristic of an intensely consumer-oriented, individualistic, and competitive society that almost completely negated the true meaning and intent of feminism. The successful woman of the late seventies was envisioned as young and beautiful, slender, highly sexual but not necessarily monogamous, highly successful in some vaguely glamorous but undefined career, and just feminist enough to want her own way. She could be seen in the commercials on television and the advertisements in popular magazines—Virginia Slims, Charley perfume, Jordache jeans, Diet Pepsi. She wore Maiden Form bras and sold perfume, sanitary products, shampoo, cars, fast food, and underwear. Her connection to the women's movement became increasingly hard to discern. Her relevance to the actual experience of most American women primarily reflected fantasy.

Women's public image was brighter, more visible, and more independent by the end of the decade. But ultimately, it was still controlled by the media which profited immensely from "women's liberation" but managed to redefine it in individualistic, market-economy terms. The real meaning of the women's movement was lost to the public. And the image that had emerged became the target of moral conservatives and the New Right which attacked the movement on the grounds that it was immoral and selfish, destructive of family and the American way of life.

CHAPTER NINE

The Spirit of Houston:
Reformers, Radicals, and Reactionaries

It is hard to imagine a more dramatic shift in the political climate than that which occurred between 1970 and 1980. If the women's movement was the unique product of the liberal-leftist politics of the 1960s, by the late 1970s, it found itself contending with a very different constituency. The New Right had taken a page out of the feminists' book of "personal politics," which it applied with great moral intensity to its own conservative objectives. The result was a resounding defeat for the most important goal of the liberal feminists the ERA—and an overall retreat from the enthusiasm and commitment of the early movement days.

The First National Women's Conference, held in Houston, Texas, in November 1977, marked the high point of the women's movement of the 1970s. The conference lasted only four days, but those days were the culmination of many months of preparation by thousands of people and years of political activism by the contemporary feminist movement. Furthermore, the adoption of a twenty-six-plank national plan of action by a large majority of the delegates appeared to reflect an impressive consensus on women's policy needs, the heart of which was the ERA.[1]

For many of the participants and observers, the conference marked a kind of coming-of-age for American women. *Time* magazine reported afterward that it was a "watershed event" in women's history and in the history of the nation. A London newspaper, the *Evening Standard*, said that mainstream feminism had evolved into a broadly based movement for egalitarianism. "The women's movement is now a truly national, unified engine of change which could conceivably become the cutting edge of the most important human issues America faces in the next decade."[2]

The impetus, the political clout, and the organization skills for the Houston conference were provided by the liberal mainstream feminist movement, but the radical feminists provided many of the issues as well as enthusiastic support. A third group of women—those of the New Right—provided the counterpoint to the conference and to the philosophy it advanced. Although the conservative, anti-ERA, antiabortion women were in a minority at Houston, they carried an ominous warning that the leaders of the women's movement were reluctant to heed. Thus, the Houston conference was both the culmination of reform feminism and a portender of a changing political climate.

The conference evolved out of the work of liberal feminists who had been active in the women's movement of the 1960s and who, by the turn of the decade, were beginning the push for the ERA. For instance, Virginia Allan, as president of the National Federation of Business and Professional Women's Clubs in 1963–64, had played an important role in the establishment of state commissions on the status of women. Then, in 1969, she was appointed to chair the President's Task Force on Women's Rights and Responsibilities, a Nixon advisory group.[3]

The President's Task Force submitted its report, *A Matter of Simple Justice*, to the president in December 1969. The tone of the report was militant in comparison to the Kennedy Commission report of a decade earlier. The Task Force recommended the establishment of an Office of Women's Rights and Responsibilities; it called for a White House conference on the same; and it proposed legislation to ensure full legal equality for women, including amendments to the Fair Labor Standards Act, the Social Security act, and the Civil Rights Acts of 1957 and 1964. Finally, it urged the president to send a message to Congress calling for the passage of the equal rights amendment.[4]

The political feminists of the early seventies were concerned with a wide range of issues, but they soon focused their attention and energies upon the passage of the ERA. The success in putting the ERA on the policy agenda of the 1970s was in large part due to the bipartisan support the amendment received within mainstream political circles. In fact, during the Nixon years, Republican women took the lead in pursuing reform. For instance, Congresswoman Martha Griffith was instrumental in getting the amendment through the House, but she worked closely with Republican Gerald Ford to have it discharged from committee. Pat Hutar, a member of the President's Task Force, was a conservative Republican, but good on women's issues. Nixon staff members Anne Armstrong and Jill Ruckelshaus worked for the ERA in the White House and, after its passage, testified in state legislatures.[5]

The most dramatic philosophical shift on the ERA occurred in the Department of Labor. The Women's Bureau had historically opposed the ERA on the grounds that its passage would mean the end of protective legislation for women in the work force. But in June 1970, when its Fiftieth Anniversary Conference was held, Elizabeth Koontz, director of the bureau, invited more than a thousand women whose views ranged from conservative-reformist to radical-feminist. The conference produced a set of strong resolutions, most of them derived from the Task Force recommendations, and it also endorsed the ERA. Koontz pressured Labor secretary George Schultz to reverse the Labor Department's historic opposition to the amendment, and he announced his support during the conference proceedings.[6]

Thus, the passage of the ERA involved the active support of mainstream political reformers in Congress, government agencies, political parties, and presidential task forces. But they had behind them the militant pressure from a whole range of women's organizations, including in particular NOW. In February 1970, Wilma Scott Heide and a group of about twenty NOW members disrupted hearings of the Senate Judiciary Committee on the eighteen-year-old vote to demand that hearings be scheduled on the ERA. Senator Birch Bayh of the Subcommittee on Constitutional Amendments promised to schedule the hearings, which were held in May 1970—the first congressional hearing on the ERA since 1956.[7]

By January 1972, when the amendment was finally passed by the Senate, it enjoyed remarkable support from a far-flung constituency. It had passed the House by a vote of 354 to 23; in the Senate, the vote was 84 to 8. Both major political parties had supported the amendment in their party platforms for years, and six presidents had endorsed it. A long list of national associations and interest groups, including almost every major women's organizations, supported the ERA. The American Bar Association had adopted a resolution of endorsement. And finally, the climate of opinion indicated an awareness of the existence of sex discrimination and a willingness to end it through legal means. In that first year twenty-two state legislatures approved the ERA.[8]

No one could have predicted in 1972 that the ERA would run into serious political difficulties and become a focus of the conservative backlash. Most liberal feminists were optimistic about the march of progress and anticipated a speedy ratification. Predicted Martha Griffiths in the spring of 1973, "ERA will be part of the Constitution long before the year's out." During that summer a coalition of thirty organizations including the League of Women Voters, the American Civil Liberties Union, the United Auto Workers, and the American Association of University Women was formed. This ERA Ratification Council began a fund-raising campaign and a low-level research and lobbying operation.[9]

But whereas the pro-ERA forces had most of the mainstream liberal organizations on their side, the opposition had Phyllis Schlafly, the individual most directly responsible for mounting the anti-ERA campaign and drawing thousands of supporters to her cause. Certainly the audience was there to be tapped, but seldom has one person played such a large role in changing the direction of a policy that seemed to be foreordained. The feminists who predicted an easy victory had not taken into account the personal force of this "Sweetheart of the Silent Majority."[10]

Except for her right-wing position on just about every imaginable issue—from government spending and welfare to defense spending and foreign policy—Schlafly could have been the perfect example of a 1970s-style liberated woman. She was intelligent, attractive, well educated, self-confident, and articulate, the mother of six children, and an influential activist in Republic party politics during the 1950s and 1960s. By the early 1970s, she had a well-established reputation based on her expertise on several public issues, including the Soviet Union, the arms race, and defense policy. She had supported the Goldwater campaign in 1964 and authored an influential piece of campaign literature about the Arizona senator entitled *A Choice, Not an Echo.*

In 1967 she lost a controversial and embittered fight for the presidency of the National Federation of Republican Women, primarily because the liberal wing of the party considered her too right wing and too hard to control. This hard-fought battle increased Schlafly's political visibility and established her as a heroine to her band of loyal supporters. It was this experience that moved Schlafly beyond traditional party politics and provided her with an organizational base from which to mount her Stop ERA campaign.[11]

It became customary for ERA advocates to portray Schlafly as a tool of the right-wing male establishment, voicing opinions that were not her own and playing on the fears and the ignorance of simple people. It was also customary for them to trivialize her power, distrust her sincerity, and therefore discount the seriousness of the threat she posed.

In fact, Schlafly's opposition to the ERA was sincere and followed naturally not only from her conservative politics but from a value system deeply embedded in her childhood education at City House, the all-girl Sacred Heart School in St. Louis, Missouri, where she grew up. Here she learned morals, discipline, hard work, and thrift—values that convinced her she could do anything. Indeed, *anyone* could do anything if he or she was willing to work and work and work. "Society's failures were not failures because they were deprived or because they were victims of racism or sexism. They were failures because they were lazy and undisciplined."[12]

As Schlafly's biographer has pointed out, these common threads of religious and moral values tied together and permeated Schlafly's political positions during her three decades of activism. There was a certain logical connection between her opposition to the SALT treaties, to the ERA, to communism, to abortion, and to the size of the defense budget. Above all, Schlafly believed she knew the difference between right and wrong, and she knew that there was a God who pronounced on that difference. That is why she was able to turn the ERA into a religious issue, and why, according to her followers, she was able to inspire such devotion.

While the ERA was being debated in Congress in 1970–71, Schlafly was busy writing about ICBMs and megatonnage and warheads, and worrying about the upcoming SALT agreements, and Nixon's policy of détente (which she opposed). She was basically apathetic about the ERA, seeing it as something between "innocuous and mildly helpful." Then, in December 1971, a friend asked her to come to Connecticut to debate a feminist on the ERA. The friend gave her some material to read, and Schlafly read it, did some research on her own, and suddenly saw the ERA as dangerous rather than innocuous. It was too late to block approval in Congress, but she decided immediately, against almost overwhelming odds, to turn the tide and defeat the amendment in the states.[13]

Schlafly's initial power was her ability to communicate to an inartic-

ulate and dispersed constituency through a monthly publication she
had launched in 1967 after her disillusionment with Republican party
politics. The *Phyllis Schlafly Report*, packed with her own opinions,
ideas, and endorsements, had become a means of consciousness-raising
among conservatives over some new concession to communism or a
curb on free enterprise. Now it was to become a means of arousing the
women who already supported her on other issues and urging them to
fight the ERA. In February 1972, the *Report* was devoted exclusively to
that issue—but it was only the first of a long line of *Reports* aimed at
defeating what appeared to be a sure thing.[14]

Schlafly started testifying before state legislatures. She testified in
Georgia, Virginia, Missouri, and Arkansas. All four states rejected the
amendment. The *Report* subscription list grew from three thousand to
thirty-five thousand, with a readership that was actually much wider.
As her biographer recounted: "That first anti-ERA *Report* became a col-
lector's item among feminists—like the first issue of *Playboy*. Women
read it and ridiculed it and howled over it until it became obvious that
state legislators were reading the *Phyllis Schlafly Report* and they weren't
laughing at all, they were just voting no."[15]

Schlafly was the first to come out with a strong, formalized stance
against the ERA. In late 1972, she established the National Committee
to Stop ERA. By mid-January 1973, the association had several thousand members in twenty-six states. It was strongest in the South and
Midwest. The organized Right also began to speak out against the
amendment. In March 1973, there was mention of the ERA and the
need for all true Americans to work for its defeat in the *Bulletin* of the
John Birch Society, and this was followed by several articles in the
American Opinion, the John Birch Society's monthly magazine. Recognized groups that took positions against the ERA in those early years
included the National Council of Catholic Women, Daughters of the
American Revolution, Conservative Caucus, Liberty Lobby, Ku Klux
Klan, and, at the other end of the political spectrum, the Communist
Party, U.S.A.[16]

Although the traditionally conservative organizations might have
been expected to take an anti-ERA stance, a more interesting development was the emergence of "alphabet soup" organizations founded for
the specific purpose of opposing the ERA. These included WWWW
(Women Who Want to Be Women), HOW (Happiness of Womanhood),
AWARE (American Women Are Richly Endowed, and also, American
Women Against the ERA), FOE (Females Opposed to Equality), and

FLAG (Family, Liberty, and God), as well as several others.[17] From 1973 onward, a cooperative spirit developed among these new groups and in relation to the well-established groups on the Right. This cooperation, or network, became more significant as the decade wore on and the Right played a larger and larger role in national politics.

In 1975, Schlafly founded the Eagle Forum and added the *Eagle Forum Newsletter* to the anti-ERA cause. The *Forum Newsletter* differed from the *Phyllis Schlafly Report* in that it was more colloquial, very heavy on local news, filled with instruction, inspiration, and advice, and directed mostly at a female readership. The *Report* was more scholarly, with a national-issues orientation and a mixed audience. The *Eagle Forum Newsletter* became a surefire means of raising money through personal appeals on the part of Schlafly. But more important, the *Newsletter* was a way of communicating a simple but essential message to women through the use of heavily moralistic language and distorted examples of feminist goals (for example, "Surely the right of parents to control the education of their children is a right of a higher order than any alleged right of, say, the two college-educated lesbian members of the Symbionese Liberation Army to teach our young people."[18]

But whereas pro-ERA advocates consistently and justifiably argued that Schlafly and the New Right intentionally distorted the meaning and the intent of the amendment, in fact, it was so open-ended that almost anything could be claimed for it. Feminists themselves were vague and unclear as to its meaning and potential application.[19] Schlafly established several grounds for her early opposition, and she continued to develop new arguments throughout the course of the campaign.

In particular, she opposed the second section of the amendment, which gave Congress the power of enforcement. Whereas the first section, according to Schlafly, would require states to make vast changes in the laws covering marriage, divorce, child custody, and adoption, the second section would give Washington the power to rewrite those laws to meet a single national standard. When Schlafly pointed out to state legislatures that Section II threatened to transfer some 70 percent of their legislative power to the federal government, it was not hard to get a majority of the legislators to agree.[20]

Schlafly was also disturbed because the ERA demanded absolute equality with no amendments, no exceptions. If the states were forced to treat men and women equally in all circumstances, the effect would be to weaken the traditional family, and in particular, it would undermine the security of the middle-aged full-time homemaker with no job skills. As Schlafly was fond of saying, the ERA did not include a "grandmother clause." Not surprisingly, it was this age group from which Schlafly drew most of her support.[21]

The potential effect on institutions—women's colleges, protective labor laws, and the military draft—was another area that Schlafly exploited successfully. The draft became one of the most hotly disputed issues of the campaign, in part because Schlafly chose to emphasize it. Not only was she horrified by the prospect of men and women sharing foxholes, but she also feared a weakened defense if women were used as combat troops.[22]

Schlafly also linked the ERA to the two most controversial issues of the women's movement—lesbianism and abortion. Some feminists sought to deny this connection, but in fact, to many if not most feminists, equal rights meant the right to control their own bodies and the right to sexual preference. This may not have been the original view of the liberal reformers, but by the mid-seventies, the movement had shifted to the left in response to the influence of radical feminists. Certainly the thrust of the women's movement was to define abortion as a woman's *right*, not as a medical issue.[23]

Opposition to abortion reform had emerged slowly and usually in response to an immediate and concrete change. For instance, New York State's Right to Life party (RTL) was started in 1970 by women who were disturbed by the impending passage of New York's abortion law. But the event that marked the real beginning of organized opposition to abortion was the Supreme Court decision, *Roe v. Wade*, on 22 January 1973. That case effectively struck down not only the nineteenth-century abortion laws, but the reform legislation of the 1960s as well. In other words, it legalized abortion on demand. The decision of the Court reflected the thinking of an entirely new constituency in the debate—the women's movement. It gave rise to another new constituency—the opposition. Both of these groups consisted overwhelmingly of women. The clash between them was not governed by the decorum that had characterized the debate during the 1960s, when it had been controlled by professionals and reformers. It became an impassioned and bitter struggle with little hope of compromise.[24]

The antiabortion movement did not produce an individual leader of the stature of Phyllis Schlafly. Rather, it was led by a number of single-issue groups, the largest of which was the National Right to Life Committee (NRLC), which claimed 11 million members by 1980. The right to life movement was the creation of the Family Life Division of the National Conference of Catholic Bishops, the directing body of the Catholic church in America. It came into existence immediately after *Roe v. Wade* and operated as a political action machine, influencing national and local elections and using the churches as an organizational base.[25]

The antiabortion groups emphasized the positive in their names and their philosophy: Concerned for Life, Right to Life, Life and Equality. Like the opposition to the ERA, they made common cause with religious groups and the profamily movement. The American Life Lobby took for a motto "for God, for Life, for the Family, for the Nation." The Minnesota Citizens Concerned for Life argued that the right to life is the basic right upon which all other issues of human rights and justice depend. Typically the prolife groups took the position that their issue was as important as slavery had been in the nineteenth century, and that it deserved to be treated as a single issue.[26]

In spite of the intensity of the abortion debate, most people were relatively indifferent to the issue during the 1970s, and the majority of the population held some kind of middle ground between the two extremes. During the 1960s, most people had been opposed to abortion, but attitudes changed quickly between the late sixties and early seventies. The shift in public opinion occurred *before* the Supreme Court decision. It was influenced by the large-scale social changes that characterized that period, and the decision merely reflected those changes.

Although the majority of Americans during the 1970s approved of abortion for one reason or another, they disapproved of casual abortion. Even the most extreme position—abortion on demand—although supported by a minority, saw an increase in support from 21 percent in 1975 to 25 percent in 1980. Thus, the prolife movement, in spite of its intense activity, did not have much impact on public opinion in the broad sense.[27]

And yet the movement experienced an impressive degree of political success. In 1976 the Republican party platform supported a constitutional amendment banning abortion, and in the same year, Congress passed the Hyde Amendment which prohibited the use of public funds to pay for the abortions of poor women. In 1978 the Supreme Court ruled that amendment to be constitutional, and Congress took action to cut off federal funding of the abortions of government employees, Peace Corps volunteers, and members of the military and their dependents.[28]

The success of the prolife movement depended not upon a ground-swell of support but on the intensity of commitment on the part of prolife activists. The dedicated activist sometimes worked thirty to forty hours a week on this issue. In fact, the very indifference of the general populace made the prolife people stand out in their intensity and gave them more influence. Also, they successfully adapted the new technologies of political activism to the life-style of the woman in the home. Telephone answering services with a roll-over feature (forward-ing the call to another number), telephone trees, which were more ef-fectively used by women in the home than by working women, and mailing lists, home computers, and electronic banking for donations were some of the devices used by prolife groups.[29]

In addition, the prolife people were active voters. They participated regularly, even in primaries, where the turnout is usually at its lowest. They tended to be single-issue voters who were willing to vote for or against a candidate on the basis of his or her stand on abortion. This was effective in the defeat of several candidates, threatened many oth-ers, and contributed to the volatility of the issue for political candi-dates.[30]

The prolife movement also reflected and was part of another new constituency that was emerging by the early 1970s. That was the New Right, a miscellaneous aggregation of special interest groups that con-tained within it several political, social, and philosophical components. Rosalind Pollack Petchesky in her study *Abortion and Woman's Choice* (1984) argues that the politics of family, sexuality, reproduction, and in particular, abortion became a primary vehicle of right-wing politicians as they sought to achieve power in the elections of the late 1970s and 1980s.[31]

Petchesky argues that by the 1970s abortion was recognized by fem-inists and their opponents alike as a condition of women's liberation. Thus, the underlying and unspoken meaning behind the abortion de-bate had more to do with sexuality, family structure, the relationship between men and women, parents and children, and women's employ-ment than it did with the fetus. The campaign against abortion in the courts, the legislatures, and political campaigns was a direct challenge to the feminist movement and only one part of the whole counterattack against feminism.[32]

It is clear that the prolife movement was part of the conservative backlash; however, it is also clear that many activists joined the move-ment out of a deep moral commitment to that single issue, and that it was *Roe v. Wade*—which appeared to make abortion on demand the "law of the land"—that served as a catalyst to their involvement. The strength of the prolife movement lay in that single-mindedness, and their refusal to make common cause with other single-issue groups, such as gun control or free enterprise. By the late seventies they had become one of the most powerful interest groups in the country. Candidates backed by the National Right to Life Committee who won in 1978 included Republican senators Roger Jepson of Iowa, Jesse Helms of North Carolina, and Rudy Boschwitz of Minnesota, and Republican congressman Larry Pressler of North Dakota.[33]

By the mid-to-late 1970s there was a tendency to view the prolife and anti-ERA movements as part of a vast New Right interlocking movement. Certainly these groups often overlapped in their worldview and in their support for one another's causes, especially at the leadership level. (Schlafly's connections with the Right have already been observed.) But the prolife movement was distinct from the individuals, organizations, publications, and political action groups that defined themselves as New Right. The New Right was not so much concerned with the life of the fetus or moral purity as with achieving political power.[34]

The political New Right was formed in 1974–75 in reaction to the liberal dominance of the Republican party. It revolved around a small core of political strategists allied with a small group of right-wing fundamentalist preachers, who acted as propagandists and fund-raisers, and a group of conservative politicians in Washington. The New Right leaders were often tied to organizations of the old Right—Young Americans for Freedom or the John Birch Society. But their goals were more far-reaching than the defensive reactionary politics of the old Right.[35]

Essentially, the New Right intended to create a national political machine directed at winning elections, initiating legislation and policy, and eventually dominating American politics and government. The means by which they pursued this aim were innovative and effective. They targeted every conservative single-issue cause in the country and attempted to fuse those causes into broad-based coalitions that could be mobilized to support right-wing candidates and issues. Finally, although the New Right was faithful to traditional conservative issues, it focused its energies on issues related to the family and sexuality rather than economic issues. In this sense, it was a direct challenge to feminism, with abortion and the ERA as prime targets.[36]

An indication of this connection was the establishment of a profamily movement in 1977. This was an attempt to build a coalition around a number of groups devoted to the preservation of the traditional social roles of the family, the churches, and the schools. The issues that fell into this category included antiabortion, anti-ERA, anti-gay rights, and antibusing. The profamily movement became the constituency for the television evangelists of the South and Southwest, who made the link with conservative politics. The Reverend Jerry Falwell, a fundamentalist preacher from Lynchburg, Virginia, was the most famous of these. Falwell created a new political organization, Moral Majority, Inc., which he used to exploit and capitalize on the social issues of the decade.[37]

The profamily movement represented a consolidation of the conservative forces that had been emerging since the early 1970s. And they came of age just in time to have an impact on the preliminaries to the Houston Conference. The National Conference on Women was the work of the National Commission on the Observance of International Women's Year (IWY Commission), which was established by President Gerald Ford on 9 January 1975 in response to the UN General Assembly's designation of 1975 as International Women's Year. The commission's home within the federal government attested to its appeal to mainstream feminists of both political parties.[38]

The commission took on the responsibility of preparing for the IWY Conference to be held in Mexico City that summer. In April 1975, Jill Ruckelshaus, a former member of the Republican National Committee, was appointed presiding officer of the IWY Commission. Other members included nationally prominent individuals who were committed to women's rights. These included Jean Stapleton, Alan Alda, Clare Boothe Luce, and Katharine Hepburn. Strong political leadership and advice was provided by former congresswoman Martha Griffith, Governor Ella Grasso of Connecticut, and other political figures. Senators Birch Bayh and Charles Percy were appointed to the commission by the president of the Senate, and Representatives Bella Abzug and Margaret Heckler were appointed by the speaker of the House.[39]

Catherine East, a senior staff officer who had worked with presidential commissions since 1962, joined the commission staff to focus on particular substantive issues. She set up thirteen committees to review progress since the Kennedy Commission and to make new recommendations. As a result, the commission was able to publish a report, "*. . .To Form a More Perfect Union . . .*," which included 115 strong recommendations, some of them critical of the executive branch, particularly with respect to the enforcement of antidiscrimination laws. This report formed the basis for the subsequent role of the commission in holding state conferences and the National Conference in Houston.[40]

The IWY Commission very early made the ERA its top priority. In fact, it went beyond the customary advisory function by establishing ERAmerica—a national umbrella organization designed to unify efforts at ratification. Much of the impetus for this organization came from Alan Alda, a cochair of the ERA Committee. Alda had agreed to serve on the commission only on the condition that he could play an activist role rather than a merely advisory role. The commission's Homemaker Committee, led by Martha Griffith, also went beyond its advisory capacity. The committee published critical monographs on the legal status of the homemaker in each state. These were used later in the state conference workshops.[41]

But in 1975, the National Conference was only a projected possibility. The Mexico City Conference was the women's movement's first attempt to go international, and as such, it was a major disappointment. About two thousand official delegates from 150 countries met in Mexico City in July 1975. But the co-optation of the movement by international politics, the harassment of certain American feminists, the control exerted by men, directly or indirectly, and the negative coverage by the media created disillusionment among many feminists and brought ridicule from the public.[42]

Mexico City was discouraging to the liberal feminists who had invested so much of themselves in the women's movement and the principle of international cooperation. But mainstream political activists are seldom utopian in their expectations, and the feminist core within the government—Virginia Allan and Mildred Marcy of the Department of State, and Catherine East, Jill Ruckelshaus, and others—already had their sights set on a national conference. In January 1975, Bella Abzug had introduced a bill in Congress directing that a national women's conference be held as part of the Bicentennial celebration. The IWY Commission was to hold the conference, which was to be preceded by state meetings open to the public for the purpose of selecting delegates.[43]

The amount of money appropriated to the commission was $5 million—about half the amount requested in the original bill. It was not made available until six months after the signing of the bill in June 1976. The commission appointed several regional coordinators to help establish the fifty-six state and territory coordinating committees, a process that was completed shortly after the election of Jimmy Carter in November 1976. During the winter and spring, the secretariat staff under Marcy was busy developing the administrative procedures for coordinating the work of the fifty-six committees.[44]

Meanwhile, the new Carter administration was ready to put its own stamp of approval on the commission. Carter expanded its size to forty-three members and appointed Bella Abzug presiding officer. Abzug replaced Elizabeth Athanasakos, who had chaired the commission from July to December 1976 (replacing Ruckelshaus), and who remained as a member to provide continuity. Sheryl Swerd, a junior staff person who worked with Catherine East from 1975 through 1977, described the process of determining the agenda for the Houston Conference as "extremely democratic." Hundreds of resolutions came into the office to be processed by the staff. If ten states mentioned a particular resolution, it was put on the agenda as part of the plan of action. "It was so democratic, when you think of it. . . . I think it was 150,000 people that participated at these meetings [the state conferences]. Nothing was devised, added or taken out. What you got was a true picture, as true as you could get, of what women were thinking about."[45]

But there were issues that were troublesome, even within the commission itself and among the people working in the secretariat. Lesbiansim was an issue that troubled many feminists, especially some of the older women who wanted to adhere more closely to traditional women's rights issues. Catherine East, who took an advanced stand on almost every issue, opposed a resolution on lesbianism because she thought it would be divisive. East was concerned that the conference be representative of "real women," and she felt that this issue got in the way. The fight to include lesbianism was led by Commissioner Jean O'Leary, a Carter appointee representing the National Gay Rights Task Force. The commission eventually went along with a "sexual preference" resolution. But East was right—it was to prove divisive.[46]

The lesbian issue reflected the growing strength of radical feminists within the mainstream movement. Radical feminists had little to do with the organization of the Houston Conference, nor did they provide much direct political clout. Nonetheless, the radicals *did* have an input. The issues that were raised at the Houston Conference covered the whole spectrum of the feminists' concerns, and the national plan of action that emerged from this four-day effort was radical in its implications. Certain of the issues would not have been discussed in "polite company" ten years earlier. They owed their place on the agenda to the consciousness-raising impact of radical feminism. These included the resolutions on battered women, rape, reproduction freedom (abortion), and sexual preference (lesbianism).

Most of the issues reflected the economic and career interests of mainstream feminism—discrimination in business, child care, credit, education, employment, and insurance. Others focused on particular constituencies that had emerged out of the social movements of the late 1960s—disabled women, homemakers, minority women, older women, offenders, rural women, and women in poverty and on welfare. But the key issue, in many ways the center of the whole plan of action, was the ERA: "At the heart of the consensus was the belief that final ratification of the Equal Rights Amendment is needed; 'to put women in the Constitution' and to establish a framework of justice for their efforts to remove remaining barriers to equality."[47]

The goal of the IWY commissioners and staff was to pass a plan of action that would show the public and the policymakers that there was a consensus among American women as to their needs. But if the state conferences of 1977 proved anything, it was that there was no real consensus—certainly not on the more controversial issues—the ERA, abortion, and lesbianism. These issues were interrelated in the minds of many women and provided the focus for the conservative backlash that was already present in 1973. Many of the reformers did not take the emerging opposition very seriously until they were confronted with its organizational strength in 1977.

That the opposition intended to have its say became apparent at the state meetings held during the spring and summer of 1977. There were spirited debates over the ERA, abortion, and other controversial issues at most of the planning conferences. In the early meetings the core resolutions were adopted, and the delegations to Houston were dedicated to equality for women. But in each state, women who were opposed to the program had attended or protested from outside. Although they attracted a lot of media attention, at first they did not elect many delegates.[48]

The first real setback to the expectations of the IWY commissioners occurred in Missouri, a state that had not ratified the ERA. Fewer than four hundred people had registered for the opening ceremonies and the workshops, but on Saturday morning, when the election for delegates was scheduled, a coalition of antiabortion and anti-ERA groups brought in more than five hundred men and women who registered at the door.

Over 861 people voted, assuring the election of the "antichange" slate. The visitors then went back to St. Louis in their chartered buses without attending any workshops or entering into dialogue with the women whose views they opposed.[49]

Although the pattern varied from state to state, liberal feminists faced a considerable amount of hostile activism on the way to Houston. During June and July the confrontation intensified. In Ohio a split among feminists enabled the right to life coalition to elect 80 percent of the delegates. In Oklahoma a church-organized group elected a conservative slate, passed a resolution calling homemaking "the most vital and rewarding career for women," and then defeated the core agenda in a single block vote before going home. Nebraska elected sixteen delegates opposed to abortion, but passed the ERA resolution in a volatile plenary session.[50]

The conservatives scored their most spectacular victory in Utah—the largest of the meetings leading up to Houston. With a total state population of little more than a million, Utah nonetheless attracted fourteen thousand men and women to the Salt Palace in Salt Lake City. They came in response to a call from the Mormon Relief Society, asking them to stand up for "correct principles"—opposition to federal funding of child care, abortion, sex education in the school, and employment "quotas" to secure equal opportunity for women. Through the sheer force of their numbers, the conservatives were able to reverse the intent of all the workshops designed by the pro-IWY state coordinating committee.[51]

The Mormons were also a powerful force in Washington State where they constituted less than 2 percent of the population, but were nearly half of those registered to vote at the state meeting. They came to vote against the ERA, but found themselves supporting the minority rights resolution. After a stormy session and recount of ballots that took days, a majority of the delegates supporting the ERA was elected.

At the Mississippi meeting, the Klu Klux Klan was one of the antichange forces, along with Stop ERA, Right to Life, the Birch Society, the Eagle Forum, the Conservative Caucus, and various local groups sympathetic to the cause of the Right. In addition, fundamentalists and other church organizations joined with dozens of antifeminist groups (like WWWW, and so on), so that the entire conference was dominated by the Right. All the delegates elected from Mississippi were white with the exception of one black woman who later resigned.[52]

The "war between women" captured the headlines and skewed the public's perception of the process of choosing delegates and establishing an agenda. Yet the meetings accomplished their basic purpose, which was to give women a forum for discussion of issues and a showcase for their talents. Exhibits of art, photography, crafts, and women's products were displayed, along with workshops on women's history, the ERA, education, employment, and health. Of the fifty-six plenary sessions, forty-three adopted all or most of the fourteen core resolutions. An additional forty-five hundred resolutions emerged from these meetings and contributed to the twenty-six resolutions that became the final plan of action.[53]

But the opposition at the state meetings brought the liberal feminists face-to-face with a backlash whose force they had previously underestimated. Mildred Marcy of the State Department said, "We began to change from our rather naive idealistic belief in inevitable progress—into realizing that we were hitting where people lived, and it was endangering the status quo and family life as they knew it."[54]

Although the majority endorsed the goals of the IMY, the organized strength of the opposition alarmed feminists and even the great "middle majority" of women who may not have defined themselves as feminists but favored improvements in the status of women. In an attempt to bring more favorable publicity to the Houston Conference, in August 1977 the American Association of University Women (AAUW) invited forty organizations to form a loose Women's Conference Network. The network consisted of national organizations with broad constituencies, although sometimes conflicting views: the National Council of Catholic Women, the National Abortion Rights Action League, the League of Women Voters, the Federation of Business and Professional Women, NOW, Girl Scouts of America, the National Women's Political Caucus, the AFL-CIO, and many other groups.[55]

The network held press conferences where "truth squads" presented data supporting the IWY Commission program and revealing the tactics used by the opposition. Jean Stapleton, television star of the popular sitcom "All in the Family" appeared on talk shows in her private capacity as an IWY commissioner. Stapleton's appearance was an unspoken but highly visible refutation of the charge that the commissioners were antifamily "misfits."[56]

Interest in the National Conference grew throughout the summer, and by the end of October, thousands of women were planning to go to Houston. In all, close to 20,000 people attended the conference, although only 2,005 were delegates. Some of the best-known women in the country were present: Bella Abzug as presiding officer, Barbara Jordan, Rosalynn Carter, Betty Ford, Lady Bird Johnson, Billie Jean King, and Margaret Mead were among the luminaries. Whatever the fears with respect to the opposition, Houston was definitely the place to be. As one junior staff person recalled, "We just wanted the whole world to come. . . . Anyone who was really interested in the women's movement did *something*. If you say 'Houston' to people, that connects you, just like that. It gives you entrée, like the 'old boys network.'"[57]

The conference was a combination of high idealism and power politics, and not all the maneuvering was between reformers and reactionaries. There were several constituencies that made their own particular demands. Minority women, which included blacks, Hispanics, native Americans, and Asian-Americans, wielded considerable power that was both moral and numerical. Minorities were overrepresented as delegates, relative to their numbers in the population. White Caucasians represented 84.4 percent of the population (as of 1976), but they were only 64.5 percent of the delegates. For many delegates the adoption of the plank on minority women was the most significant event of the conference.[58]

At least one observer attributed a similar importance to the plank on sexual preference. "It opened a channel of compassion in women long separated by their sexual allegiances." The view of most delegates was probably less sublime. The sexual preference plank had not been one of the recommendations originally submitted by the IWY Commission to the states, but lesbians and other feminists had succeeded in getting it adopted in thirty state meetings. At Houston, Catherine East spoke against it, and Dorris Holmes, a leader of the ERA struggle in Georgia called it an "albatross." Speaking in favor of the resolution were Ellie Smeal, Charlotte Bunch, and surprisingly, Betty Friedan, who had always opposed lesbianism but was willing to accept it as a human rights issue.[59]

The reproduction freedom resolution probably stirred up more emotion than any other issue on the agenda. The depth of feelings represented more than a polarization of views. Many people who voted for the resolution did so with mixed feelings and might have desired some middle ground. The standing vote on the issue was about five to one, but the celebration was subdued, as many prochoice delegates realized for the first time the depth of the commitment of the prolife delegates.[60]

The centerpiece of the conference was the ERA. By 1977, it had become clear that the proposed amendment was in trouble. In fact, it had been dying a slow death ever since 1973. Only three states ratified the amendment in 1974, one more in 1975, and the last one, Indiana, ratified on 18 January 1977. Furthermore, the ERA had suffered two major setbacks in 1975 when New York and New Jersey, both of which had already ratified, rejected referenda on the amendment. These two losses were major political upsets because they suggested that despite favorable public opinion polls, the voters did not actually support the ERA.[61]

Thus, the success of the Houston Conference was closely linked to the ratification of the ERA. The majority of the delegates, even among the conservatives, favored the ERA resolution, and it was adopted by a standing vote of about five to one. Nonetheless, it was an emotionally charged issue on both sides. Supporters chanted and sang pro-ERA slogans and chain-danced through the aisles, while commissioners smiled and embraced each other. But the opposition sat silent, some of them weeping. The division on this issue, although more one-sided, was in some ways even more intense than the division over abortion.[62]

Some participants left Houston feeling exhilarated and some disillusioned, but the great majority of the delegates went home convinced that they would continue to work on the issues they had supported. There was considerable variation in the degree of commitment, but 74 percent of the delegates claimed that they would be actively involved in the ERA ratification campaign. Issues that affect women's overall status in society, such as employment, education, and political life, as well as the resolutions on battered women and minority women, also headed the list of activist concerns, with over 70 percent of the delegates intending to work for their implementation. There was no resolution that attracted less than 30 percent active support. And only those delegates identified with the anti-plan caucus expressed any intention of working against any of the resolutions.[63]

One of the major criticisms directed at the Houston Conference by the right wing was that it was not representative of American women. Phyllis Schlafly's counterconference—the Pro-Family Rally—held in another part of Houston that same weekend, underscored this critique. It did not attract as much attention as liberals had feared it might, and given the unity at the establishment conference, Schlafly's efforts seemed peculiarly out of step with the times. And yet it represented a discontent that was brewing among the "stay-at-homes" at least, who saw the reform efforts of feminists as threats to their way of life.

The complaints of the Right were not entirely unfounded. The IWY Commission sincerely tried to run inclusive, representative meetings at the state level to ensure participation of a diversity by race, age, class, and locale. To a great extent, it succeeded, particularly in terms of racial composition. But the women who went to Houston, not surprisingly, were the reformers and activists. Over 40 percent of the delegates belonged to NOW, about 30 percent belonged to the League of Women Voters, and roughly 20 percent belonged to the National Abortion Rights Action League, AAUW, or BWP. And there was a great deal of overlap in membership.[64]

Certainly the concerns of the reformers were diverse and affected the lives of all American women, but the issues that got the most media attention and, therefore, projected a particular image to the woman watching bits and pieces of the proceeding on television were issues that were threatening to many nonactivists. Lesbiansim, in particular, was an alienating life-style to most Americans and may have contributed to a negative perception of the conference that was out of proportion to the actual significance of the issue within the total conference proceedings and plan of action. A *Washington Star* editorial observed in an exaggerated, but not totally inaccurate commentary:

> There's a certain amount of liberal tsk-tsking over the way the anti-ERA forces have organized their campaign around the idea that a vote for equal rights is a vote for lesbian quotas on school faculties, junior-high abortion clinics, compulsory round-the-clock day care, and the overthrow of capitalism. But the fact is that Phyllis Schlafly didn't have to make it up. Leaders of the National Commission on the Observance of International Women's Year, an official body set up by Congress and paid for with federal funds, have put the package together for her.[65]

Of course, the media was eager to exploit any displays of radical exuberance at the IWY Conference, and many feminists took this opportunity to express their feelings through the wearing of T-shirts and buttons and in speeches and general celebratory activity. The response to the sexual preference plank, which was endorsed on a Sunday afternoon, consisted of hundreds of young women hugging, cheering, and raising clenched fists while gas-filled balloons proclaiming "We Are

Everywhere" filled the balcony. The television cameras zoomed in on inflammatory buttons—"Mother Nature is Lesbian"—and indeed, to the casual viewer, lesbianism *did* seem to be everywhere.[66]

Whatever the Houston Conference meant to the television viewer, the "spirit of Houston" had real meaning for most of the women who participated as delegates, staff people, commissioners, or observers. The symbolic significance of the meetings was perhaps best expressed by the Torch Relay, a cross-country run that began two months before the conference. About one thousand people, mostly young women but some men and some people in their fifties and sixties, passed a lighted torch hand-to-hand across 2,600 miles and fourteen states from Seneca Falls, New York, to Houston, where it was carried to the welcoming ceremonies at the Convention Center. The runners wore T-shirts emblazoned with the slogan "Women on the Move." Thousands of observers came out to cheer them on their way.[67]

For many women, the entire conference was an emotional high—an exhilarating combination of sisterhood, love, empathy, and compassion, offering all the best potential of the women's movement compressed into four days.[68] The speeches by the distinguished, the exhibits, entertainment, workshops, clinics, and briefings led by the lesser-knowns, the networking and politicking engaged in by almost all—this was Houston, not as expressed in a plan of action nor as reported by the press, but as experienced by those who were there.

In many ways, the plan of action was the least significant accomplishment of the conference, at least in terms of its practical impact over the next decade. It established an agenda for the women's movement that would have had broad implications for social change had it been implemented. But it never became the program of a major political party. The attempts to move ahead on women's issues within the Carter administration met with frustrations that were publicly revealed when Carter fired Bella Abzug from her position as cochair of the National Advisory Committee on Women. The leadership of the committee fell into the hands of moderate feminists who were concerned with the legal issue of women's rights rather than the more radical concerns expressed by Abzug, such as the economics of women's oppression, Medicaid abortion, wage-earning women, and inflation.[69]

Meanwhile, the leading feminist organization in the country, NOW, turned its full attention to the drive for the ratification of the ERA, as did most feminist reformers of the late seventies. And the conservative backlash, which was already having its impact on the presidential politics of the Carter administration, culminated in the election of Ronald Reagan and the concerted effort to roll back the gains made by reformers in the 1960s and 1970s.

It could be said that the battle lines were drawn at Houston for the final struggle over the ERA. The reformers and feminists had won the first round. The second round was to be won by a persuasive, vocal, well-organized, and well-financed minority that was able to halt the political thrust of the organized women's movement.

EPILOGUE

By the 1980s, although women had made great strides in education, opened up new employment possibilities, and gained a brand new public image, the movement as an organized force for social change was a lackluster imitation of its former self. The term *postfeminist* had been snatched up by the media to characterize the "liberated, dress-for-success, you've-come-along-way, baby, superwoman" of the 1980s, but the social ideals of feminism were not a part of this media image.[1]

If the result was a disappointment to liberal and radical activists, it should have come as no surprise to those with a sense of history. Another cycle of reform had run its course. It had fallen short of the ideals of its most advanced and committed devotées, and yet it had contributed to a change in women's status and a changing consciousness on the part of the nation as a whole. The women's movement may have been temporarily in retreat, but as with the civil rights movement of the 1960s, changes had occurred that could not be retracted. The most intangible and difficult to measure was the change in public consciousness and the consciousness of women—especially young women who now assumed responsibility for their own future in a way that could not have been matched by their mothers and grandmothers. The concrete change was that women had entered the political debate of the 1980s, and the "gender gap," although it proved to be a disappointment in the election of 1984, remained as a threat that most politicians could not ignore.

The issues of the eighties reflected the importance of women as a political constituency and, to some extent, even reflected a feminist perspective of some social issues. Unfortunately, they also confirmed, and even accentuated, the resistance to women's attempt to move be-

197

yond traditional roles. The struggle for the ERA, which was the major focus of the mainstream women's movement from 1977 through 1982, offers an excellent example of women's political coming of age placed in juxtaposition to resistance by a powerful minority.

By the time of the Houston Conference of 1977, it was becoming increasingly apparent that the ratification of the ERA was not going to occur before the 1979 deadline. Therefore, over the next several years, there was a major effort to obtain an extension of the deadline. The drive was led by NOW president Ellie Smeal, in cooperation with ERAmerica, the coalition organization established by the IWY Commission in 1976.[2]

The extension was achieved, but the victory was short-lived and primarily psychological; in the end, it may have been more damaging than helpful to the cause of feminism. Nonetheless, it had the effect of mobilizing many women on both sides of the issue, and it even created a new feminist heroine, Sonia Johnson, the Utah Mormon who evolved from "housewife to heretic" within a few short years. Johnson described in her autobiography the impact of the political struggle on women: "Women of all political hues are initiated into the secrets of power now and are loving it. Women on both sides of the ERA battle share in that. We are women who know and understand the importance of our presence in politics and intend to stay there."[3]

A retrospective analysis of the ERA campaign raises questions about the nature of the feminist movement in relation to the amendment. Joan Hoff-Wilson's anthology *Rights of Passage: The Past and Future of the ERA* (1986) attempts to place the amendment and the ratification campaign into historical and cultural context. An essay by Edith Mayo and Jerry K. Frye argues that the ERA supporters were unable to impress upon the public mind a clear distinction between "political and legal equality" and "sexual sameness." The opponents of the amendment skillfully exploited this confusion. The point is pursued a step further when the authors argue that the ERA was not separated from the rhetoric of the women's movement nor differentiated from the controversial issues of homosexuality and abortion: "The negative image of 'libbers' and their perceived attack on the family and traditional social and personal relationships was transferred to the ERA and firmly and irrevocably fixed in the public mind. . . . 'women's lib' rhetoric made an excellent target of attack for opponents of Stop ERA."[4]

The confusion over the meaning of the ERA and its relationship to the feminist movement was inevitable, since without feminism there would have *been* no ERA, and by the mid-1970s, many feminists *did* place a radical interpretation on the full intent of the amendment. But the liberal feminists viewed the ERA as a political reform that would guarantee women's legal equality under the Constitution as citizens of the United States. They argued that the amendment was only a natural extension to women of the political rights that men had always taken for granted. The strategy of the liberal ERA campaign was to downplay any significant change in sex roles and to argue that the conservative opposition's use of controversial issues was irrelevant and/or ridiculous.[5]

In particular, ERA proponents tried to deny any connection between the amendment and the abortion issue—a connection that had been skillfully exploited by Phyllis Schlafly and other ERA opponents. Liberal Catholics who supported the ERA took it upon themselves to declare the two issues to be "separate and distinct." Abortion, according to the liberal perspective, was a situation arising from a unique physical characteristic that could not be shared with the other sex. "Since it is impossible to treat men and women equally in this area, there can be no showing of a purpose or intent to discriminate." The Supreme Court, during the 1970s, based its abortion decisions on due process grounds and went out of its way to avoid defining pregnancy as an issue of sex discrimination.[6]

If one accepted the narrow interpretation of the liberal feminists, which they applied not only to abortion but to other social issues as well, in particular, lesbianism, the tendency might be to wonder whether the struggle was worth all the fuss. And in fact, many women, feminist or otherwise, felt that the attention given the ERA in the latter years of the drive for ratification detracted from more pressing social and economic issues. Women who did not identify so readily with the white middle-class career-oriented women of the liberal feminist movement, especially ethnic and minority women, were apt to show little enthusiasm for the amendment. They complained that ERA organizations failed to develop policy around the whole issue of racism/sexism, and they were insensitive to minority participation within the reform structure. These women felt left out of the network that ERA proponents had developed between 1972 and 1979.[7]

Thus, another perspective on the ERA was that it was irrelevant to the pressing concerns of working-class and minority women, a position also taken by some radical feminists, especially lesbian separatists, who may have given the amendment lukewarm support but refused to see it as an essential feminist issue. Extreme radicals (like Mary Daly, who defines radicalism as an "inner voyage"—a retreat from political struggle) would refuse to enter the patriarchal struggle on any terms. But even many activist feminists attached little importance to the ratification of the ERA.[8]

On the other hand, it was possible to apply a radical interpretation to the amendment and see it as a means of undermining the patriarchy. This perspective accepts the New Right interpretation of the potential "dangers" of the ERA and turns it on its head. Sonia Johnson's crusade for the ERA was just that—a crusade in a righteous cause. To her, the amendment meant much more than simply civil rights for women; it was a revolutionary statement that would affect those very issues that were considered so controversial: abortion, lesbian rights—"everything that women needed." Johnson argued that the ERA could be interpreted to cover those issues and that there was no point in putting so much energy into it unless it did.[9]

The confusion over the meaning and importance of the ERA was never satisfactorily resolved. Its impact on the women's movement was also ambiguous. As a crusade for justice, it was a great force for mobilization. But crusades that are lost become a source of disillusionment, and the ERA struggle was no different from other crusades in that respect. After its defeat there was a marked tendency for women, even feminists, to back off from their demands for equality, or at least to redefine equality in less threatening, less strident terms than those of the 1970s. Indeed, a whole new debate about the "nature" of women began to appear in the scholarly feminist literature of the late 1970s and early 1980s.

A controversial essay by Alice Rossi, "A Biosocial Perspective on Parenting," appeared in a 1977 special issue of *Daedalus* on the family.[10] Rossi was attempting to restore biology to a central place in feminist and social science thinking. She argued that the basic facts of any family system are biological, and that women are more naturally suited than men to the tasks of child care, food preparation, and other domestic work. Equity between mothers and fathers in their relationship to the young infant and toddler is not easily attained, according to this biosocial perspective. The mother may continue to be emotionally the most important parent even in the self-consciously androgynous household.[11]

Although Rossi claimed she did not intend to justify the conservative status quo—that is, traditional family and work roles for men and women—her attempt to synthesize biological and sociological theory brought her dangerously close to the trap of biological determinism, and provided ammunition for antifeminists.[12] Ironically, it was feminists themselves, the so-called neofeminists, who addressed the issue the most directly and persistently. Betty Friedan, in *The Second Stage* (1981), called upon feminists to make the family the "new frontier." The primary failure of the first stage of feminism was "our blind spot about the family." The new goal was to avoid polarization between men and women and between feminists and antifeminists by avoiding the controversial sexual issues such as lesbianism and abortion on demand. Friedan envisioned "the quiet movement among American men" to be the cutting edge of the second stage of liberation.[13]

Friedan was arguing from an activist, reformist perspective—that of a liberal feminist responding to the failures of liberal feminism. But Jean Bethke Elshtain adopted a theoretical point of view. During the early 1980s she produced a body of writing that included her book *Public Man, Private Woman* (1981) and several articles and exchanges with other writers, most notably Barbara Ehrenreich. Essentially, Elshtain calls for a "social feminism" that places children at the center of feminist concern, preserves traditional families and communities, maintains a clear boundary between public and private life, and sustains gender differentiation when necessary to social life.[14]

Perhaps the most distinctive characteristic of the neofeminist point of view is that it ignores man's culpability in the "war between the sexes" and, indeed, places almost the entire responsibility for resolving the polarization of men and women and the breakdown of the family upon women or, more specifically, feminists. In placing family first and equality for women second, if not last, the neofeminists reflect the backlash that has characterized the social-political milieu of the 1980s.

Nonetheless, the gains of the seventies should not be devalued or trivialized. Although the degree of liberation has been limited by the realities of the patriarchal capitalistic system, and the new problems of postfeminism have emerged to replace the old problems of the "feminine mystique," young women growing up in America today face a set of options very different from those that were available to earlier generations. Whether the issue is work, education, sexuality, motherhood, family life, friendship, or autonomy, it has been redefined so that for many women the problem has become choice rather than channeling. Likewise, the politics of the 1980s have reflected the centrality of wom-

en's issues. Abortion, pornography, feminization of poverty, comparable worth, the gender gap—these were nonissues in the premovement
years. And the feminist assault on the arts has made it impossible to
ignore any longer the woman writer, artist, or musician, even though
the debate rages on as to the relationship between gender and creativity.

But any attempt to measure the gains of the seventies has to acknowledge the reaffirmation of prefeminist values that has characterized
the 1980s. Today, marriage continues to present women with the age-
old dilemma of family versus career, and the biological time clock
ticks louder for women than for men—whether they are seeking a
mate or trying to decide when to have a baby. In spite of the many
advances on all fronts, the politics of family have taken a heavier toll
on women than on men, and a satisfactory individual solution to the
public sphere–private sphere dilemma is difficult if not impossible to
achieve.[15]

If there is one lesson to be learned from the experience of the seventies, it is that real progress toward equality for women can be
achieved only through a collective effort. The breakthroughs of the decade were the result of hard work, persistent struggle, and personal
sacrifice. The legacy of that decade of women on the move has shaped
the politics and culture of the last years of the century to an extent
unrivaled by any recent social movement. The long-term impact is yet
to be measured, but the women's movement is a process, not a conclusion, and as such, its story deserves to be accepted on its own terms.

NOTES AND REFERENCES

Introduction

1. See Arthur H. Miller, et al., "A Majority Party in Disarray: Policy Polarization in the 1972 Election," *American Political Science Review* 70 (September 1976): 753–78, for a political interpretation of the sixties and seventies that notes the emergence of issue politics.

2. Quote taken from interview with Professor Joan Roberts, Department of Child and Family Studies, Syracuse University, 28 July 1985. Comment on consensus taken from interview with Frances Kolb, NOW activist, 17 July 1985.

3. This basic distinction is made by nearly all those who have written on the women's movement, although occasionally different labels are used. See Judith Hole and Ellen Levine, *Rebirth of Feminism* (New York: Quadrangle Books, 1971), chap. 1, which covers the activities and accomplishments of reformers, and chap. 2, which discusses the various groups within the women's liberation movement that emerged from the New Left.

4. See Irene Tinker, ed., *Women in Washington: Advocates for Public Policy*, Sage Yearbooks in Women's Policy Studies, vol. 7 (Beverly Hills: Sage Publications, 1963), for a sense of the breadth of issues and the impact of women's groups on public policy in the sixties and seventies.

5. See Esther Peterson, "The Kennedy Commission," in Tinker, ed., *Women in Washington*, pp. 21–34; and Cynthia E. Harrison, "A 'New Frontier' for Women: The Public Policy of the Kennedy Administration," *Journal of American History* 67 (December 1980): 630–46.

6. Marlene Dixon, "The Rise and Demise of Women's Liberation," in *The Future of Women* (San Francisco: Synthesis Publications, 1978), pp. 79–82.

7. See Betty Friedan, *The Feminine Mystique* (New York: Dell Publishing Co., 1962).

8. See Jo Freeman, *The Politics of Women's Liberation: A Case Study of an Emerging Social Movement and Its Relation to the Policy Process* (New York: David McKay Co., 1975), chap. 5.

9. This critique was offered in 1979 by two feminist intellectuals who noted the emphasis on the personal to the detriment of the political, a tendency they felt characterized the later years of the movement. See Barbara Haber, "Is Personal Life Still a Political Issue?" *Feminist Studies* 5, no. 3 (Fall 1979: 417–30, and Elizabeth Fox-Genovese, "Personal Is Not Political Enough," *Marxist Perspectives* (Winter 1979–80): 94–113.

10. See Alan Crawford, *Thunder on the Right: The "New Right" and the Politics of Resentment* (New York: Pantheon Books, 1980), esp. chap. 5, "Protecting Hearth and Home: The Women's Place," pp. 144–60.

11. Interview with Professor Joan Roberts, 28 July 1985.

12. See Zillah R. Eisenstein, *Feminism and Sexual Equality: Crisis in Liberal America* (New York: Monthly Review Press, 1984), and Pamela Conover and Virginia Gray, *Feminism and the New Right* (New York: Praeger, 1983).

13. Richard Hofstadter, *Age of Reform* (New York: Vintage, 1948).

14. See Andrea Dworkin, *Right-Wing Women* (New York: G. P. Putnam's Sons, 1978), p. 2.

15. See William H. Chafe, *The American Woman: Her Social, Economic, and Political Roles* (Oxford: Oxford University Press, 1973).

Chapter One

1. Abe Peck, *Uncovering the Sixties: The Life and Times of the Underground Press* (New York: Pantheon Books, 1985), p. 213. For Robin Morgan's interpretation, see *Going Too Far: The Personal Chronicle of a Feminist* (New York: Random House, 1977), pp. 115–20. See also Jane Alpert, *Growing Up Underground* (New York: William Morrow & Co., 1981), pp. 243–44.

2. Sara Evans, *Personal Politics: The Roots of Women's Liberation in the Civil Rights Movement and the New Left* (New York: Random House, 1979), traces that history. See Robin Morgan, "Good-Bye to All That," in Morgan, *Going Too Far*, pp. 121–30, and Marge Piercy, "The Grand Coolie Dam," in Robin Morgan, ed., *Sisterhood Is Powerful: An Anthology of Writings from the Women's Liberation Movement* (New York: Random House, 1970), pp. 421–38.

3. Judith Hole and Ellen Levine, *Rebirth of Feminism* (New York: Quadrangle Books, 1971), pp. 110–11, and Evans, *Personal Politics*, pp. 85–88.

4. Hole and Levine, *Rebirth*, pp. 111–13, and Evans, *Personal Politics*, pp. 196–99.

5. Hole and Levine, *Rebirth*, pp. 113–14.

6. See Gail Paradise Kelly, "Women's Liberation and the New Left," in Edith Hoshino Altback, ed., *From Feminism to Liberation* (Cambridge, Mass.: Schenkman Publishing Co., 1971), pp. 39–46.

7. Thomas Powers, *Diana: The Making of a Terrorist* (Boston: Houghton Mifflin Co., 1971), p. 126.

8. Kelly, *Women's Liberation*, pp. 42–43. For a discussion of the differ-

ences between women in the New Left and those in the Old Left, see Ellen Kay Trimberger, "Women in the Old and New Left: The Evolution of a Politics of Personal Life," and a response by Peggy Dennis in *Feminist Studies* 5 (Fall 1979): 432–61.

9. March Lockwood Carden, *The New Feminist Movement* (New York: Russell Sage Foundation, 1974), pp. 69–70.

10. Ellen Willis, "Women and the Left," reprinted in *Notes from the Second Year: Women's Liberation—Major Writings of the Radical Feminists*, April 1970, p. 55.

11. Willis, "Sequel: Letter to a Critic," in *Notes from the Second Year*, pp. 57–58.

12. Hole and Levine, *Rebirth*, pp. 115–18, and Carden, *New Feminist Movement*, p. 61.

13. Hole and Levine, *Rebirth*, pp. 119–22, and 126–29.

14. Ibid., pp. 136–37. See "Redstockings Manifesto," in Morgan, *Sisterhood Is Powerful*, pp. 533–36.

15. "Women's Group Splits over Meaning of Feminism," *Washington Post*, October (no day) 1968, in Charlotte Bunch Collection, Schlesinger Library, Radcliffe College, Carton 1, Folder 7.

16. Ibid. See also Andrew H. Merton, *Enemies of Choice: The Right-to-Life Movement and Its Threat to Abortion* (Boston: Beacon Press, 1981), pp. 106–7, for a discussion of Bill Baird.

17. See "The Feminists: A Political Organization to Annihilate Sex Roles," in Ann Koedt, ed., *Radical Feminism* (New York: Quadrangle Books, 1973), pp. 368–69.

18. Ibid., pp. 370–74.

19. For a discussion of consciousness-raising, see Judith Brown and Carol Giandina, "Deadend Consciousness-Raising and Ideological Scabbing: Roadblocks to Revolutions," unpublished paper, June 1971, in Charlotte Bunch Collection, Carton 1, Folder 5.

20. Lynn Ellen O'Connor, "Prison Guards," *Women's Page*, n.d., in Charlotte Bunch Collection, Carton 1, Folder 5.

21. Jennifer Gardner, "The Small Group," *Women's Page*, n.d.; Jeanne Arrow, "Dangers in the Pro-Women Line and Consciousness-Raising," unpublished paper from the ideas of the Feminists, November 1969, pp. 4–6; and Gardner, "Gallstones: A Case in Point," *Women's Page*, n.d., all in Charlotte Bunch Collection, Carton 1, Folder 5.

22. Arrow, "Dangers in the Pro-Women Line."

23. "The Politics of Ego: A Manifesto for New York Radical Feminists," in Koedt, *Radical Feminism*, pp. 379–83.

24. Power, *Diana*. See also Ellen Frankfort, *Kathy Boudin and the Dance of Death* (Briarcliff, N.Y.: Stein & Day, 1983).

25. Power, p. 126.

26. Ibid., pp. 72–73, 101.

27. Susan Stern, *With the Weatherman: The Personal Journal of a Revolutionary Woman* (Garden City, N.Y.: Doubleday, 1975).

28. Kenneth Keniston, *The Uncommitted: Alienated Youth in American Society* (New York: Harcourt Brace Jovanovich, 1960), p. 349.

29. Stern, *With the Weatherman*, pp. 256–58, 9–12.

30. Ibid., p. 65.

31. Ibid., p. 72.

32. Ibid., pp. 39, 143–44.

33. Ibid., pp. 73, 93.

34. Alpert, *Growing Up Underground*, chaps. 1 and 2.

35. Ibid., pp. 122–24.

36. Ibid., pp. 134–35.

37. Ibid., p. 185.

38. Ibid., pp. 242–43.

39. Ibid., pp. 243–44.

40. See n. 2 above.

41. Jane Alpert, "Forum: Mother Right—A New Feminist Theory," *MS.* 2 (August 1973): 53. See also Alpert, *Growing Up Underground*, chap. 16.

42. Alpert, "Mother Right."

43. Judith Coburn, "The Issue That's Splitting Feminists," reprinted in Flo Kennedy, *Color Me Flo: My Life and Good Times* (Englewood Cliffs, N.J.: Prentice-Hall, 1976).

44. Ibid.

45. Letter to Charlotte Bunch from Pamela Kearon and Mary E. Lutz, 12 September 1975, in Bunch Collection, Carton 4, Folder 15.

46. Activists who attested to the interaction among feminists in their personal interviews included Yvette Oldendorf, Minnesota Democratic Farmer-Labor party feminist caucus, St. Paul, Minn.; Francis Kolb, NOW historian and activist, Boston, Mass.; Joan Roberts, chair, Department of Child and Family Studies, Syracuse University; and Donna Allen, Women's Institute for Freedom of the Press, Washington, D.C.

Chapter Two

1. For an especially upbeat interpretation of the early Kennedy years, see Arthur M. Schlesinger, Jr., *A Thousand Days: John F. Kennedy in the White House* (Boston: Houghton Mifflin Co., 1965), and Theodore C. Sorensen, *Kennedy* (New York: Harper & Row, 1965). For later, more detached interpretations, see Jim Heath, *Decade of Disillusionment: The Kennedy–Johnson Years* (Bloomington: Indiana University Press, 1975), and Herbert S. Parmet, *JFK: The Presidency of John F. Kennedy* (New York: Dial, 1983).

2. Interview with Esther Peterson, March 1971, quoted in Judith Hole and Ellen Levine, *Rebirth of Feminism* (New York: Quadrangle Books, 1971), p.

19. See also Cynthia E. Harrison, "A New Frontier for Women: The Public Policy of the Kennedy Administration," *Journal of American History* 67 (December 1980): 630–46; Esther Peterson, "The Kennedy Commission," and Catherine East, "Newer Commissions," in Irene Tinker, ed., *Women in Washington: Advocates for Public Policy*, Sage Yearbooks in Women's Policy Studies, vol. 7 (Beverly Hills, Calif.: Sage Publications, 1983).

3. Interview with Catherine East, Ithaca, New York, 5 July 1985; and Catherine East, "Newer Commissions," in Tinker, ed., *Women in Washington*, p. 35.

4. Ibid., pp. 35–36. See also Ethel Klein, *Gender Politics: From Consciousness to Mass Politics* (Cambridge: Harvard University Press, 1984), pp. 22–23.

5. Myra Marx Ferree and Beth B. Hess, *Controversy and Coalition: The New Feminist Movement* (Boston: Twayne Publishers, 1985), pp. 53–54.

6. Klein, *Gender Politics*, p. 23.

7. Ferree and Hess, *Controversy and Coalition*, p. 54. See also Hole and Levine, *Rebirth*, pp. 82–83. See chapter 3 of this book for a more detailed analysis of the early history of NOW.

8. East, "Newer Commissions," pp. 36–37; Hole and Levine, *Rebirth*, pp. 24–28.

9. Hole and Levine, *Rebirth*, pp. 25–26, and East, "Newer Commissions," pp. 36–37.

10. Interview with Arvonne Fraser, Hubert Humphrey Institute for Public Affairs, University of Minnesota, 27 August 1985. See also Arvonne S. Fraser, "Insiders and Outsiders: Women in the Political Arena," in Tinker, ed., *Women in Washington*, pp. 120–39.

11. See Arlene Daniels, "W.E.A.L.: The Growth of a Feminist Organization," in Bernice Cummings and Victoria Schuck, eds., *Women Organizing: An Anthology* (Metuchen, N.J.: Scarecrow Press, 1979), pp. 133–51; and Hole and Levine, *Rebirth*, pp. 95–98.

12. See Arthur H. Miller, Warren E. Miller, Alden S. Raine, and Thad A. Brown, "A Majority Party in Disarray: Policy Polarization in the 1972 Election," *American Political Science Review* 70 (September 1976): 753–78.

13. Ibid., pp. 753–54.

14. See Byron E. Shafer, *Quiet Revolution: The Struggle for the Democratic Party and the Shaping of Post-Reform Politics* (New York: Russell Sage Foundation, 1983), esp. chap. 17.

15. Herbert S. Parmet, *The Democrats: The Years after FDR* (New York: Macmillan, 1976), pp. 292–94. For a more thorough analysis of the whole process of party reform through the McGovern Commission, see Shafer, *Quiet Revolution*, chaps. 4 and 5. See also "The Commission on Party Structure and Delegate Selection to the Democratic National Committee," in Report of the Commission, *Mandate for Reform* (Washington, D.C., April 1970), p. 34, quoted in Stephen C. Schlesinger, *The New Reformers: Forces for Change in American Politics* (Boston: Houghton Mifflin Co., 1975), p. 3.

16. Parmet, *The Democrats*, p. 284. See also Kevin Phillips, *The Emerging Republican Majority* (New Rochelle, N.Y.: Arlington House, 1969).

17. Schlesinger, *New Reformers*, pp. 10–11.

18. Ibid., pp. 24–26.

19. Bella S. Abzug, *Bella! Ms. Abzug Goes to Washington* (New York: Saturday Review Press, 1972), pp. 160–61, 163–64.

20. Ibid., pp. 177, 198–200. See also Rona F. Feit, "Organizing for Political Power: The National Women's Political Caucus," in Cummings and Schuck, eds., *Women Organizing*, p. 185.

21. Feit, "Organizing," p. 185. There was still tension between Abzug and Friedan as to priorities—women's rights or social issues.

22. Shafer, *Quiet Revolution*, p. 461.

23. Ibid., p. 481.

24. See ibid., pp. 473–86, for an explanation and description of the main actors in this drama.

25. Shafer, *Quiet Revolution*, chap. 17 and esp. Conclusion.

26. Theodore H. White, *The Making of the President: 1972* (New York: Atheneum, 1973), chap. 7.

27. See esp. Germaine Greer, "McGovern, the Big Tease," *Harper's*, October 1972, pp. 56–71; Shana Alexander, "The Politics of Abortion," *Newsweek*, 2 October 1972; and Nora Ephron, "Women," *Esquire* 78 (November 1972): 10. For the radical leftist critique, see Linda Jenness and Richard Gottfried, "McGovern and the Democratic Party: The Way to Radical Change?" *International Socialist Review* 33 (September 1972): 6–9, 38–39, and Betsy Stone, "Women and the 1972 Election," *International Socialist Review* 33 (February 1972): 15–19, 39.

28. See Abzug, *Bella*, p. 241, for her description of the friction between Friedan and herself in terms of class and political affiliation. See also Schlesinger, *New Reformers*, pp. 28–29.

29. Fraser, "Insiders," p. 134.

30. Abzug, *Bella*, pp. 219–20, and Shirley Chisholm, *The Good Fight* (New York: Harper & Row, 1973), p. 74

31. Quoted in Schlesinger, *New Reformers*, p. 35.

32. Chisholm, *Good Fight*, pp. 75–76.

33. Ibid.

34. Gloria Steinem, *Outrageous Acts and Everyday Rebellions* (New York: Holt, Rinehart & Winston, 1983), p. 105.

35. Chisholm, *Good Fight*, p. 77.

36. Steinem, *Outrageous Acts*, p. 104. Gary Hart, McGovern's campaign manager, in particular seemed to be unsympathetic to the role of women at the convention. See quote by Jean Westwood, in Susan and Martin Tolchin, *Clout: Womanpower and Politics* (New York: Coward, McCann & Geoghegan, 1974), p. 39.

37. Tolchin, *Clout*, pp. 32–33. On the symbolic importance of the co-chair issue, see pp. 40–41.

38. Tolchin, *Clout*, p. 33.

39. See ibid., pp. 41–43, and Denis G. Sullivan et al., *The Politics of Representation: The Democratic Convention, 1972* (New York: St. Martin's Press, 1974), pp. 53, 69*n* 11.

40. See Shirley MacLaine, "Women, the Convention and Brown Paper Bags," *New York Times Magazine* 30 July 1972, p. 14. See Tolchin, *Clout*, p. 37, for the reaction of feminists to the MacLaine appointment, and a defense of MacLaine by Rick Stearns, a McGovern lieutenant.

41. Tolchin, *Clout*, p. 48.

42. MacLaine, "Women, the Convention, and Brown Paper Bags," and Schlesinger, *New Reformers*, p. 38.

43. Tolchin, *Clout*, pp. 44–46.

44. The New Right did not emerge until 1974–75, when it formed in reaction to what was perceived as liberals dominating the Republican party. The Moral Majority emerged much later. Although the right-to-life movement began as early as 1970, when the Catholic church began to organize right-to-life committees, it did not launch a full-scale campaign until after *Roe* v. *Wade* in 1973.

45. Shana Alexander, "The Politics of Abortion," *Newsweek*, 2 October 1972.

46. Jeane Kirkpatrick had a more cynical interpretation that was ultimately more accurate. See Kirkpatrick, "The Revolt of the Masses," *Commentary* 55 (February 1973): 58–62.

47. See Elizabeth Frappollo, "The Ticket That Might Have Been . . . Vice-President Farenthold," *Ms.*, January 1973, pp. 74–75. See also Tolchin, *Clout*, pp. 49–53, and MacLaine, "Women, the Convention, and Brown Paper Bags."

48. See Frappollo, "The Ticket," p. 74.

49. Greer, "McGovern," pp. 62–63.

50. Sullivan, *Politics of Representation*, p. 86.

51. Schlesinger, *New Reformers*, pp. 43–44.

52. Ibid., pp. 44–45.

53. Klein, *Gender Politics*, pp. 30–31, 81.

54. Ruth B. Mandel, *In the Running: The New Woman Candidate* (New York: Ticknor & Fields, 1981), pp. 135–37, and Klein, *Gender Politics*, p. 31.

55. Interview with Yvette Oldendorf, Working Opportunities for Women, St. Paul, Minnesota, 26 August 1985.

56. Schlesinger, *New Reformers*, pp. 46–47.

57. Fraser, "Insiders," pp. 136–37.

58. Ibid., pp. 135, 137–38.

59. Schlesinger, *New Reformers*, pp. 49–50.

60. See Tolchin, *Clout*, chap. 6, and pp. 245–46.

61. Klein, *Gender Politics*, p. 31, and Tolchin, *Clout*, pp. 197–98.

Chapter Three

1. Barbara J. Nelson, "Women's Poverty and Women's Citizenship: Some Political Consequences of Economic Marginality," *Signs: Journal of Women in Culture and Society* 10 (Winter 1984): 225–26.

2. Jo Freeman, *The Politics of Women's Liberation: A Case Study of an Emerging Social Movement and Its Relation to the Policy Process* (New York: David McKay Co., 1975), pp. 49–55.

3. See Aileen S. Kraditor, *The Ideas of the Woman Suffrage Movement, 1890–1920* (New York: Columbia University Press, 1965), esp. pp. 231–48. For a recent interpretation, see Nancy F. Cott, "Feminist Politics in the 1920s: The National Woman's Party," *Journal of American History* 71 (June 1984): 43–68.

4. Freeman, *Politics of Women's Liberation*, p. 72.

5. See Hole and Levine, *Rebirth*, pp. 81–84, for a description of the founding of NOW. See also Maren Lockwood Carden, *The New Feminist Movement* (New York: Russell Sage Foundation, 1974), pp. 103–5, and Ethel Klein, *Gender Politics: From Consciousness to Mass Politics* (Cambridge: Harvard University Press, 1984), p. 23. Betty Friedan gives a colorful personal account in *It Changed My Life: Writings on the Women's Movement* (New York: Dell Publishing Co., 1977), pp. 109–23, in which she notes the key contributions of Catharine East, Richard Graham, and others.

6. Hole and Levine, *Rebirth*, pp. 84–85. See pp. 85–86 for a statement of principles and goals. The twenty-four-member board, a distinguished group, included seven university professors or administrators, four federal and local government officials, five state and national labor union officials, and four business executives.

7. Zillah R. Eisenstein, *The Radical Future of Liberal Feminism* (New York: Longman, 1981), pp. 177–78, 181–82.

8. Friedan, *It Changed My Life*, p. 103, quoted in Eisenstein, *Radical Future*, p. 185.

9. Freeman, *Politics of Women's Liberation*, p. 75.

10. Hole and Levine, *Rebirth*, pp. 86–87.

11. Ibid., p. 88. See also Friedan, *It Changed My Life*, pp. 143–45.

12. Hole and Levine, *Rebirth*, p. 88. See also Freeman, *Politics of Women's Liberation*, p. 80.

13. Hole and Levine, *Rebirth*, pp. 95–96, and Freeman, *Politics of Women's Liberation*, p. 81.

14. Interview with Mary Jean Collins, former vice president of NOW, Washington, D.C., 15 October 1985. Collins, a long-time activist and NOW board member pointed out that NOW was always slightly ahead of the general

population and led on issues such as the ERA and abortion. But the organization also had a certain pragmatic adaptability that allowed it to survive through the seventies, when more radical organizations disappeared.

15. See news article, "Friedan: Feminism Faces a Backlash," *Washington Post*, n.d., 1968, in Charlotte Bunch Collection, Carton 1, Folder 7, in the Schlesinger Library, Radcliffe College, Cambridge, Massachusetts.

16. For a negative interpretation of Atkinson, her split with NOW, and her impact on the movement, see Leah Fritz, *Dreamers and Dealers: An Intimate Appraisal of the Women's Movement* (Boston: Beacon Press, 1979), esp. pp. 37–49 and also pp. 61–66, 92–100. See also Ti-Grace Atkinson, *Amazon Odysseus* (New York: Links Books, 1974).

17. See, for example, Joan Cassell, *A Group Called Women: Sisterhood and Symbolism in the Feminist Movement* (New York: David McKay Co., 1977), p. 7. Cassell also contrasts the women's liberation "uniform" with the NOW "uniform" (pp. 84–85) and relates the differences in dress style to differences in philosophy and hierarchical style (pp. 94–95).

18. Interview with Lois Galgay Reckitt, vice president–executive, NOW, Washington, D.C., 25 June 1985.

19. Interview with Frances Kolb, former NOW activist and board member, Cambridge, Mass., 17 July 1985.

20. Hole and Levine, *Rebirth*, pp. 150–52, and Friedan, *It Changed My Life*, pp. 185–87.

21. Friedan, *It Changed My Life*, pp. 189–90.

22. Ibid., pp. 190–91.

23. Ibid., pp. 207–9. See Klein, *Gender Politics*, pp. 1, 25, for an analysis of the political impact of the strike. Klein notes that after the strike, 80 percent of American adults were aware of the women's movement. See also, Hole and Levine, *Rebirth*, p. 93.

24. Hole and Levine, *Rebirth*, pp. 93–94.

25. Freeman, *Politics of Women's Liberation*, pp. 99–100.

26. For a statement of Heide's feminist philosophy and a brief biographical sketch, see Wilma Scott Heide, *Feminism for the Health of It* (Buffalo, N.Y.: Margaretdaughters, 1985), with a foreword by Jessie Bernard. See also Eleanor Humes Haney, *A Feminist Legacy: The Ethics of Wilma Scott Heide and Company* (Buffalo, N.Y.: Margaretdaughters, 1985).

27. See Heide, *Feminism*, pp. 59–60, for her statement on lesbianism. See also Haney, *Feminist Legacy*, pp. 108–11. See Friedan, *It Changed My Life*, pp. 189–90, 215, 478–79.

28. For examples of Heide's concern, see correspondence from Wilma Scott Heide to Sherry Smith, 26 December 1971, NOW Papers, Carton 3, File: President Heide, 1973–74; and memo from Betsy Hogan to Massachusetts Chapter Presidents and Convenors, 22 August 1972, NOW Papers, Carton 3, File: Bylaws; and memo from President Wilma Scott Heide to NOW Chapter Presidents, November 1972, NOW Papers, Carton 3, File: Bylaws.

29. Correspondence from Ann Scott to Wilma Scott Heide, n.d., 1971, in NOW Papers, Carton 3, File: President Heide. See also Scott to Heide, 16 September 1971, NOW Papers, Carton 3, File: President Heide.

30. Freeman, *Politics of Women's Liberation*, p. 100. Carden also describes the movement toward more humanizing and radical goals in the early seventies (*New Feminist Movement*, p. 118).

31. Correspondence from President Heide to Sen. George McGovern, 5 October 1971, NOW Papers, Carton 3, File: President Heide.

32. Correspondence from President Heide to President Richard M. Nixon, 1 January 1973; and Correspondence from President Heide to Dr. Henry Kissinger, Secretary of State, U.S. Department of State, 30 September 1973, NOW Papers, Carton 3, File: President Heide.

33. Correspondence from Heide to Irene Tinker, Ph.D., Presiding Officer, Federation of Organizations for Professional Women, 17 October 1973; and Correspondence from Heide to Carmen R. Maymi, Director of Women's Bureau, Employment Standards Administration, U.S. Department of Labor, 28 December 1973, NOW Papers, File: President Heide.

34. Correspondence to Tinker. See also Friedan, *It Changed My Life*, pp. 135–36.

35. Carden, *New Feminist Movement*, pp. 119–22.

36. Ibid., p. 122.

37. Ibid., p. 123. These figures are approximate, and somewhat understate the case. For more specific figures, see NOW Papers, Carton 3, File: Financial Vice President.

38. "Dues-Sharing Proposal of Boston NOW," for consideration by National Board Meeting, Denver, 16–18 April 1972, NOW Papers, Carton 3, File: Financial Vice President.

39. Carden, *New Feminist Movement*, pp. 125–26. See also Freeman, *Politics of Women's Liberation*, pp. 88–90.

40. Report of NOW President Heide to the Board of Directors, 23–25 February 1974, p. 2. See also Haney, *Feminist Legacy*, p. 128.

41. Ibid., p. 126. Also interview with Karen DeCrow, former NOW President, Syracuse, N.Y., 8 August 1985.

42. Interview with De Crow.

43. "Chicago NOW POWER New Directions," in NOW Papers, Carton 5, File: 1974 National Conference.

44. News from the National Public Information Office, NOW, 28 May 1974, NOW Papers, Carton 5, File: 1974 National Conference. See Haney, *Feminist Legacy*, p. 126, for a description of the conference.

45. Correspondence from President Karen DeCrow to NOW Budget Committee, 12 July 1974, NOW Papers, Box 15: File: Plitt Controversy.

46. Correspondence from Jane Plitt, Executive Officer, to Karen DeCrow, NOW President, two letters, both dated 17 September 1974, NOW Papers, Box

15, File: Plitt Controversy. There were also letters in October and November that voiced the same concern.

47. Interview with DeCrow.

48. Information is contained in the NOW Papers, Box 15, File: Plitt Controversy. See also Haney, *Feminist Legacy*, pp. 127–29. For written complaints from NOW members, see the papers of Mary Ann Sedey, Midwest Regional Director, NOW Papers, Box 16, File: Mary Ann Sedey.

49. Karen DeCrow, "A Call to Conference," *Electric Circle* 1, no. 1 (August 1975): 1.

50. See Bev Jones, "Leveling the Hierarchy," and Ann Pride, "Growing Up with the Movement," *Electric Circle* 1, no. 1 (August 1975). See also *Electric Circle* 1, no. 2 (October 1975), for conference news.

51. Interviews with Kolb and Collins. It is interesting that although Kolb and Collins were on opposite sides of the political fence in 1975, they both saw the conference as a disgrace and an embarrassment to NOW. See also Haney, *Feminist Legacy*, p. 117.

52. See ibid., pp. 127–28, for Heide's reaction to the conference. Heide tried hard to remain neutral. She was torn philosophically and personally by the division, and some NOW members were critical of her nonalignment.

53. Interview with Kolb.

54. Interviews with Kolb, Collins, and Reckitt.

55. Kay Whitlock, "Moving toward Autocracy: Power Brokerage and Single Issue Politics in NOW," *Quest* 5 (Spring 1979): 36–55.

56. Letter to *Gay Community News* from Charlotte Bunch, 13 November 1979, in Charlotte Bunch Collection, Carton 2, File 52, Schlesinger Library.

57. Nancy Day, "Black Women Turn Down NOW Offer," *San Francisco Examiner*, 16 October 1979; unpublished manuscript in Bunch Collection, Carton 2, File 52.

Chapter Four

1. Interview with Karen DeCrow, August 1985.

2. See Marilyn Frye, *The Politics of Reality: Essays in Feminist Theory* (Trumansberg, N.Y.: Crossing Press, 1983), esp. the essays, "Oppression," pp. 1–16, and "Some Reflections on Separatism and Power," pp. 95–109.

3. Carol P. Christ and Judith Plaskow, eds., *Womanspirit Rising: A Feminist Reader in Religion* (New York: Harper & Row, 1979), pp. 19–20.

4. In an interview with Sonia Johnson, I used the term *visionary feminism* several times, until Johnson pointed out that she had run for president in 1984, which she understandably viewed as a pretty high level of political activism.

5. See Sidney Abbott and Barbara Love, *Sappho Was a Right-on Woman: A Liberated View of Lesbianism* (New York: Stein & Day, 1972), p. 151.

6. Hole and Levine, *Rebirth*, pp. 373–74.

7. See Christ and Plaskow, *Womanspirit*, "Introduction," pp. 1–17, for a thoughtful overview of the feminist critique of traditional religion.

8. Christ and Plaskow, *Womanspirit*, p. 193.

9. Valerie Saiving, "The Human Situation: A Feminine View," *Journal of Religion* (April 1960); also reprinted in Christ and Plaskow, *Womanspirit*, pp. 25–42.

10. See Anne Barstow Driver, "Review Essay: Religion," *Signs: A Journal of Women in Culture and Society* 2 (Winter 1976): 435.

11. Ruether, "Motherearth and the Megamachine: A Theology of Liberation in a Feminine, Somatic, and Ecological Perspective," reprinted in Christ and Plaskow, *Womanspirit*, pp. 43–52, originally published in *Christianity and Crisis*, 12 April 1972.

12. Driver, "Religion," p. 436. See Fay H. Ellison, "A Modest Proposal," *Theological Education* (Winter 1975): 106–11. See also Emily Hewitt and Susan Hiatt, *Women Priests: Yes or No?* (New York: Seabury Press, 1973), and Carter Heyward, *A Priest Forever* (New York: Harper & Row, 1976).

13. Heyward, *Priest Forever*, pp. 2–3.

14. Ibid., pp. 32–33. See also Jeanne Richie, "Church, Caste and Women," *Christian Century*, 21 January 1970, pp. 73–77.

15. "Proposal Regarding the Status of Women in the Roman Catholic Church to Be Presented to the National Conference of Catholic Bishops," 20 August 1970, in the Charlotte Bunch Papers, Carton 1, Folder 16, at the Schlesinger Women's History Library, Cambridge, Massachusetts.

16. Mary Daly, *The Church and the Second Sex: With a New Feminist Post-Christian Introduction* (New York: Harper Colophon Books, 1968, 1975), p. 5.

17. Ibid., pp. 10–12.

18. See Daly, "After the Death of God the Father," reprinted in Christ and Plaskow, *Womanspirit*, pp. 53–62. For editorial comment, see pp. 22–24.

19. Daly, *Beyond God the Father: Toward a Philosophy of Women's Liberation* (Boston: Beacon Press, 1973), p. 29.

20. Ibid., pp. 13–14.

21. Daly, *The Church and the Second Sex*, p. 42.

22. Daly, *Gyn/Ecology: The Metaphysics of Radical Feminism* (Boston: Beacon Press, 1979), reviewed by Ross S. Kraemer in *Signs* 5 (Winter 1979): 354–56.

23. See Letty M. Russell, *Human Liberation in a Feminist Perspective—a Theology* (Philadelphia: Westminster Press, 1974); and essays in Christ and Plaskow, *Womanspirit*, in part 3, "Reconstructing Tradition," and part 4, "Creating New Traditions." See also Charlene Spretnak, ed., *The Politics of Women's Spirituality: Essays on the Rise of Spiritual Power within the Feminist Movement* (New York: Doubleday, 1982), pp. xi–xxiv.

24. See Spretnak, *Women's Spirituality*, especially essays by Merlin Stone, Carol P. Christ, Adrienne Rich, Naomi Goldenberg, and Sabrina Sojourner, whose essay reclaims the African tradition of a black goddess.

25. Quoted in Gayle Graham Yates, "Spirituality and the American Fem-

inist Experience," *Signs* 9 (Autumn 1983): 60, from Eleanor Humes Haney, "What Is Feminist Ethics? A Proposal for Continuing Discussion," *Journal of Religious Ethics* 8 (Spring 1980): 115–24.

26. For an extreme interpretation of a women-controlled universe, see Sally Miller Gearhart, "The Future—If There is One—Is Female," in Pam McAllister, *Reweaving the Web of Life: Feminism and Nonviolence* (Philadelphia: New Society Publishers, 1982).

27. Alix Kates Shulman, "Sex and Power: Sexual Bases of Radical Feminism," *Signs* 5 (Summer 1980): 590–91.

28. Ibid., p. 592.

29. Ibid., p. 597. Koedt's article was reprinted in Leslie Tanner, ed., *Voices from Women's Liberation* (New York: New American Library/Mentor Books, 1970).

30. See Ti-Grace Atkinson, "The Institution of Sexual Intercourse," in *Notes from the Second Year*, pp. 45–46; and Dana Densmore, "On Celibacy," in Tanner, pp. 164–68.

31. Robin Morgan, *Going Too Far: The Personal Chronicle of a Feminist* (New York: Random House, 1977), pp. 21–56.

32. Susan Braudy, *Between Marriage and Divorce: A Woman's Diary* (New York: William Morrow, 1975), p. 235.

33. Lillian Faderman, *Surpassing the Love of Men: Romantic Friendship and Love between Women from the Renaissance to the Present* (New York: William Morrow, 1981), pp. 377–78. See also Carol Smith-Rosenberg's landmark essay "The Female World of Love and Ritual: Relations Between Women in Nineteenth Century America," *Signs* 1 (Autumn 1975): 1–29.

34. Abbott and Love, *Sappho*, p. 110, and Friedan, *It Changed My Life*, pp. 189–90, 210–13.

35. Abbott and Love, *Sappho*, pp. 110–11.

36. Ibid., pp. 111–13.

37. Ibid., p. 113, and Donn Teal, *The Gay Militants* (New York: Stein & Day, 1971), p. 183. For another early statement, see Martha Shelly, "Notes of a Radical Lesbian," in Morgan, ed., *Sisterhood Is Powerful*, pp. 306–11.

38. Radicalesbians, "The Woman-Identified Woman," in Koedt, *Radical Feminism*, p. 243, and Shelly, "Notes," p. 308.

39. Abbott and Love, *Sappho*, pp. 113–14. See also Teal, *Gay Militants*, pp. 179–80.

40. "Women's Lib: A Second Look," *Time*, 14 December 1970, p. 50, quoted in Abbott and Love, *Sappho*, p. 121.

41. Abbott and Love, *Sappho*, pp. 123–25.

42. Ibid., p. 129.

43. Ibid., pp. 133–34. For a sense of the extent to which the lesbian issue became a political football in 1975, see Correspondence: Sidney Abbott to Mary Ann Sedley, 24 November 1975, and accompanying article, "NOW Leaders form a Dissident 'Network,'" *New York Times*, 15 November 1975, p. 1, in

NOW Papers, Box 16, Sedley Correspondence, Oct. 1974–Nov. 1976, at the Schlesinger Library.

44. Kerry Lobel and Jeanne Cordovo, "NOW Convention: Out of the Revolution, into the Mainstream," *Lesbian Tide,* November-December 1979, p. 20.

45. Morgan, "Lesbianism and Feminism: Synonyms or Contradictions?" in *Good-Bye to All That,* p. 178.

46. Joreen, "Forum: Trashing, The Dark Side of Sisterhood," *Ms.,* April 1976, pp. 49–51. Joreen was a pen name used by Jo Freeman.

47. Ibid., p. 97.

48. See Gayle Kimball, "Women's Culture: Themes and Images," in *Women's Culture: The Women's Renaissance of the Seventies* (Metuchen, N.J.: Scarecrow Press, 1981). For an overview of developments in the field of literary criticism, see Elaine Showalter, "The Feminist Critical Revolution," in *The New Feminist Criticism: Essays on Women, Literature, and Theory* (New York: Pantheon Books, 1985), pp. 3–18.

49. Kate Millett, *Sexual Politics* (New York: Doubleday, 1970), and Millett, *Sita* (New York: Random House, 1976).

50. Rosalind Coward, "Are Women's Novels Feminist Novels?" in Showalter, *New Feminist Criticism,* pp. 225–39.

51. Erica Jong, *Fear of Flying* (New York: New American Library, 1973).

52. Ann Barr Snitow, "The Front Line: Notes on Sex in Novels by Women, 1969–1979," *Signs* 5 (Summer 1980).

53. Marge Piercy, in "Symposium: From the 60s to the 80s," *Cultural Correspondence* 12–14 (Summer 1981): 37–38.

54. Carol Burr Megibow, "The Use of Story in Women's Novels of the Seventies," in Kimball, *Women's Culture,* p. 200. See also Marge Piercy, "Mirror Images," in the same book, p. 192.

55. See Morgan, *Anatomy of Freedom,* p. 283.

56. See Margaret A. Simons, "Racism and Feminism: A Schism in the Sisterhood," *Feminist Studies* 5 (Summer 1979): 384–401.

57. Bonnie Thornton Dill, "Race, Class, and Gender: Prospects for an All-Inclusive Sisterhood," *Feminist Studies* 9 (Spring 1983): 131–50. See also Angela Davis, "Reflections on the Black Woman's Role in the Community of Slaves," *Black Scholar* 2 (December 1971). See also Elizabeth Fox-Genovese, "The Personal Is Not Political Enough," *Marxist Perspectives* (Winter 1979–80): 94–113.

58. Alice Walker, "A Talk: Convocation 1972," in *In Search of Our Mothers' Gardens* (New York: Harcourt Brace Jovanovich, 1983), p. 36.

59. Barbara Smith, "Toward a Black Feminist Criticism," in Showalter, *New Feminist Criticism,* p. 169.

60. Ibid., pp. 174–75.

61. See Michelle Wallace, "Black Macho and the Myth of Superwoman," *Ms.,* January 1979, p. 87, adapted from the book of the same title. Wallace's book had a number of problems with respect to perspective, scholarship, and

method, and she has been taken to task by critics. See, in particular, Linda Powell, "Black Macho and Black Feminism," *Radical America* 14 (March-April 1980): 57–63, and Alice Walker, "To the Black Scholar," in *In Search of Our Mothers' Gardens*, pp. 320–25.

62. Walker, *In Search of Our Mothers' Gardens*, pp. xi–xii.

63. Ibid., "Looking to the Side and Back," pp. 313–19. See also Audre Lorde, "Scratching the Surface: Some Notes on Barriers to Women and Loving," *Black Scholar* (April 1978): 31–35, in which Lorde analyzes attitudes toward black lesbians in the black community and describes women-identified women in Africa.

64. The most widely read of Sarton's journals are *Journal of a Solitude* (1973) and *Plant Dreaming Deep* (1967), both of which recount her life in Nelson, New Hampshire, and *The House by the Sea* (1977), which describes her first year in her new home by the ocean in Maine.

65. For critical reviews of Sarton's novels, see Kathleen Gregory Klein, "Aging and Dying in the Novels of May Sarton," *Critique: Studies in Modern Fiction* 24 (Spring 1983): 150–57; and Jane S. Bakerman, "'Kinds of Love': Love and Friendship in Novels of May Sarton," *Critique* 20 (Winter 1978): 83–91.

66. Adrienne Rich, "When We Dead Awaken: Writing as Re-Vision," *College English* 34 (October 1972): 18–25, reprinted in Rich, *On Lies, Secrets, and Silences: Selected Prose, 1966–1978* (New York: W. W. Norton & Co., 1979), p. 42. For a biographical account of Rich's life which includes a literary analysis, see Wendy Martin, *An American Triptych: Anne Bradstreet, Emily Dickinson, Adrienne Rich* (Chapel Hill: University of North Carolina Press, 1984), esp. pp. 167–72.

67. Martin, ibid., p. 168.

68. Rich, *On Lies, Secrets, and Silences*, p. 17.

69. Martin, *American Triptych*, pp. 217–21.

70. Adrienne Rich, "Compulsory Heterosexuality and Lesbian Existence," *Signs* 5 (Summer 1980): 647.

71. Ibid., pp. 648–50.

72. Susan Griffin, *Made from This Earth: An Anthology of Writing* (New York: Harper & Row, 1982), p. 8.

73. See Anna Ferguson, Jacquelyn N. Zita, and Kathyrne Pyne Addelson, "On 'Compulsory Heterosexuality and Lesbian Existence': Defining the Issues," *Signs* (1981–82): 147–88.

74. See Hester Eisenstein, *Contemporary Feminist Thought* (Boston: G. K. Hall & Co., 1983), pp. 125–35, for a discussion of metaphysical feminism. See also Robin Morgan, "Metaphysical Feminism," in *Going Too Far*, pp. 290–310.

75. See Elaine Showalter, "Women Who Write Are Women," *New York Times Book Review*, 16 December 1984, and "Letters to the Editor" during January 1985.

Chapter Five

1. Interviews: Norma Swenson, and Judy Norsigian, Boston Women's Health Book Collective, 17 September 1985. See also Wendy Coppedge Sanford, "Working Together, Growing Together: A Brief History of the Women's Health Book Collective," *heresies* 2, no. 3 (1979): 83–92.

2. See Jo Freeman, *The Politics of Women's Liberation* (New York: David McKay Co., 1975), chap. 4.

3. Ibid., pp. 103–5. For a critique of the nonhierarchical approach to organization, see Freeman, "The Tyranny of Structurelessness," in Jane Jaquette, ed., *Women in Politics* (New York: Wiley, 1974), pp. 202–14.

4. Sanford, "Working Together," p. 84.

5. Interview: Norma Swenson, 17 September 1985.

6. Claudia Dreifus, ed., *Seizing Our Bodies: The Politics of Women's Health* (New York: Random House, 1977), pp. xxiv–xxv.

7. There have been several recent studies on the evolution of the abortion reform movement in America. See Rosalind Pollack Petchesky, *Abortion and Woman's Choice: The State, Sexuality, and Reproductive Freedom* (New York: Longman, 1984); Kristin Luker, *Abortion and the Politics of Motherhood* (Berkeley: University of California Press, 1984); Eva R. Rubin, *Abortion, Politics, and the Courts: Roe v. Wade and Its Aftermath* (Westport, Conn.: Greenwood Press, 1982).

8. Pauline Bart and Melinda Bart Schlesinger, "Collective Work and Self-Identity: The Effect of Working in a Feminist Illegal Abortion Collective," in Frank Lindenfeld and Joyce Rothschild-Whitt, eds., *Workplace Democracy and Social Change* (Boston: Porter Sargent, 1980), pp. 139–53.

9. Bart and Schlesinger, "Collective Work," pp. 141–42.

10. Ibid., pp. 144–49.

11. Ibid., p. 147.

12. Rachel Gillet Fruchter et al. of the Healthright Collective, "The Women's Health Movement: Where Are We Now?" in Dreifus, *Seizing Our Bodies*, pp. 271–78. See also Sheryl Burt Ruzek, *The Women's Health Movement: Feminist Alternatives to Medical Control* (New York: Praeger, 1978). For a critique of the medical profession in relation to women, see Gena Corea, *The Hidden Malpractice: How American Medicine Treats Women as Patients and Professionals* (New York: William Morrow, 1977).

13. Interview: Swenson. See Claudia Dreifus, "Abortion: This Piece Is for Remembrance," in *Seizing Our Bodies*, for a description of the legal battle over abortion in New York State.

14. Sanford, "Working Together."

15. Ibid., p. 84.

16. Ibid., pp. 88–89. See also "A New Look for a Best-Seller," *Boston Globe*, 26 September 1984, p. 61. *Our Body, Ourselves*, as of 1984, had gone

through four commercially published editions with sales of 2.25 million English-language copies and twelve foreign editions, with two more on the way.

17. Interview: Swenson.

18. Quoted in "A New Look for a Best-Seller."

19. Fruchter et al., "Women's Health Movement," pp. 273–74.

20. "Northeast Alliance of Women Health Activists Holds 'Founding Weekend' in New Hampshire," *WomanWise*, Fall 1978. For a good discussion of the National Network, its founders, and activism, see Ruzek, *Women's Health Movement*, pp. 155–57.

21. Ruzek, ibid., p. 155.

22. Interview: Swenson.

23. Helen I. Marieskind and Barbara Ehrenreich, "Toward Socialist Medicine: The Women's Health Movement," *Social Policy*, September-October 1975, p. 38.

24. Ibid., p. 39.

25. Ibid., p. 40. See also Corea, *Hidden Malpractice*, pp. 257–66.

26. Frances Hornstein, "An Interview on Women's Health Politics," pt. 2 *Quest* 1 (Fall 1974): 75–76. See also Hornstein, pt. 2 in *Quest* 1 (Summer 1974): 27–36.

27. Ibid., pt. 1, pp. 32–33.

28. Audrey Gartner, "A Typology of Women's Self-Help Groups," *Social Policy*, Winter 1985, pp. 25–30. The full range of self-help groups is much too broad to describe in this context, but the Gartner article gives a good overview.

29. The Feminist Counseling Collective, "Feminist Psychotherapy," *Social Policy*, September-October 1975, pp. 54–62.

30. Susan E. Bell, "Feminist Self-Help: The Case of Fertility Consciousness/Women Controlled Natural Birth Control Groups," *Radical Teacher* 19 (1982): 17–20.

31. Pamela S. Eakins, "The Rise of the Free Standing Birth Center: Principles and Practice," *Women and Health* 9 (Winter 1984): 49–63.

32. Miriam Galper and Carolyn Cott Washburne, "A Women's Self-Help Program in Action," *Social Policy*, March-April 1976, p. 48.

33. Ibid., pp. 48–50.

34. Ibid., p. 51.

35. Ibid., p. 52. For a general critique of the self-help movement, as well as some of the internal problems of feminist collectives, see Anne Withorn, "Helping Ourselves: The Limits and Potential of Self-Help," *Radical America* 14 (1980): 25–38.

36. Susan Griffin, "The Politics of Rape," in *Made from This Earth: An Anthology of Writings* (New York: Harper & Row, 1982), pp. 39–58; first published as "Rape—The All-American Crime," *Ramparts*, September 1971.

37. Ibid., p. 55.

38. Susan Brownmiller, *Against Our Will: Men, Women, and Rape* (New York: Simon & Schuster, 1975), p. 15. Brownmiller went beyond the issue of

men raping women to explore other kinds of violent sexual behavior, such as homosexual rape in prisons and the sexual exploitation of children.

39. Bell Hooks, *Ain't I a Woman: Black Women and Feminism* (Boston: South End Press, 1981), p. 52. See also Deb Friedman, "Rape, Racism—and Reality," *FAAR and NCN Newsletter*, July-August 1978, pp. 17–26. This article discusses black women's critique of Susan Brownmiller. (The publication has changed its name to *Aegis: Magazine on Ending Violence against Women.*). See also Gerda Lerner, "The Rape of Black Women as a Weapon of Terror," in *Black Women in White America: A Documentary History* (New York: Vintage Books, 1972), pp. 172–93.

40. Angela Davis notes that of the 455 men executed between 1930 and 1967 on the basis of rape convictions, 405 of them were black. See Davis, "Rape, Racism and the Myth of the Black Rapist," in *Women, Race, and Class* (New York: Random House, 1981), p. 172.

41. Ibid., p. 174. Davis points out that the feminists who supported Joanne Little did not respond to her appeal to support Delbert Tibbs, a black man falsely charged with rape. See also Davis, "The Dialectic of Rape," *Ms.*, June 1975, pp. 74ff.

42. Susan Schechter, *Women and Male Violence: The Visions and Struggles of the Battered Women's Movement* (Boston: South End Press, 1982), pp. 35–38. Much of my material on the antirape and battered women's movements is taken from this excellent study.

43. Ibid., p. 38.

44. "The Feminist Workplace: Interview with Nancy McDonald," in *Building Feminist Theory: Essays from Quest*, ed. Charlotte Bunch (New York: Longman, 1981), pp. 253–54.

45. Ibid., p. 255.

46. Schechter, *Women and Male Violence*, p. 42.

47. Ibid., p. 43.

48. Ibid., pp. 43–54. This is a good discussion of the ideological diversity of the movement.

49. Joyce Gelb, "The Politics of Wife Abuse," in Irene Diamond, ed., *Families, Politics, and Public Polities: A Feminist Dialogue on Women and the State* (New York: Longman, 1983), pp. 250–51. Schechter has a good description of the philosophy, formation, funding, and operational procedures of women's advocates, pp. 62–65.

50. Schechter, *Women and Male Violence*, pp. 93–98, 111.

51. Karen Kollias, "Spiral of Change: An Introduction to Quest," *Quest: A Feminist Quarterly* 1 (Summer 1974): 8.

52. *Building Feminist Theory*, pp. xv–xvi.

53. See Lucia Valeska, "The Future of Female Separatism," *Quest* 2 (Fall 1975). See also in the same volume Charlotte Bunch, "Not for Lesbians Only." Both are reprinted in *Building Feminist Theory*. Another anthology, indispensa-

ble to an understanding of the issue of lesbian feminism, is Nancy Myron and Charlotte Bunch, *Lesbianism and the Women's Movement* (Baltimore: Diana Press, 1979).

54. Valeska, "The Future of Female Separatism."

55. For an excellent description of the development of the San Francisco lesbian community during the years 1972–75, see Deborah Goleman Wolf, *The Lesbian Community* (Berkeley: University of California Press, 1979, 1980).

56. Ibid., "Afterword."

57. June Arnold, "Feminist Presses and Feminist Politics," *Quest* 3 (Summer 1976): 18.

58. "Critique & Commentary: The Female Journalism Debate," *Quest* 3 (Fall 1976): 31–40. See also Alexa Freeman and Valle Jones, "Creating Feminist Communications," *Quest* 3 (Fall 1976): 3–10.

59. Judy Chicago, *Through the Flower: My Struggle as a Woman Artist*, rev. ed. (Garden City, N.Y.: Doubleday, 1982). See also Paula Harper, "The First Feminist Art Program: A View from the 1980s," *Signs* 10 (Summer 1985): 762–81.

60. Chicago, *Through the Flower*, p. 65.

61. Harper, "First Feminist Art Program," pp. 762–65. Harper, as an art historian, was also a teacher at FAP.

62. Ibid., p. 766, from a 1982 interview.

63. Ibid., pp. 766–68. Chicago describes in detail the experience of building Womanhouse, as well as some of the exhibits and performances that were held there. See Chicago, *Through the Flower*, pp. 107–32.

64. Harper, "First Feminist Art Program," p. 774. Chicago's own interpretation of her problems with the younger women was that women have trouble accepting another woman as an "authority figure" or role model, and that they need to reject the figure that has helped them to develop. See Chicago, *Through the Flower*, pp. 108–10.

65. Harper, "First Feminist Art Program," pp. 777–78.

66. Ibid., pp. 778–79.

67. Interview: Judith Bush, artist, Fly Creek, New York, 9 February 1986.

68. Ibid.

Chapter Six

1. For an overview of women's impact on education in the 1970s, see Joan N. Burstyn and Polly Welts Kaufman, "Women and Education," in Barbara Haber, ed., *The Women's Annual, 1980: The Year in Review* (Boston: G. K. Hall & Co., 1981), pp. 23–41.

2. Sonia Johnson, panel discussion on Wilma Scott Heide, National Women's Studies Association Conference, University of Illinois, 14 June 1986.

See also Adrienne Rich, "Toward a Woman-Centered University," in Florence Howe, ed., *Women and the Power to Change* (Berkeley, Calif.: Carnegie Commission on Higher Education, 1975), pp. 15–46.

3. Diane Ravitch, *The Troubled Crusade: American Education, 1945–1980* (New York: Basic Books, 1983), pp. 228–38.

4. Ibid., pp. 267–68.

5. There was a number of critiques of America's educational system and the impact of sexism upon young children. See Barbara Grizzuti Harrison, *Unlearning the Lie: Sexism in the School* (New York: William Morrow, 1974), and Judith Stacey, Susan Béreaud, and Joan Daniels, eds., *And Jill Came Tumbling After* (New York: Dell Publishing Co., 1974).

6. Ravitch, *Troubled Crusade*, pp. 294–95.

7. Jo Freeman, "Women on the Move: The Roots of Revolt," in Alice S. Rossi and Ann Calderwood, eds., *Academic Women on the Move* (New York: Russell Sage Foundation, 1973), p. 28, and Interview: Bernice Sandler, Project on the Status and Education of Women, Washington, D.C., June 1985.

8. Ibid. See also Bernice Sandler, "A Little Help from Our Government: WEAL and Contract Compliance," in Rossi and Calderwood, *Academic Women*, pp. 439–40.

9. Sandler, "A Little Help from Our Government," pp. 440–41.

10. Interview: Joan Roberts, Syracuse University, 1 August 1985. See also Hole and Levine, *Rebirth*, p. 97, for quote by Washington reporter.

11. Interview: Sandler. See also Sandler, "A Little Help from Our Government," p. 453.

12. Interview: Sandler; and Ravitch, *Troubled Crusade*, pp. 294–95. For the Green hearings, see Edith Green and others, *Discrimination Against Women*, Hearings before the Special Subcommittee on Education of the Committee on Education and Labor, House of Representatives, 91st Congress, 2nd Session, on Section 805 of HR 16098. (Washington, D.C.: U.S. Government Printing Office, 1970).

13. Ravitch, *Troubled Crusade*, pp. 294–95. See also "An Interview on Title IX with Shirley Chisholm, Holly Knox, Leslie R. Wolfe, Cynthia G. Grown, and Mary Kaaren Jolly," *Harvard Educational Review* 49 (November 1979): 504–5.

14. See unpublished paper, "Background Information," in NCRWED Collection, Box 1, File 1, at the Schlesinger Library, Radcliffe College, Cambridge, Massachusetts.

15. See "The National Coalition for Research on Women's Education and Development, Inc.: Purposes, Activities, Organization," in NCRWED Collection, Box 1, File 1.

16. Susan Hartmann, "Allies of the Women's Movement," unpublished paper prepared for the 1986 Annual Meeting of the Organization of American Historians and the National Council on Public History, April 1986, New York, New York.

17. See "An Interview on Title IX," p. 526, for a brief discussion of PEER.

18. See the AAC brochure, *Project on the Status and Education of Women*, available at the AAC office in Washington, D.C.

19. Interview: Sandler.

20. Joan Abramson, *The Invisible Woman: Discrimination in the Academic Profession* (San Francisco: Jossey-Bass, 1975), p. vii. See also Abramson, *Old Boys, New Women: The Politics of Sex Discrimination* (New York: Praeger Publishers, 1979), and Gloria DeSole and Leonore Hoffman, eds., *Rocking the Boat: Academic Women and Academic Processes* (New York: Modern Language Association of America, 1981), for more individual accounts of sex discrimination.

21. "HEW Reveals Sex Bias in GSD Hiring Practices," *Harvard Crimson*, 25 September 1972. See also "The Job Scene," *Bay State Banner*, 9 November 1972, and "Sex Bias in Hiring Hit at Harvard Design School," *Christian Science Monitor*, 20 September 1972. Newspaper clippings taken from NOW Papers, Box 17, Compliance; File: Harvard University.

22. "GSD Analysis," *Harvard Crimson*, 25 September 1972. NOW Papers, Box 17, Compliance.

23. See "The Job Scene"; and press release, Hosken, 28 August 1972.

24. Susan F. Kingsley, "What Are Harvard's Admissions Plans?" *Harvard Crimson*, 13 December 1972. NOW Papers, Box 17, Compliance.

25. Ibid.

26. Ann E. Juergens, "Inequality Persists in GSAS Policies," *Harvard Crimson*, 27 March 1973, and Susan F. Kingsley, "Affirmative Action Troubles," *Harvard Crimson*, 30 March 1973. NOW Papers, Box 17, Compliance.

27. Abramson, *Invisible Woman*, p. 22.

28. Richard M. Weintraub, "US Commission Charges Tufts with Hiring Bias," *Boston Globe*, 20 September 1973. NOW Papers, Box 17, Compliance, File: Tufts University.

29. Bill Abrams, "Prof Charges 'Political Firing,'" news article (source not given); and see "Fine Arts Head Supports Joost," "Moxey Claims Harassment," and "750 Sign Petition." NOW Papers, Box 17, File: Tufts University.

30. "Joost Firing Case: Not Unique," by the Committee to Rehire Ms. Joost, n.d., in NOW Papers, Box 17, Tufts University. This article uses several interesting cases as examples, including Mary Daly's famous case at Boston College.

31. Emily Abel, "Collective Protest and the Meritocracy: Faculty Women and Sex Discrimination Lawsuits," *Feminist Studies* 7 (Fall 1981): 505.

32. Ibid., pp. 510–11.

33. Ibid., pp. 521–25. Abel claims that of the twenty women whom she interviewed, few fought for equity as a group. "For most, protesting sex discrimination in academia remained a lonely pursuit" (p. 525).

34. Interview: Joan Roberts. See also Roberts, "The Ramifications of the Study of Women," in *Beyond Intellectual Sexism: A New Woman, A New Reality* (New York: David McKay Co., 1976), pp. 3–13.

35. Sarah Slavin and Jacqueline Macaulay, "Joan Roberts and the University," in Desole and Hoffman, eds., *Rocking the Boat*, pp. 39–40.

36. Ibid., pp. 41–45.

37. Interview: Roberts. Roberts noted the influence of writers such as Dale Spender, Susan Griffith, and Joanna Russ in developing the concept of breaking silence.

38. Ibid. See also Slavin and Macaulay, "Joan Roberts," pp. 46–48.

39. Interview: Judith Long, Syracuse University, 22 August 1985. See also "Equality Is an Uphill Climb for Judith Long Laws," *Syracuse Post-Standard*, 18 December 1980, p. A–11.

40. Memorandum from Donald P. Hayes, chairman, Department of Sociology, to Dean Harry Levin, College of Arts and Sciences, Cornell University, on the negative department vote on Judith Long Laws's tenure, 29 December 1976. Also, correspondence from Donald P. Hayes, chairman, to Professor Judith Long Laws, 27 February 1976. Both are in the private files of Judith Long, Syracuse University.

41. See Laws, with Pepper Schwartz, *The Social Construction of Female Sexuality* (New York: Dryden Press, 1976), and Laws, *The Second XX* (New York: Elsevier Publishers, 1976). In addition, Laws wrote two chapters on the AT&T case, as well as articles which appeared in *Signs*, *Psychology of Women*, *Journal of Marriage and the Family*, and *Sex Roles*.

42. See "Equality Is an Uphill Climb," and "Cornell University Charged with Nine Sex Discrimination Offenses," *Ithaca Times*, 25–31 January 1979, p. 1. See also Charlotte Williams Conable, *Women at Cornell: The Myth of Equal Education* (Ithaca: Cornell University Press, 1977), pp. 147–50.

43. Interview, Judith Long; and "Cornell University Charged."

44. "Judge Finds No Sex Discrimination in Case of 'Cornell 11,'" *Syracuse Post-Standard*, 29 March 1983, p. 1.

45. Interview: Long.

46. Deborah Shapley, "University Women's Rights: Whose Feet Are Dragging?" *Science* 14 (January 1972): 151–54. See also Burstyn and Kaufman, "Women and Education," p. 23.

47. Marilyn Gittell, "The Illusion of Affirmation Action," *Change* 7 (October 1975), p. 40.

48. Public address given by Lois Black, director of affirmative action, Syracuse University, at Cornell University, 10 October 1975.

49. Ibid.

50. Abramson, *Old Boys, New Women*, pp. 82–83.

51. Ibid., pp. 83–84. In 1974–75, 31.2 percent of all faculty men and 41.4 percent of faculty women were at the assistant professor rank. By 1977–78, the figures were 27.3 percent for men and 41.6 percent for women. Men were seldom employed as instructors or lecturers: 8.2 percent were employed at those levels in 1974–75 and 8.4 percent in 1977–78. Over 25 percent of all women were at these two low ranks in each year of the AAUP survey. See also

Lilli S. Hornig, "Untenured and Tenuous: The Status of Women Faculty," *Annals, AAPSS* 48 (March 1980): 115–25.

52. Constance M. Carroll, "Three's a Crowd: The Dilemma of the Black Woman in Higher Education," in Rossi and Calderwood, *Academic Women,* p. 179.

53. See Cora Bagley Marrett and Westina Matthews, "The Participation of Minority Women in Higher Education," in Elizabeth Fennema and M. Jane Ayer, eds., *Women and Education: Equity or Equality* (Berkeley, Calif.: McCutchan Publishing Corp., 1984), pp. 197–220.

54. Ruth Fischer, "Black, Female—and Qualified," *Change* 6 (Winter 1974–75): 13–15.

55. Ibid., pp. 13–14.

56. Gittell, "Illusion," pp. 42–43.

57. Interview: Gretchen Kreuter, University of Minnesota, 23 August 1985.

58. Joyce Gelb and Marian Lief Palley, *Women and Public Policies* (Princeton: Princeton University Press, 1982), pp. 96–97.

59. Ibid., pp. 105–6. See also Judith Miller, "Collegiate Sports and Other Title IX Controversies," *Change* 6 (Winter 1974–75): 20–23.

60. Ibid., pp. 103–4, 112–13.

61. Burstyn and Kaufman, "Women and Education," pp. 26–27.

62. See Mary Lou Randour, "Research Report: Women in Higher Education: Trends in Enrollments and Degrees Earned," *Harvard Educational Review* 52 (May 1982): 191–201, for a balanced and thorough analysis of recent data on women students.

63. Ibid., pp. 198–200.

64. Interview: Sandler. See Ravitch, *Troubled Crusade,* p. 304, for a discussion of sexual harassment, which emerges as an issue in the late 1970s.

65. Interview: Anne Truax, director of Women's Center, 27 August 1985.

66. Interview: Roberts. See also Slavin and Macaulay, "Joan Roberts," pp. 42–43.

67. Lorelei R. Brush, Alice Ross Gold, and Marni Goldstein White, "The Paradox of Intention and Effect: A Women's Studies Course," *Signs* 3 (Summer 1978): 870–71.

68. Florence Howe and Paul Lauter, *The Impact of Women's Studies on the Campuses and the Disciplines* (Washington, D.C.: U.S. Department of Health, Education and Welfare, 1980), p. 1. See also Howe's *Myths of Coeducation: Selected Essays, 1964–1983* (Bloomington: Indiana University Press, 1984).

69. Marilyn J. Boxer, "Review Essay: For and About Women: The Theory and Practice of Women's Studies in the United States," *Signs* 7 (Spring 1982): 663–64. See also Howe, *Myths of Coeducation,* pp. 78–110.

70. See Shelia Tobias, *Female Studies I* (Pittsburgh: Know, Inc., 1970); and Florence Howe, ed., *Female Studies II* (Pittsburgh: Know, Inc., 1970).

71. Boxer, "For and About Women," pp. 665–66. See also Howe and Lau-

ter, *The Impact of Women's Studies*, and Howe, *Seven Years Later: Women's Studies Programs in 1976* (Washington, D.C.: National Advisory Council on Women's Educational Programs, 1977).

72. Interview: Joan Burstyn, dean of the College of Education, Syracuse University, 28 March 1986.

73. Ellen Carol Dubois et al., *Feminist Scholarship: Kindling in the Groves of Academe* (Chicago: University of Illinois Press, 1985), p. 3. See also Roberts, ed., *Beyond Intellectual Sexism*; Elizabeth Langland and Walter Gove, eds., *A Feminist Perspective in the Academy: The Difference It Makes* (Chicago: University of Chicago Press, 1981); and Dale Spender, ed., *Men's Studies Modified: The Impact of Feminism on the Academic Disciplines* (New York: Pergamon Press, 1981).

74. Interview: Burstyn.

75. Interview: Kreuter. For a more general statement of this pattern, see Donna Martin, "The Wives of Academe," *Change*, Winter 1972–73, pp. 67–69.

76. Interview: Kreuter. For a list of women's groups within professional associations and an analysis of their emergence, see Kay Klotzburger, "Political Action by Academic Women," in Rossi and Calderwood, pp. 359–91. Political science and sociology also had strong women's action groups. Between 1968 and the end of 1971 at least fifty such groups were formed. See *Sociologists for Women in Society New York* 14 (November 1985), for a history of the professional organization of women in sociology.

77. Boxer, "For and About Women," pp. 673–74.

78. Ibid., pp. 674–80.

79. Ibid., pp. 669–70.

80. Interview: Gayle Graham Yates, associate professor of American studies, University of Minnesota, 27 August 1986. Yates described some of the internal problems of the women's studies program at the University of Minnesota that were present from the beginning but became particularly difficult in the late 1970s. Also interview: Roberts.

81. Boxer, "For and About Women," pp. 680–82. For a discussion of black women in relation to women's studies, see "Special Feature: Black Studies and Women's Studies: Search for a Long Overdue Partnership," *Women's Studies Quarterly* 10 (Summer 1982): 10–16.

Chapter Seven

1. Lynn Weiner, *From Working Girl to Working Mother: The Female Labor Force in the United States, 1820–1980* (Chapel Hill: University of North Carolina Press, 1985), p. 3

2. Kathleen Gerson, *Hard Choices: How Women Decide about Work, Career, and Motherhood* (Berkeley: University of California Press, 1985), pp. 1–2.

3. See David Cooper, *The Death of the Family* (New York: Random House, 1970); and R. D. Laing, *The Politics of the Family and Other Essays* (New

York: Random House, 1969), for examples of radical critiques of modern family life that came out of the general cultural critique of the 1960s.

4. Carl N. Degler, *At Odds: Women and Family in America from the Revolution to the Present* (New York: Oxford University Press, 1980), pp. 448–49.

5. U.S. Department of Labor, *1975 Handbook on Women Workers*, Women's Bureau Bulletin 297 (Washington, D.C.: U.S. Government Printing Office, 1975), pp. 89–91, table 38.

6. Ibid., chart L, p. 124; and p. 137.

7. See Clair Vickery, "Women's Economic Contribution to the Family," in Ralph E. Smith, ed., *The Subtle Revolution: Women at Work* (Washington, D.C.: Urban Institute, 1979), pp. 159–65; and fig. 13, p. 168; and Elizabeth Waldman, Allyson Sherman Grossman, Howard Hayghe, and Beverly L. Johnson, "Working Mothers in the 1970s: A Look at the Statistics," *Monthly Labor Review* (October 1979): 39.

8. Waldman, Grossman, Hayghe, and Johnson, "Working Mothers," pp. 39–40. See also Ellen Ross, "Review Essay: The Love Crisis: Couples' Advice Books of the late 1970s," *Signs* 6 (Autumn 1980): 109–22.

9. Waldman, Grossman, Hayghe, and Johnson, "Working Mothers," p. 40.

10. Judith A. Baer, "Sexual Equality and the Burger Court," *Western Political Quarterly* 13 (December 1978): 470.

11. Ibid., pp. 490–91. An example of the Court's nonfeminist stance was *General Electric Co.* v. *Gilbert* in December 1976. The Court reversed the EEOC and six U.S. courts of appeals to hold that an employee sickness and accident benefits plan that excluded from its coverage disabilities related to pregnancy did not violate Title VII of the Civil Rights Act of 1964. See also Ruth Sidel, *Women and Children Last: The Plight of Poor Women in Affluent America* (New York: Viking Press, 1985).

12. Gerson, *Hard Choices*, pp. 205–7.

13. Margaret Gates, "Homemakers into Widows and Divorcées: Can the Law Provide Economic Protection?" in Jane Roberts Chapman and Margaret Gates, eds., *Women into Wives: The Legal and Economic Impact of Marriage* (Beverly Hills, Calif.: Sage Publications, 1977), p. 222.

14. Betty Berry, "Report of NOW-NY, Marriage and Divorce Committee," September 1970. NOW Papers, Box 9, Task Forces; File: Marriage and Divorce Task Force.

15. Ibid.

16. Lenore J. Weitzman, *The Divorce Revolution: The Unexpected Social and Economic Consequences for Women and Children in America* (New York: Free Press, 1985), pp. x–xi.

17. Barbara Ehrenreich, "Poor Mom, a Review of *Women and Children Last: The Plight of Poor Women in Affluent America*, by Ruth Sidel," *Atlantic*, April 1986, pp. 125–30.

18. Ellen Sim Dewey, "Nebraska Women's Legal Status Needs More Light," *World Herald* (Omaha), 22 July 1973, p. 11B.

19. Barbara Ehrenreich, *Hearts of Men: American Dreams and the Flight from Commitment* (Garden City, N.Y.: Doubleday, 1983), pp. 117–19.

20. Ibid., p. 120.

21. Ibid., p. 121.

22. This term was coined by Diana Pearce, "The Feminization of Poverty: Women, Work, and Welfare," *Urban and Social Change Review*, February 1978.

23. Beverly L. Johnson, "Women Who Head Families, 1970–1977: Their Numbers Rose, Income Lagged," *Monthly Labor Review* (February 1978): 32.

24. Ibid., and Weitzman, *Divorce Revolution*, pp. 350–51.

25. Weitzman, *Divorce Revolution*, p. 323.

26. Ibid., pp. 340–43.

27. Johnson, "Women Who Head Families," pp. 32–33.

28. There have been many studies of the black family over the past few decades. For an interpretation that places the family within the historical-cultural context of post–World War II, see the two-part series by Nicholas Lemann, "The Origins of the Underclass," *Atlantic*, May 1986, pp. 31–55, and June 1986, pp. 54–68.

29. Lemann, "Origins of the Underclass," *Atlantic*, June 1986, p. 58.

30. Ibid.

31. See Linda Burnham, "Has Poverty Been Feminized in Black America?" *Black Scholar* 16 (March-April 1985): 22. See also in the same issue, Julianne Malveaux, "Current Economic Trends and Black Feminist Consciousness," pp. 26–31.

32. See Elizabeth M. Almquist and Juanita L. Wehrie-Einhorn, "The Doubly-Disadvantaged: Minority Women in the Labor Force," in Ann H. Stromberg and Shirley Harkneww, eds., *Women Working: Theories and Facts in Perspective* (Palo Alto, Calif.: Mayfield Publishing Co., 1978), pp. 63–88. This study analyzes status differences among several minority groups relative to whites: black, Mexican, Puerto Rican, Cuban, American Indian, Japanese, Chinese, and Filipino.

33. Phyllis A. Wallace, Linda Datcher, and Julianne Malveaux, *Black Women in the Labor Force* (Cambridge, Mass.: MIT Press, 1980), pp. 23–25.

34. Ibid., pp. 24–25.

35. Ibid.

36. Mary Frank Fox and Sharlene Hesse-Biber, *Women at Work* (Palo Alto, Calif.: Mayfield Publishing Co., 1984), pp. 160–66.

37. Fox and Hesse-Biber, *Women at Work*, p. 169.

38. See especially Joyce A. Ladner, *Tomorrow's Tomorrow: The Black Woman* (Garden City, N.Y.: Doubleday, 1971); and Carol B. Stack, *All Our Kin: Strategies for Survival in a Black Community* (New York: Harper & Row, 1974).

39. Barbara Smith, "Home Truths on the Contemporary Black Feminist

Movement," *Black Scholar* 16 (March-April 1985): 8. See also Barbara Smith, ed., *Home Girls: A Black Feminist Anthology* (New York: Kitchen Table, Women of Color Press, 1983).

40. Jeanne-Marie A. Miller, "Black Women Playwrights from Grimké to Shange: Selected Synopses of Their Works," in Gloria T. Hull, Patricia Bell Scott, and Barbara Smith, eds., *All the Women Are White, All the Blacks Are Men, But Some of Us Are Brave: Black Women's Studies* (Old Westbury, N.Y.: Feminist Press, 1982), pp. 280–96.

41. See Smith, "Home Truths," especially pp. 5–6, 11. See also Carol Stack, *All Our Kin*, chap. 7, which offers an interesting insight into the ambivalence of black women toward the men in their lives.

42. Beth Richie, "Battered Black Women: A Challenge for the Black Community," *Black Scholar* 16 (March-April 1985): 41.

43. Ibid., pp. 41–42.

44. Ibid., pp. 42–43.

45. See Sandra Wexler, "Battered Women and Public Policy," in Ellen Boneparth, ed., *Women, Power and Policy* (New York: Pergamon Press, 1982), pp. 184–86. Although wife abuse crosses class lines, it is not equally distributed. There are higher occurrences among lower socioeconomic and minority populations, which suggest the influence of societal stress factors (p. 188).

46. Faith McNulty, *The Burning Bed: The True Story of an Abused Wife* (New York: Harcourt Brace Jovanovich, 1980), pp. 23–24.

47. Ibid.

48. Susan Schecter, *Women and Male Violence: The Visions and Struggles of the Battered Women's Movement* (Boston: South End Press, 1982), p. 29.

49. McNulty, *Burning Bed*, pp. 286–87. See Richard J. Gelles, *The Violent Home: A Study of Physical Aggression between Husbands and Wives* (Beverly Hills, Calif.: Sage Publications, 1974).

50. See Elizabeth M. Schneider, "Equal Rights to Trial for Women: Sex Bias in the Law of Self-Defense," *Harvard Civil Rights–Civil Liberties Law Review* 15 (Winter 1980): 624–26, quoted in Rosemary Tong, *Women, Sex, and the Law* (Totowa, N.J.: Rowman & Allanheld, 1984), p. 124. See also William A. Stacey and Anson Shape, *The Family Secret: Domestic Violence in America* (Boston: Beacon Press, 1983), p. 3, which makes the analogy with a national epidemic.

51. Ellen Dunwoody, "The National Coalition against Domestic Violence: A Grass-Roots Movement," *Response: To Violence in the Family*, Winter 1982, p. 15.

52. For a representative collection of Griffin's writings, most of them done in the seventies, see *Made from This Earth: An Anthology of Writings* (New York: Harper & Row, 1982). See also Adrienne Rich, "Husband-Right and Father-Right," in *On Lies, Secrets and Silence: Selected Prose, 1966–1978* (New York: W. W. Norton, 1979), p. 218.

53. Stacey and Shape, *Family Secret*, pp. 202–3.

54. See Letty Cottin Pogrebin, *Family Politics: Love and Power on the Inti-*

mate Frontier (New York: McGraw-Hill, 1983), which, although written in the 1980s, contains many of the arguments and refers to much of the literature of the 1970s. See also Brigitte Berger and Peter L. Berger, *The War over the Family: Capturing the Middle Ground* (New York: Doubleday, Anchor Press, 1983).

55. See especially Adrienne Rich, *Of Woman Born: Motherhood as Experience and Institution* (New York: W. W. Norton, 1976), p. 56.

56. Alvin Toffler, *Future Shock* (New York: Random House, 1970), p. 2

57. Ibid., p. 251.

58. Nena O'Neill and George O'Neill, *Open Marriage: A New Lifestyle for Couples* (New York: Avon Books, 1972).

59. Pogrebin, *Family Politics*, p. 25.

60. Ibid., pp. 143–44, and Pat Mainardi, "The Politics of Housework," in *Sisterhood Is Powerful* (New York: Vintage Books, 1970), pp. 447–554.

61. Maxine L. Margolis, *Mothers and Such: Views of American Women and Why They Changed* (Berkeley: University of California Press, 1984), pp. 176–77.

62. Ibid., pp. 177–78.

63. Joseph H. Pleck, *Working Wives/Working Husbands* (Beverly Hills, Calif.: Sage Publications, 1985), chaps. 6 and 7.

64. Ibid., p. 156.

65. See Ehrenreich, *Hearts of Men*, chap. 9, for a discussion of men's liberation in the 1970s and 1980s.

66. See "The Fathering Instinct," *Ms.*, May 1974.

67. See Nancy D. Polikoff, "Gender and Child-Custody Determinations: Exploding the Myths," in Diamond, ed., *Family, Politics, and Public Policy*, pp. 184–85.

68. Weitzman, *Divorce Revolution*, pp. 242–43. See also Andrew Hacker, "Farewell to the Family?" *New York Review of Books*, 18 March 1982, p. 37, for a discussion of paternal custody.

69. Dorothy Dinnerstein, *The Mermaid and the Minotaur: Sexual Arrangements and Human Malaise* (New York: Harper & Row, 1976).

70. Nancy Chodorow, *The Reproduction of Mothering: Psychoanalysis and the Sociology of Gender* (Berkeley: University of California Press, 1978), p. 51.

71. Letty Cottin Pogrebin, "Can Women Really Have It All: Should We?" *Ms.*, March 1978, p. 47.

72. See Barbara Easton, "Feminism and the Contemporary Family," *Socialist Review*, May 1978, pp. 11–36.

Chapter Eight

1. Billie Jean King, with Kim Chapin, *Billie Jean* (New York: Harper & Row, 1974), pp. 147, 164–69. See also "How Bobby Runs and Talks, Talks, Talks," *Time*, 10 September 1973, pp. 54–60.

2. John T. Talamini and Charles H. Page, eds., *Sport and Society: An Anthology* (Boston: Little, Brown & Co., 1973), pp. 415–18.

3. William Johnson, "TV Made It All a New Game," in ibid., p. 460.
4. Ibid., pp. 461–62.
5. King, *Billie Jean*, pp. 78–91.
6. Ibid., pp. 99–101.
7. Ibid., p. 106.
8. Ibid., pp. 142–47. See also an interview by Bud Collins, "Billie Jean King Evens the Score," *Ms.*, July 1973, pp. 37–43, for King's concerns on the eve of the match with Riggs.
9. See "How Bobby Runs."
10. King, *Billie Jean*, p. 185.
11. Ibid., pp. 181–85.
12. Ibid.
13. Collins, "Billie Jean King," p. 40.
14. Michaele Weissman, "Popular Culture," in Barbara Haber, ed., *The Women's Annual, 1981: The Year in Review* (Boston: G. K. Hall & Co., 1982), pp. 193–94. The critique referred to an interview in an April 1981 *Playboy* article, but it clearly reflected the treatment of women's liberation by popular culture and the mass media during the previous decade.
15. John H. Davis, *The Kennedys: Dynasty and Disaster* (New York: Mc-Graw-Hill, 1984), pp. 567–74. See also Peter Collier and David Horowitz, *The Kennedys: An American Drama* (New York: Summit Books, 1984), pp. 366–67.
16. See "Gloria Steinem on Jacqueline Onassis," *Ms.*, March 1979, and reactions to that article in *Ms.*, July 1979.
17. Ellen Goodman, "Jacqueline Onassis: Tripping on Her Past," in *Close to Home* (New York: Simon & Schuster, 1979), pp. 64–65.
18. See "The Relentless Ordeal of Political Wives," *Time*, 7 October 1974, pp. 15–22.
19. These impressions are carried through numerous articles that appeared in the popular press from 1969 through the mid-seventies. The articles talked about Pat Nixon's role as a first lady, her style in the White House, and the "private Pat Nixon." By the mid-seventies, Pat Nixon's "ordeal" became a focus of attention.
20. See Lester David, *The Lonely Lady at San Clemente: The Story of Pat Nixon* (New York: Thomas Y. Crowell, 1978). See also Fawn Brodie, *Richard Nixon: The Shaping of His Character* (Cambridge: Harvard University Press, 1983), especially chaps. 11, 17, and 31.
21. See Bob Woodward and Carl Bernstein, *All the President's Men* (New York: Simon & Schuster, 1976), pp. 164–66, for a sad account of Pat Nixon's activities in the spring of 1974.
22. Betty Ford, with Chris Chase, *The Times of My Life* (New York: Harper & Row, 1978), p. 194.
23. Ford, *Times of My Life*, pp. 206–7. See also the account by Betty Ford's press secretary, Shelia Robb Weidenfeld, *First Lady's Lady: With the Fords at the White House* (New York: G. P. Putnam's Sons, 1979), pp. 149–50, 160–70.

24. "Woman of the Year," *Newsweek*, 29 December 1975, pp. 19–23. See also Ford, *Times of My Life*, p. 208. Weidenfeld, as the first lady's press secretary, was constantly concerned with image and popularity, and discusses this issue throughout her account.

25. Weidenfeld, *First Lady's Lady*, p. 136.

26. Ford, *Times of My Life*, p. 202. Mrs. Ford had wanted Anne Armstrong as a vice presidential candidate in 1976, and she had also wanted a woman on the Supreme Court, but she was not able to influence her husband on these issues.

27. Ibid., pp. 204–5.

28. Ibid., pp. 280–92.

29. Rosalynn Carter, *First Lady from Plains* (Boston: Houghton Mifflin Co., 1984), p. 164.

30. "Rosalynn: So Many Goals," *Time*, 10 January 1977, pp. 11–12.

31. Carter, *First Lady*, p. 173.

32. "Rosalynn on the Road: With Mrs. Carter in Latin America," *New Republic*, 18 June 1977, pp. 13–14.

33. Ibid.

34. Meg Greenfield, "Mrs. President," *Newsweek*, 20 June 1977.

35. John Osborne, "White House Watch: Rosalynn," *New Republic*, 19 August 1978, pp. 8–9. See also Hugh Sidney, "The Presidency: Second Most Powerful Person," *Time*, 7 May 1979, p. 22; "Mrs. President," *Newsweek*, 6 August 1979, pp. 22–24; and "The President's Partner," *Newsweek*, 5 November 1979, pp. 36–47.

36. See Sidney, "The Presidency," p. 22; and "Advocate-in-Chief," *Newsweek*, 4 September 1978, p. 18.

37. "The President's Partner," p. 36. See also "Mrs. President," p. 22.

38. Bella Abzug, with Mim Kelber, *Gender Gap: Bella Abzug's Guide to Political Power for American Women* (Boston: Houghton Mifflin Co., 1984), pp. 19–20.

39. Ibid., pp. 20–21.

40. "Requiem for a Heavyweight," *New Republic*, 4 March 1978, p. 14.

41. Ibid.

42. "Bella," *Newsweek*, 5 October 1970, pp. 28–29.

43. "Requiem for a Heavyweight," p. 13.

44. Ellen Goodman, "Bella Abzug: She's Hot and the Times Are Cool," in *Close to Home*, p. 69.

45. Gloria Steinem, "The Ticket that Might Have Been: President Chisholm," *Ms.*, January 1973, pp. 73, 120.

46. Ibid.

47. Ibid.

48. Elizabeth Frappollo, "The Ticket that Might Have Been: Vice-President Farenthold," *Ms.*, January 1973, pp. 74–76, 116–20. Frappollo notes that Nicholas Von Hoffman of the *Washington Post* was an exception, along with a couple of New York City reporters.

49. B. J. Phillips, "Recognizing the Gentleladies of the Judiciary Committee," *Ms.*, November 1974, pp. 70–74.

50. "Rep. Holtzman a Chief Nixon Critic," *Philadelphia Bulletin*, Special Series: Biography News, August 1974, in Charlotte Bunch Papers, Carton 4, Folder 152, Schlesinger Library, Radcliffe College.

51. Charlotte Bunch, unpublished article written for *Ms.*, 1979, p. 2, in Bunch Papers, Carton 4, Folder 152.

52. Ibid., pp. 4–5.

53. Ibid., p. 9.

54. Ibid., pp. 10–11.

55. Arlie Scott, NOW vice president-action, quoted in Bunch, p. 11.

56. See James Haskins, *Barbara Jordan* (New York: Dial Press, 1977), and Barbara Jordan and Shelby Hearon, *Barbara Jordan: A Self-Portrait* (Garden City, N.Y.: Doubleday & Co., 1979).

57. Haskins, *Barbara Jordan*, pp. 159–60.

58. Ibid., pp. 160–66.

59. Ibid., pp. 188–91.

60. There has been a great deal written on the impact of the modern media. See, in particular, John M. Phelan, *Mediaworld: Programming the Public* (New York: Seabury Press, 1977), and Ray Elden Hiebert and Carol Reuss, *Impact of Mass Media: Current Issues* (New York: Longman, 1985). For a special focus on women, see Helen Baehr, ed., *Women and the Media* (New York: Pergamon Press, 1980), and Maurine Beasley and Shelia Silver, eds., *Women in the Media: A Documentary Sourcebook* (Washington, D.C.: Women's Institute for Freedom of the Press, 1977).

61. Editors of *Ms.*, "How *Ms.* Magazine Got Started," in Francine Klagsbrun, ed., *The First Ms. Reader* (1973), reprinted in Fredric Rissover and David C. Birch, eds., *Mass Media and the Popular Arts* (New York: McGraw-Hill, 1977), pp. 238–43.

62. Gail Rock, "Same Time, Same Station, Same Sexism," *Ms.*, December 1973, p. 24.

63. Ibid., pp. 24–25.

64. Ibid., pp. 24–28. *Ms.* magazine did a number of articles on television stars of the 1970s and 1980s. See Lee Israel, "Lily Tomlin: Good-Bye to Duddiness," *Ms.*, January 1974, pp. 46–49, and "Prime Time Comes of Age," *Ms.*, November 1975, pp. 61–65. For an interesting article on Carol Burnett, see Susan Dworkin, "Carol Burnett: Getting On with It," *Ms.*, September 1983, pp. 43–45.

65. Margaret Drabble, "Jane Fonda: Her Own Woman . . . At Last?" *Ms.*, October 1977, p. 88.

66. Harriet Lyons and Susan Braudy, "'Julia' and Lillian and Jane and Vanessa: Such Good Friends?" *Ms.*, October 1977, p. 55.

67. Marjorie Rosen, "'The Turning Point': A Tearjerker—Just Like Life," *Ms.*, January 1978, p. 29.

68. "Little Women," *Newsweek*, 29 August 1978.

69. Drabble, "Jane Fonda," p. 88.

70. See Kim Chernin, *The Obsession: Reflections on the Tyranny of Slenderness* (New York: Harper & Row, 1981).

Chapter Nine

1. National Commission on the Observance of International Women's Year, *The Spirit of Houston: The First National Women's Conference* (Washington, D.C., March 1978), p. 11.

2. Quoted in Abzug, *Gender Gap*, p. 57.

3. Catherine East, "Newer Commissions," in Irene Tinker, ed., *Women in Washington: Advocates for Public Policy*, Sage Yearbooks in Women's Policy Studies, vol. 7 (Beverly Hills, Calif.: Sage Publications, 1983), pp. 37–38.

4. *A Matter of Simple Justice*, Report of the President's Task Force on Women's Rights and Responsibilities, (Washington, D.C.: U.S. Government Printing Office, April 1970.). See also East, "Newer Commissions," pp. 37–38, and Janet K. Boles, *The Politics of the Equal Rights Amendment: Conflict and the Decision Process* (New York: Longman, 1979), pp. 44–45.

5. Interview: Catherine East, 5 July 1985. See also Citizen's Advisory Council on the Status of Women, "The Proposed Equal Rights Amendment to the Constitution: A Memorandum" (Washington, D.C.: March 1970). For Griffith's role, see Hole and Levine, *Rebirth*, p. 56.

6. Hole and Levine, *Rebirth*, pp. 52–53.

7. For a description of the hearings, see Boles, *Politics of the ERA*, pp. 38–39. See also Berenice Carroll, "Direct Action and Constitutional Rights: The Case of ERA," in Joan Hoff-Wilson, ed., *Rights of Passage: The Past and Future of the ERA* (Bloomington: Indiana University Press, 1986), p. 68.

8. Boles, *Politics of the ERA*, pp. 1–2. For a more in-depth discussion of American public opinion on women's rights, see pp. 51–56.

9. Myra Marx Ferree and Beth B. Hess, *Controversy and Coalition: The New Feminist Movement* (Boston: Twayne, 1985), p. 128.

10. See Carol Felsenthal, *The Sweetheart of the Silent Majority: The Biography of Phyllis Schlafly* (Garden City, N.Y.: Doubleday, 1981).

11. See Felsenthal, *Sweetheart*, chap. 12, for an interesting description of Schlafly's defeat within the Republican party.

12. Ibid., p. 34.

13. Felsenthal, *Sweetheart*, pp. 239–40.

14. Ibid., p. 269.

15. Ibid.

16. Boles, *Politics of the ERA*, p. 68, and "Outline of Remarks about the 'Right Wing' and ERA," made by Marilyn D. Heath, BPW/ERA coordinator, 22 March 1979, in the ERAmerica Papers, Box 124, File: Right Wing; Library of Congress Manuscript Division, Washington, D.C.

17. Ibid. See Boles, *Politics of the ERA*, pp. 200–202, for a list of organizations opposing ERA.

18. Felsenthal, *Sweetheart*, pp. 272–73.

19. This is a point that Janet J. Mansbridge makes in her analysis of the ERA campaign, *Why We Lost the ERA* (Chicago: Chicago University Press, 1986).

20. Felsenthal, *Sweetheart*, pp. 235–36.

21. Ibid., pp. 236–37.

22. Ibid., pp. 237–38. See also Boles, *Politics of the ERA*, p. 34, for a discussion of the intent of the amendment with respect to military service.

23. For examples of a feminist stance on abortion, see Ellen Willis, "Abortion: Is a Woman a Person?" in *Beginning to See the Light: Pieces of a Decade* (New York: Alfred A. Knopf, 1981), pp. 205–11, and Lucinda Cisler, "Abortion Law Repeal (Sort of): A Warning to Women," in Edith Hosino Altbach, ed., *From Feminism to Liberation* (Cambridge, Mass.: Schenkman, 1971), pp. 241–49. See also Beverly Wildung Harrison, *Our Right to Choose: A New Ethic of Abortion* (Boston: Beacon Press, 1983). There have been several recent studies of the abortion reform movement and the conservative reaction. See Rosalind Pollack Petchesky, *Abortion and Women's Choice: The State, Sexuality, and Reproductive Freedom* (New York: Longman, 1984); Kristin Luker, *Abortion and the Politics of Motherhood* (Berkeley: University of California Press, 1984); and Eva R. Rubin, *Abortion, Politics and the Courts: Roe v. Wade and Its Aftermath* (Westport, Conn.: Greenwood Press, 1982).

24. Pamela Johnston Conover and Virginia Gray, *Feminism and the New Right: Conflict over the American Family* (New York: Praeger, 1983), pp. 87–92.

25. Petchesky, *Abortion and Women's Choice*, p. 252.

26. Conover and Gray, *Feminism*, p. 87.

27. Luker, *Abortion and Politics of Motherhood*, pp. 225–26. See also Lucy M. Tedrow and E. R. Mahoney, "Trends in Attitudes toward Abortion: 1972–1976," *Public Opinion Quarterly* (Summer 1979): 181–89.

28. Luker, *Abortion and Politics of Motherhood*, pp. 216–17. As Luker notes, in the 1980s the Senate Judiciary Committee has held hearings on a human life statute that would outlaw virtually all abortions by declaring that human life begins at conception. Several antiabortion bills have also been under congressional consideration.

29. Ibid., pp. 219–22.

30. Ibid., pp. 223–24.

31. Petchesky, *Abortion and Women's Choice*, pp. 242–52. See also Peter Skerry, "The Class Conflict over Abortion," *Public Interest* 52 (Summer 1978): 69–84.

32. Petchesky, *Abortion and Women's Choice*, p. 252. See also Susan Harding, "Family Reform Movements: Recent Feminism and Its Opposition," *Feminist Studies* 7 (Spring 1981): 57–75.

33. Alan Crawford, *Thunder on the Right: The "New Right" and the Politics of Appeasement* (New York: Pantheon Books, 1980), pp. 34–36.

34. Petchesky, *Abortion and Women's Choice*, p. 254.

35. Ibid.

36. Ibid., pp. 254–55. See also Linda Gordon and Allen Hunter, "Sex,

Family, and the New Right: Anti-Feminism as a Political Force," *Radical America* 11–12 (November 1977–February 1978): 9–25; and Donald Granbery, "Pro-life or Reflection of Conservative Ideology? An Analysis of Opposition to Legalized Abortion," *Sociology and Social Research* 62 (April 1978): 414–29.

37. Crawford, *Thunder on the Right*, p. 38. See also Carol Virginia Pohli, "Church Closets and Back Doors: A Feminist View of Moral Majority Women," *Feminist Studies* 9 (Fall 1983): 529–58.

38. East, "Newer Commissions," p. 41.

39. Interview: Mildred Marcy, 24 June 1985, and Catherine East, *American Women: 1963, 1983, 2003* (Washington, D.C.: National Federation of Business and Professional Women's Clubs, 1983), p. 18.

40. Ibid., p. 19.

41. Ibid.

42. Friedan, *It Changed My Life*, pp. 466–67.

43. East, "Newer Commissions," pp. 42–43; and East, *American Women*, p. 20. See also Alice S. Rossi, *Feminists in Politics: A Panel Analysis of the First National Women's Conference* (New York: Academic Press, 1982), pp. 25–26.

44. Rossi, *Feminists*, pp. 25–26; and East, *American Women*, p. 20.

45. Interview: Sheryl Swerd, former junior staff person, IWY Commission, 15 October 1985.

46. Interview: Swerd.

47. See *The Spirit of Houston*, which contains the entire national plan of action, p. 1 for the quote on the ERA, and pp. 13–97 for the resolutions.

48. *The Spirit of Houston*, p. 104.

49. Ibid., pp. 104–105.

50. Ibid., p. 109.

51. Ibid.

52. Ibid., pp. 109–10.

53. Ibid., pp. 110–11.

54. Interview: Marcy.

55. *The Spirit of Houston*, p. 112. Alice Rossi claims that 57 percent of the delegates reported high levels of concern that political opponents of the conference would disrupt it. At its last meeting before the conference, the IWY Commission greatly increased its budgeting for security guards in Houston. See Rossi, *Feminists*, p. 28.

56. *The Spirit of Houston*, p. 113.

57. Interview: Swerd.

58. Rossi, *Feminists*, p. 32, table 1.2; and *The Spirit of Houston*, p. 157. See also Anne Taylor Fleming, "That Week in Houston," *New York Times Magazine*, 25 December 1977.

59. Fleming, "That Week," p. 33; *The Spirit of Houston*, pp. 165–66; and Interviews: Swerd and Marcy.

60. Rossi, *Feminists*, pp. 186–87; and *Spirit of Houston*, pp. 162–63.

61. Elizabeth Pleck, "Failed Strategies; Renewed Hope," in Hoff-Wilson, ed., *Rights of Passage*, p. 112.

62. *The Spirit of Houston*, pp. 149–53.
63. Rossi, *Feminists*, pp. 313–17, 336–37.
64. Ibid., pp. 82–84.
65. Quoted in Felsenthal, *Sweetheart*, p. 291.
66. Ibid., p. 290.
67. See *The Spirit of Houston*, pp. 193–203, for a colorful detailed description of the torch relay.
68. See Fleming, "That Week in Houston," for the emotional impact on a journalist-observer.
69. Zillah R. Eisenstein, *The Radical Future of Liberal Feminism* (New York: Longman, 1981), pp. 246–48.

Epilogue

1. See Susan Bolotin, "Voices from the Post-Feminist Generation," *New York Times Magazine*, 17 October 1982, pp. 28–31, 103.
2. ERAmerica Files, in the Manuscript Reading Room of the Library of Congress, Washington, D.C.
3. Sonia Johnson, *From Housewife to Heretic* (Garden City, N.Y.: Doubleday, Anchor Press, 1983), p. 158. Johnson ran for NOW president in 1982 in an attempt to move the organization to the left. In 1984, she ran for president of the United States on the Citizen's party ticket.
4. Edith Mayo and Jerry K. Frye, "ERA: Postmortem of a Failure in Political Communication," in Hoff-Wilson, ed., *Rights of Passage*, p. 86.
5. See Eisenstein, *Radical Future of Liberal Feminism*, pp. 232–33, for an interesting discussion of the ERA as a symbolic reform that could also be used to fight oppression.
6. Elizabeth Alexander and Maureen Fiedler, "The Equal Rights Amendment and Abortion: Separate and Distinct," *America*, 12 April 1980, pp. 314–18.
7. See Newtonia V. Harris, "ERA and Ethnic Minority Women," *Response: United Methodist Women Journal*, March 1980, pp. 16–17, 33; "The Equal Rights Amendment—Impact on Black America," *Black Woman's Voice*, April 1980, pp. 3, 8; and Liz Wheaton, "ERA:Black Women Ask 'What's in It for Us?'" *Women's Rights Report*, Fall 1979, p. 3, for examples of black women trying to educate their own constituency as to the value of the amendment.
8. Hester Eisenstein, *Contemporary Feminist Thought* (Boston: G. K. Hall, 1983), p. 136.
9. Interview: Sonia Johnson, Arlington, Virginia, 16 October 1985.
10. Alice Rossi, "A Biosocial Perspective on Parenting," *Daedalus* 106 (Spring 1977): 1–32. For a critique of the Rossi essay and others, see Wini Breines, Margaret Cerullo, and Judith Stacey, "Social Biology, Family Studies, and Antifeminist Backlash," *Feminist Studies* 4 (February 1978): 43–67.
11. Rossi, "Biosocial Perspective," p. 24.
12. Breines, Cerullo, and Stacey, "Social Biology," p. 51.

13. Betty Friedan, *The Second Stage* (New York: Summit Books, 1981). For a critique of Friedan, see Judith Stacey, "The New Conservative Feminism," *Feminist Studies* 9 (Fall 1983): 559–83.

14. See Jean Elshtain, *Public Man, Private Woman: Women in Social and Political Thought* (Princeton: Princeton University Press, 1981), and a discussion of her work in Stacey, "New Conservative Feminism."

15. For a particularly depressing update on the status of married women, see Anne Taylor Fleming, "The American Wife," *New York Times Magazine*, 26 October 1986, pp. 28–35.

A NOTE ON SOURCES

The manuscript sources used in this study are only representative of the large range of primary sources located in archives across the country. The decade of the seventies witnessed an outpouring of studies on women, as well as a tremendous growth of women's organizations locally, regionally, and nationally. The Schlesinger Library at Radcliffe College contains organizational papers that were particularly valuable to me. The most important collection for my purposes was the National Organization of Women papers, which include records from 1966 into the 1980s, and records of the Joint Committee of Organizations Concerned about the Status of Women in the Catholic Church; the Ecumenical Task Force on Women and Religion; the Catholic Caucus; and the NOW Legal Defense and Education Fund Public Service Advertising Campaign. The Schlesinger also has the following relevant collections: the National Women's Political Caucus; the National Abortion Rights Action League; the World Population Conference; the Women's Equity Action League; the Committee on the Status of Women at Harvard (1969–71); the Black Women Oral History Project; Women in the Federal Government interviews; and the papers of Betty Friedan, Charlotte Bunch, and Mildred Marcy. The papers of Virginia Allan are at the Bentley Library, University of Michigan.

The papers and other materials of the IWY Commission are at the Smithsonian and the Women's Bureau collection at the National Archives. The Women's Bureau also has reports on women's employment status during the 1970s. The ERAmerica collection is at the Library of Congress. The Center for Women Policy Studies in Washington, D.C., is an invaluable resource for material on women's social and economic status. The Project on the Status and Education of Women of the As-

sociation of American Colleges publishes *On Campus with Women* and is
another source for policy on women. The Henry A. Murray Research
Center of Radcliffe College serves as an archive for social science data
about women's lives. The Boston Women's Health Book Collective,
Watertown, Massachusetts, is an important repository of information
on women's health policy and concerns of the 1970s and 1980s.

The Women's Collection of the Special Collections Department,
Northwestern University Library, contains papers of the women's liberation movement from the late 1960s to the present, as well as the
largest feminist periodical collection here or abroad. Bethune Museum
Archives, Inc., Washington, D.C., contains archival collections on
black women's twentieth-century history, including the Record of the
National Council of Negro Women. The Sophia Smith Collection,
Women's History Archives, Smith College, contains primary sources
on birth control, education, professions, humanities and the fine arts,
women in industry, and women's rights. The State Historical Society
of Wisconsin has a Women's History Sources collection, which contains
the papers of the Women's National Abortion Action Coalition as well
as the papers of several activists.

The Women's Institute for Freedom of the Press has published several directories of women and the media that encompass all aspects of
the media—periodicals, presses, publishers, film, bookstores, library
collections, and so on. See *Directory of Women's Media* (1985); *Media Report to Women: Annotated Index of Media Activities and Research* (1977); and
The Second Five-Year Index to Media Report to Women (1981). The large
numbers of journals, periodicals, and newsletters that appeared during
the decade of the seventies are too numerous to list. The ones I found
most helpful were *Signs, Feminist Studies, Quest, Women's Studies Quarterly, The Women's Review of Books,* and *Women's Political Times. Ms.* magazine is also an invaluable source for the evolution of the women's
movement in the context of popular culture and trends. See, in addition
to the monthly publications, *The Decade of Women: A Ms. History of the
Seventies in Words and Pictures* (New York, 1980).

Reference material on women of the seventies includes *American
Women: Three Decades of Change,* Special Demographic Analysis (U.S.
Department of Commerce, Bureau of the Census, 1984); *Women in Pub-
lic Office: A Biographical Dictionary and Statistical Analysis,* compiled by
the Center for American Woman and Politics, Eagleton Institute of
Politics, 2nd ed. (Metuchen, N.J.: Scarecrow Press, 1978); Barbara J.
Nelson, *American Women and Politics: A Selected Bibliography and Resource*

Guide (New York: Garland Publishing, 1984); Katherine Fishburn, *Women in Popular Culture: A Reference Guide* (Westport, Conn.: Greenwood Press, 1982); and Barbara Haber, ed., *The Women's Annual*, no. 1 (Boston: G. K. Hall, 1980), a comprehensive survey of current women's history using a topical approach.

The decade of the seventies is too recent to have attracted a significant amount of historical analysis, but there are several important studies of the emergence of the women's movement during the 1960s and early 1970s. Sara Evans's ground-breaking study, *Personal Politics: The Roots of Women's Liberation in the Civil Rights Movement and the New Left*, traces the history of the movement in the sixties as an outgrowth of New Left politics. For the evolution of the movement in the early seventies, see Judith Hole and Ellen Levine, *Rebirth of Feminism* (New York: Quadrangle Books, 1971); Maren Lockwood Carden, *The New Feminist Movement* (New York: Russell Sage Foundation, 1974); and Jo Freeman, *The Politics of Women's Liberation* (New York: David McKay, 1975). Absolutely essential to an understanding of the emergence of liberal feminism is Betty Friedan's *Feminine Mystique* (New York: W. W. Norton Co., 1963).

The relationship of the radical branch of the New Left to the women's liberation movement can be found in several key essays in Harold Jacobs, ed., *Weatherman* (Palo Alto, Calif.: Ramparts Press, 1970), and Abe Peck, *Uncovering the Sixties: The Life and Times of the Underground Press* (New York: Pantheon Books, 1985). See also Robin Morgan, ed., *Sisterhood Is Powerful: An Anthology of Writing from the Women's Liberation Movement* (New York: Vintage Books, 1970); and Morgan, *Going Too Far: The Personal Chronicle of a Feminist* (New York: Random House, 1977). The relationship between Marxism and feminism is analyzed in Lydia Sargent, ed., *Women and Revolution: A Discussion of the Unhappy Marriage of Marxism and Feminism* (Boston: South End Press, 1981).

The emergence of radical feminism as a political and intellectual movement distinct and separate from the New Left can be seen in the writings of various feminists. See especially Shulamith Firestone and Anne Koedt, eds., *Notes from the Second Year: Women's Liberation* (New York: Radical Feminists, 1970); and Firestone, *The Dialectic of Sex: The Case for a Feminist Revolution* (New York: William Morrow, 1970). See also Anne Koedt, Ellen Levine, and Anita Rapone, eds., *Radical Feminism* (New York: Quadrangle, 1973).

Mary Lou Thompson, ed., *Voices of the New Feminism* (Boston: Beacon Press, 1970), is a collection of early statements by liberal feminists.

Other similar collections of greater range and with policy implications are Vivian Gornick and Barbara Moran, eds., *Woman in Sexist Society* (New York: New American Library, 1972); and Joan Haber, ed., *Changing Women in a Changing Society* (Chicago: University of Chicago Press, 1973). The brand of feminism espoused by NOW can be found in Lucy Komisar, *The New Feminism* (New York: Franklin Watts, 1971); Komisar and Ann Scott, *And Justice for All* (Chicago: National Organization for Women, 1971); and a recent biography by Eleanor Humes Haney, *A Feminist Legacy: The Ethics of Wilma Scott Heide and Company* (Buffalo, N.Y.: Margaretdaughters, 1985). See also Betty Friedan, *It Changed My Life: Writings on the Women's Movement* (New York: Dell Publishing Co., 1976), for Friedan's view of NOW politics.

For women's role in the reform politics of the early seventies, see Byron Shafer, *Quiet Revolution: The Struggle for the Democratic Party and the Shaping of Post-Reform Politics* (New York: Russell Sage Foundation, 1983); and Stephen Schlesinger, *The New Reformers: Forces for Change in American Politics* (Boston: Houghton Mifflin Co., 1975).

Women's political role changed dramatically during the 1970s with respect to organizational activity, party politics, office-holding, and policy-making. The following publications analyze this change. See Jane Jaquette, ed., *Women in Politics* (New York: Wiley, 1974); Susan and Martin Tolchin, *Clout: Womanpower and Politics* (New York: Coward, McCann & Geoghegan, 1974); M. Githens and J. L. Prestage, eds., *A Portrait of Marginality: The Political Behavior of the American Woman* (New York: Longman, 1977); Ruth B. Mandel, *In the Running: The New Woman Candidate* (New Haven: Ticknor & Fields, 1981); Virginia Sapiro, *The Political Integration of Women: Roles, Socialization, and Politics* (Urbana: University of Illinois Press, 1983); Ethel Klein, *Gender Politics: From Consciousness to Mass Politics* (Cambridge, Mass.: Harvard University Press, 1984); and Myra Marx Ferree and Beth B. Hess, *Controversy and Coalition: The New Feminist Movement* (Boston: G. K. Hall, 1985).

For biographies of political figures of the decade, see Ralph Nader Congress Projects: Citizens Look at Congress, *Bella Abzug, Democratic Representative from New York* (Washington, D.C.: Grossman, 1972). The Nader group also published biographies of Edith Green, Ella Grasso, and others. See also Bella S. Abzug, *Bella! Ms Abzug Goes to Washington*, ed. Mel Ziegler (New York: Saturday Review Press, 1972); Shirley Chisholm, *Unbought and Unbossed* (Boston: Houghton Mifflin Co., 1970); Chisholm, *The Good Fight* (New York: Harper & Row, 1973);

Barbara Jordan and Shelby Hearon, *Barbara Jordan: A Self-Portrait* (Garden City, N.Y.: Doubleday & Co., 1979); and James Haskins, *Barbara Jordan* (New York: Dial Press, 1977).

Women became a major focus of public policy during the 1970s, particularly with respect to the issue of equal rights. See "Symposium: Women's Rights," *Hastings Law Journal* 23 (November 1971), which contains articles on domestic violence, abortion, employment rights, the draft, and sex discrimination. See also Joyce Gelb and Marian Lief, *Women and Public Policies* (Princeton: Princeton University Press, 1982), and Irene Tinker, ed., *Women in Washington: Advocates for Public Policy*, Sage Yearbooks in Women's Policy Studies, vol. 7 (Beverly Hills, Calif.: Sage Publications, 1983).

On the struggle over the equal rights amendment, see Janet K. Boles, *The Politics of the Equal Rights Amendment: Conflict and Decision Process* (New York: Longman, 1979); Joan Hoff-Wilson, ed., *Rights of Passage: The Past and Future of the ERA* (Bloomington: Indiana University Press, 1986); Mary Frances Berry, *Why ERA Failed* (Bloomington: Indiana University Press, 1986); Jane Mansbridge, *Why We Lost the ERA* (Chicago: University of Chicago Press, 1986); and Carol Felsenthal, *The Sweetheart of the Silent Majority* (Garden City, N.Y.: Doubleday & Co., 1981).

Women made some of their most significant advances in the field of education. For a historical interpretation of educational reform since World War II, which places women's role into a broader context, see Diane Ravitch, *The Troubled Crusade: American Education, 1945–1980* (New York: Basic Books, 1983). For an early feminist critique, see Barbara Grizzuti Harrison, *Unlearning the Lie: Sexism in School* (New York: William Morrow Co., 1974). For an overview of women's impact on education in the 1970s, see Joan N. Burstyn and Polly Welts Kaufman, "Women and Education," in Barbara Haber, ed., *The Women's Annual, 1980: The Year in Review* (Boston: G. K. Hall & Co., 1981), pp. 23–41. For women in higher education, see Alice S. Rossi and A. Calderwook, eds., *Academic Women on the Move* (New York: Russell Sage Foundation, 1973); Joan Abramson, *The Invisible Woman: Discrimination in the Academic Profession* (San Francisco: Jossey-Bass, 1975); Saul D. Feldman, *Escape from the Doll's House: Women in Graduate and Professional School Education* (New York: McGraw-Hill, 1974); and Gloria Desole and Leonore Hoffmann, eds., *Rocking the Boat: Academic Women and Academic Processes* (New York: Modern Language Association of America, 1981).

The impact of women's studies on the curriculum is the subject of several important publications. For a general overview, good for classroom use, see Hunter College Women's Studies Collective, *Women's Realities, Women's Choices: An Introduction to Women's Studies* (New York: Oxford University Press, 1983). See also Marilyn J. Boxer, "Review Essay: For and About Women: The Theory and Practice of Women's Studies in the United States," *Signs* 7 (Spring 1982); Elizabeth Langland and Walter Gover, eds., *A Feminist Perspective in the Academy: The Difference It Makes* (Chicago: University of Chicago Press, 1983); Ellen Carol Dubois, Gail Paradise Kelly, Elizabeth Lapovsky Kennedy, Carolyn W. Korsmeyer, and Lillian S. Robinson, *Feminist Scholarship: Kindling in the Groves of Academe* (Chicago: University of Illinois Press, 1985); and Marilyn R. Schuster and Susan R. Van Dyne, *Women's Place in the Academy: Transforming the Liberal Arts Curriculum* (Totowa, N.J.: Rowman & Allanheld, 1985). For a radical feminist discussion of women's studies, see Charlotte Bunch and Sandra Pollack, eds., *Learning Our Way: Essays in Feminist Education* (Trumansburg, N.Y.: Crossing Press, 1983).

The intellectual revolution underlying the women's studies movement was part of a broader cultural development. Kate Millet's *Sexual Politics* (New York: Doubleday & Co., 1970), offered a devastating critique of male literature from a feminist perspective. For general surveys and criticism of the period, see Elaine Showalter, *Women's Liberation and Literature* (New York: Harcourt Brace Jovanovich, 1971); Carol Fairbanks, *More Women in Literature: Criticism of the Seventies* (Metuchen, N.J.: Scarecrow Press, 1979); and Showalter, ed., *The New Feminist Criticism: Essays on Women, Literature, and Theory* (New York: Pantheon Books, 1985). For women and the arts, see Judy Chicago, *Through the Flower: My Struggle as a Woman Artist* (Garden City, N.Y.: Doubleday, 1977); Germaine Greer, *The Obstacle Race: The Fortunes of Women Painters and Their Work* (New York: Farrar, Straus & Giroux, 1979); and Elaine Hedges and Ingrid Wendt, eds., *In Her Own Image: Women Working in the Arts* (Old Westbury, N.Y.: Feminist Press; New York: McGraw-Hill, 1980).

For other feminist statements on women's nature and the whole issue of gender, culture, and society, see Elizabeth Janeway, *Man's World, Women's Place: A Study in Social Mythology* (New York: Dell Publishing, 1971); Germaine Greer, *The Female Eunuch* (New York: Bantam Books, 1972); Carolyn G. Heilbrun, *Toward a Recognition of Androgyny* (New York: Alfred A. Knopf, 1973); and Ti-Grace Atkinson, *Amazon Odyssey* (New York: Link Books, 1974). The importance of the mothering role, and its impact on men, women, and children was treated in Adrienne Rich, *Of Woman Born: Motherhood as Experience and Institution* (New York: W. W. Norton, 1976); Dorothy Dinnerstein, *The Mermaid and the Minotaur: Sexual Arrangements and Human Malaise* (New York: Harper & Row, 1977); and Nancy Chodorow, *The Reproduction of Mothering: Psychoanalysis and the Sociology of Gender* (Berkeley: University of California Press, 1978). See also Susan Griffin, *Woman and Nature: The Roaring Inside Her* (New York: Harper & Row, 1978).

The feminist inquiry into the psychology of women also emerged in the early 1970s. See Judith M. Bardwick, *Psychology of Women: A Study of Bio-cultural Conflicts* (New York: Harper & Row, 1971); Phyllis Chesler, *Women and Madness* (Garden City, N.Y.: Doubleday, 1972); Juliet Mitchell, *Psychoanalysis and Feminism: Freud, Reich, Laing, and Women* (New York: Random House, 1974); Jean Strouse, ed., *Women and Analysis: Dialogues on Psychoanalytic Views of Femininity* (New York: Grossman Publishers, 1974); and, in particular, Jean Baker Miller, *Toward a Psychology of Women* (Boston: Beacon Press, 1976).

Much of the writing on the nature of women addressed the issue of lesbianism. Jill Johnston, *Lesbian Nation: The Feminist Solution* (New York: Simon & Schuster, 1974), offered an early angry statement. Sidney Abbott and Barbara Love, *Sappho Was a Right-on Woman: A Liberated View of Lesbianism* (New York: Stein & Day, 1972), placed the issue into the context of the politics of the women's movement and especially NOW politics. See also Del Martin and Phyllis Lyon, *Lesbian/Woman* (New York: Bantam Books, 1972). The classic article by Adrienne Rich, "Compulsory Heterosexuality and Lesbian Existence," *Signs* 5 (1980), is perhaps the most thoughtful justification for a woman-centered emotional and sexual life-style.

Relationships with men was not a particularly popular topic with many feminists of the seventies, but Shere Hite's controversial best-seller, *The Hite Report* (New York: Dell Publishing Co., 1976), was indicative of the impact of the sexual revolution upon at least *some* American women. A more negative account of sexual relationships was Susan Brownmiller's *Against Our Will: Men, Women, and Rape* (New York: Simon & Schuster, 1975). Brownmiller's basic thesis—that all men are potential rapists—was not particularly well received, but rape became a public policy issue of the seventies because of the attention that feminists brought to the issue. Male violence against women—in particular, the problem of battered wives—became another policy issue that was generated by the women's movement. See Susan Schechter,

Women and Male Violence: The Visions and Struggles of the Battered Women's Movement (Boston: South End Press, 1982). See also Jane Roberts Chapman and Margaret Gates, eds., *The Victimization of Women*, Sage Yearbooks in Women's Policy Studies, vol. 3 (Beverly Hills, Calif.: Sage Publications, 1978). The U.S. Commission on Civil Rights has also done several studies of this issue: *Battered Women: Issues of Public Policy*, a consultation (Washington, D.C.: U.S. Government Printing Office, 30–31 January 1978); *The Federal Response to Domestic Violence* (Washington, D.C.: GPO, 1982); and G. Gerebenies, *Under the Rule of Thumb: Battered Women and the Administration of Justice* (Washington, D.C.: GPO, 1982).

The changing relationship between women and organized religion was another important aspect of women's experience in the 1970s. In the years after 1965, thousands of nuns left their orders in America. See Mary Griffin, *The Courage to Choose: An American Nun's Story* (Boston: Little, Brown & Co., 1975); and Nancy Henderson, *Out of the Curtained World: The Story of an American Nun Who Left the Convent* (Garden City, N.Y.: Doubleday, 1972). See also Sarah Bentley Doely, ed., *Women's Liberation and the Church: The New Demand for Freedom in the Life of the Christian Church* (New York: Association Press, 1970). Rosemary Ruether's two most important studies are *New Woman/New Earth: Sexist Ideologies and Human Liberation* (New York: Seabury, 1975); and Ruether, ed., *Religion and Sexism: Images of Woman in the Jewish and Christian Traditions* (New York: Simon & Schuster, 1974). The strongest indictment against the Catholic church came from Mary Daly: *The Church and the Second Sex* (New York: Harper & Row, 1975), and *Beyond God the Father: Toward a Philosophy of Women's Liberation* (Boston: Beacon Press, 1973). For other radical feminist approaches to religion, see Carol P. Christ and Judith Plaskow, eds., *Womanspirit Rising: A Feminist Reader in Religion* (New York: Harper & Row, 1979); and Naomi Goldenberg, *Changing of the Gods: Feminism and the End of Traditional Religions* (Boston: Beacon Press, 1979).

The best source on the feminist perspective of women's health issues is undoubtedly the Boston Women's Health Book Collective, *The New Our Bodies, Ourselves* (New York: Simon & Schuster, 1984). This revised version of the 1976 edition contains a wealth of information. It also includes a useful bibliography at the end of each chapter. In addition, see Helen Roberts, ed., *Women, Health, and Reproduction* (Boston: Routledge & Kegan Paul, 1981); and Gena Corea, *The Hidden Malpractice:*

How American Medicine Treats Women as Patients and Professionals (New York: William Morrow, 1977).

Black women offered a significant critique of feminism as movement and ideology. Most of the important historical and theoretical writings appeared in the 1980s: G. Auzaldua and C. Moraga, eds., *This Bridge Called My Back: Writings by Radical Women of Color* (Watertown, Mass.: Persephone Press, 1981); Bell Hooks, *Ain't I a Woman: Black Women and Feminism* (Boston: South End Press, 1981); Hooks, *Feminist Theory: From Margin to Center* (Boston: South End Press, 1984); and Jacqueline Jones, *Labor of Love, Labor of Sorrow* (New York: Basic Books, 1985). For black women's studies, see Gloria Hull, Patricia Bell Scott, and Barbara Smith, eds., *All the Women Are White, All the Blacks Are Men, But Some of Us Are Brave: Black Women's Studies* (Old Westbury, N.Y.: Feminist Press, 1983). *Social Science Quarterly* 56 (June 1975), contains several articles on the status of black women. Early in the decade there were two studies of women in the black family: Joyce Ladner, *Tomorrow's Tomorrow* (Garden City, N.Y.: Doubleday & Co., 1971); and Carol Stack, *All Our Kin: Strategies for Survival in a Black Community* (New York: Harper & Row, 1975). See also Toni Cade, ed., *The Black Woman: An Anthology* (New York: New American Library, 1970), for an early collection of writings by black women; and the writings of Alice Walker, Toni Morrison, and Maya Angelou for black literature and autobiographical writings. For a more recent interpretation, see Roseann Bell, Bettye Parker, and Beverley Guy-Sheftall, *Sturdy Black Bridges: Visions of Black Women in Literature* (New York: Doubleday, Anchor Press, 1979).

Perhaps the most significant occurrence of the seventies, and the one that to many Americans was virtually synonymous with women's liberation was the movement of women into the labor force. There is an enormous amount of material on the subject, of which only a few titles will be mentioned here. For statistical accounts of women's economic status, see *1975 Handbook on Women Workers*, Women's Bureau Bulletin 297 (Washington, D.C.: Department of Labor, 1975); and U.S. Department of Labor, Women's Bureau, *20 Facts on Women Workers* (Washington, D.C.: GPO, 1982). See Ralph E. Smith, ed., *The Subtle Revolution: Women at Work* (Washington, D.C.: Urban Institute, 1979), for an analysis of several aspects of women's work and family life. Rosabeth Moss Kanter has written the standard account of women in corporations, *Men and Women of the Corporation* (New York: Basic Books,

1977), as well as a study of the relationship between work and family, *Work and Family in the United States: A Critical Review and Agenda for Research and Policy* (New York: Russell Sage Foundation, 1977). See also Mary Jo Bane, *Here to Stay: American Families in the Twentieth Century* (New York: Basic Books, 1976).

Right-wing reaction to changes in family life is analyzed in Pamela Johnston Conover and Virginia Gray, *Feminism and the New Right: Conflict over the American Family* (New York: Praeger, 1983); and in Walda Katz Fishman, *The New Right: Unravelling the Opposition to Women's Equality* (New York: Praeger, 1982). The backlash to the women's movement was first expressed in the writings of Midge Decter, *The New Chastity and Other Arguments against Women's Liberation* (New York: Coward, McCann & Geoghegan, 1972), and *The Liberated Woman and Other Americans* (New York: Coward, McCann & Geoghegan, 1971).

The profamily thrust of the New Right was met by the neofeminist writings of Betty Friedan, *The Second Stage* (New York: Summit Books, 1981), and Jean Bethke Elshtain, *Public Man, Private Woman: Woman in Social and Political Thought* (Princeton: Princeton University Press, 1981). For a feminist analysis of these issues, see Zillah Eisenstein, *The Radical Future of Liberal Feminism* (New York: Longman, 1981); and *Feminism and the State: Reagan, Neoconservatism, and Revisionist Feminism* (New York: Monthly Review, 1984). See also Elizabeth Janeway, *Cross-Sections from a Decade of Change* (New York: William Morrow, 1982), and Hester Eisenstein, *Contemporary Feminist Thought* (Boston: G. K. Hall, 1983).

One of the joys of writing contemporary history is that it provides one with the opportunity to do oral history. The following women gave generously of their time and added a unique dimension to my understanding of the activism of the seventies: Virginia Allan, Donna Allen, Lois Black, Joan Burstyn, Judith Bush, Joan Roberts Chapman, Mary Jean Collins, Karen DeCrow, Catherine East, Arvonne Fraser, Mary Jane Gillespie, Sonia Johnson, Frances Kolb, Gretchen Kreuter, Judith Long, Mildred Marcy, Judith Norsigian, Yvette Oldendorf, Lois Galgay Reckitt, Joan Roberts, Bernice Sandler, Betty Bone Schiess, Sheryl Swerd, Norma Swenson, Irene Tinker, Anne Truax, and Gayle Graham Yates.

INDEX

Abbott, Sidney, 67
Abel, Emily, 111, 223n33
abortion, xiii, xiv, 19, 28–32, 40, 52, 88, 158, 162, 182, *183–85*, 189, 193, 199, 202
Abortion and Women's Choice (Petchesky), 184
abortion reform movement, *82–84*, 87, 218n7
Abramson, Joan, 107–108, 109
Abzug, Bella, 22, 23, 24, 25, 27, 28, 29, 34, 35, 163–64, 165, 167, 169, 186, 187, 188, 192, 195
affirmative action, 21, 108–10, 115–20, 126
AFL-CIO, 191
Against Our Will: Men, Women, and Rape (Brownmiller), 91–92
Alda, Alan, 186, 187
Alexander, Shana, 30
"Alice Doesn't . . . Day," 51
"All in the Family," 170, 191
Allan, Virginia, 176, 187
Allen, Donna, 97
Allen, Pam, 5
Alpert, Jane, 1, 11–14
Alther, Lisa, 70
Amatniek (Sarachild), Kathie, 5, 12
American Academy of Religion, Women's Caucus, 57
American Association of University Professors (AAUP), 119

American Association of University Women (AAUW), 33, 119, 178, 191, 194
American Bar Association (ABA), 177
American Civil Liberties Union (ACLU), 178
American Council on Education (ACE), 119
Amis, Kingsley, 70
anti-feminism, 35, 184, 185, 189, 235–236n36
anti-rape movement, 92–94
anti-war movement, 5, 20, 21, 81
Armstrong, Anne, 158–59, 177
Arnow, Harriet, 69
Arthur, Bea, 170
Association of American Colleges (AAC), 107
Association of Faculty Women (AFW), 112
As We Are Now (Sarton), 75
Athanasakos, Elizabeth, 188
Atkinson, Ti-Grace, 6, 14, 41, 63, 67, 211, 211n16
Ayers, Bill, 9, 10

Baird, Bill, 6
Bancroft, Anne, 170, 171
Battered Minority Women (BMW), 139–40
battered women, 94–95, 141, 229

battered women's centers, 56, 81, 94–95, 141, 220n49
battered women's movement, 94–95, 141, 220n42
Bay Area Women Against Rape, 92
Bayh, Birch, 177, 186
Beach Area Women's Clinic, 86
Beauvoir, Simone de, 71
Bellamy, Carol, 35
Berkshire Conference on Women's History, 124
Berry, Mary Francis, 117–18
Beyond God the Father (Daly), 60
Bill of Rights for Women, 40
biosocial perspective, 77, 200–201, 237n10
Bird, Caroline, 67
birth control, 19, 82, 89
Birth Project, The (Chicago), 98, 99
Black American Political Association of California, 54
Black family, 134–36, 137–39, 228n28
Black feminism, 72, 138, 228–29
Black Macho and the Myth of Superwoman, (Wallace), 73, 138
Black power, 4
Black revolution, 103
Black women, 71–74, 116–18, 133, 134–40, 228
Black women's literature, 72–74
Bok, Derek C., 108, 109
Bolt, Molly, 70
Boschwitz, Rudy, 185
Boston College, 59–60
Boston Women's Health Book Collective, 79, 80–81, 84–85
Boudin, Kathy, 9, 11
Boyer, Elizabeth, 19
Bradlee, Ben, 26
Braudy, Susan, 63
Brewster, Kingman, 109
Brown, Rita Mae, 14, 65, 68
Brownmiller, Susan, 67, 91–92
Budapest, Z., 62
Bunch, Charlotte, 14, 53, 192
Burger Court, 130, 227n11
Burnett, Carol, 170
Burstyn, Joan, 122–23
Bush, Judith, 100, 101

Carnegie Corporation, 106
Carpenter, Liz, 26
Carroll, Constance M., 117
Carter Administration, 34, 159, 161–62, 188, 195, 196
Carter, Jimmy, 24, 162, 188
Carter, Rosalyn, 156, 159–62, 192
Casals, Rosie, 152
Catcher in the Rye (Salinger), 70
Cellar, Emanuel, 166
Chafe, William, xv
Change of World, A (Rich), 76
Chicago, Judy, 98–100, 221n63, n64
Chicago NOW, 49, 50
Chicago, University of, 82, 104
Chicago, University of Chicago Press, 123
child abuse, xiv, 142
child care centers, 56
child custody, 19, 147
Chisholm for President, 26
Chisholm, Shirley, 22, 25–27, 30, 31, 35, 164–65, 169
Chiswick Women's Aid, 94
Chodorow, Nancy, 147
Choice, Not an Echo, A (Schlafly), 178
Chopin, Kate, 69
Christ, Carol, 56, 62
Christian Century, 62
Church and the Second Sex, The (Daly), 59, 60
Citizens' Advisory Council on the Status of Women (CACSW), 18–19
Civil Rights Act of 1957, 176
Civil Rights Act of 1964, 18, 103, 104, 105, 176
Civil Rights Commission, 31
civil rights movement, 2, 20, 39, 73, 137
Clarenbach, Kathryn, 18, 38
Coalition for Women's Appointments, 34
College Entrance Examination Board, 106
Collins, Mary Jean, 49, 50, 210–11n14, 213n51
Color Purple, The (Walker), 74
Columbia University, 105
Columbia Women's Liberation, 66

Combahee River Collective, 138
Comment, 106
Committee for a Rational Alternative, 115
Community Action Programs, 135
Communist Party, USA, 180
comparable worth, 202
Comprehensive Employment and Training Act of 1973 (CETA), 130
"Compulsory Heterosexuality and Lesbian Existence," 76
Congress to Unite Women, 43, 66
Congresswomen's Caucus, 166
consciousness-raising, 6, 7, 9, 55, 56, 62–63, 65, 71, 93, 99, 205n19, n21
Conservative Caucus, 180
Coordinating Council for Women in Higher Education (CCWHE), 112
"Cornell 11," 114
Cornell School of Veterinary Medicine, 120
Cornell University, 113–15, 122
Court, Margaret, 153
Cronkite, Walter, 31

Daly, Mary, 57, 59–61, 62, 71, 77, 200
Dance the Eagle to Sleep (Piercy), 71
Daughters of the American Revolution, 180
Davidson, Sara, 70
Dean, Pat, 165
DeCrow, Karen, 14, 49–53
Democratic Farmer-Labor Party (DFL) of Minnesota, 33
Democratic National Committee, 21, 23
Democratic National Convention, 1968, 20, 22, 31, 41
Democratic National Convention, 1972, 24–32
Democratic National Convention, 1976, 87, 168
Democratic Party, ix, 20–22, 31
Densmore, Dana, 63
DFL Feminist Caucus, 33
Diamond Cutters (Rich), 76
Dinner Party, The (Chicago), 98, 99
Dinnerstein, Dorothy, 147
divorce, 19, 90, 129, 130–33, 135

Divorce Revolution, The (Weitzman), 133–34
Dixon, Marlene, xi
Do IT NOW, 48
Dohrn, Bernardine, 11
Dowd, Nancy F., 104
Downer, Carol, 87–88
Durr, Frankie, 152
Dworkin, Andrea, xiv

Eagle Forum, 181
Eagle Forum Newsletter, 181
Eagleton, Tom, 30, 31, 165
East, Catherine, 16, 18, 186, 187, 188, 192
East New York Alliance, 14
eating disorders, 173
education, 102–26
Education Amendments of 1976, 119
Ehlstain, Jean Bethke, 77, 201
Ehrenreich, Barbara, 132, 144, 201
Eisenstein, Zillah, 38–39
employment, 116–18, 127–30, 136–37
Equal Employment Opportunity Act, 1972 Amendment, 46, 129
Equal Employment Opportunity Commission (EEOC), 18, 38, 44, 110, 111, 116
Equal Pay Act, 17–18, 31, 129
Equal Rights Amendment (ERA), x, xiv, 16, 31, 40, 46, 47, 52–53, 54, 68, 120, 158, 159, 162, 175, 176–78, 179, 187, 189, 192–93, 195–96, 198–200
ERAmerica, 187, 198
ERA Extension, 166, 198
Evening Standard, 176
Executive Order 11375, 104
Exxon Education Foundation, 106

Fair Labor Standards Act, 176
Falwell, Jerry, 186
family violence, 130, 139–42
family wage system, 132
Farenthold, Frances "Sissy," 28, 30–31, 165, 232n48
fathering, 130, 146–47
Fear of Flying, 70
Federally Employed Women (FEW), xi
female-headed households, 134, 135–36

Female Studies I, II, 122
Feminine Mystique, The (Friedan), 10
feminism, xii, 35, 39, 83–84, 120, 137–38, 167
Feminist Alliance Against Rape (FAAR), 93
Feminist Art Program, 98–100
feminist consciousness, 8, 9, 10, 16, 17, 33, 35, 81, 83–84, 91, 98, 100, 111, 120, 171
Feminist Counseling Collective (FCC), 89
Feminist Press, 122
feminist scholarship, 102, 112, 113, 123, 126
feminist spirituality, 56–62
Feminist Studies, 71, 122
Feminist Women's Health Centers (FWHC), 86, 87–88
Feminists, The (October 17th Movement), 6–7, 8
feminization of poverty, 130, 133–36, 202, 228
Ferris, Charlotte, 114
fertility, 127
Fertility Consciousness/Women-Controlled Natural Birth Control Groups (FC/WCNBC), 89
Field, Sally, 170
film, 170–72
Fiorenze, Elizabeth, 61
Firestone, Shulamith, 3, 5
Fischer, Ruth, 117
"fitness craze," 172–73
Fonda, Henry, 171
Fonda, Jane, 171, 172
Fonda, Peter, 171
Ford Administration, 34, 157
Ford, Betty, 156, 157–59, 192, 232n24, n26
Ford Foundation, 106
Ford, Gerald, 157, 158, 177, 186
Forest Hills, 11, 150, 152
Fox, Alma, 26
Fraser, Arvonne, 19, 24
Fraser, Don, 19, 23
free standing birth centers, (FSBC), 89–90
Freeman, Jo, 3, 15, 36–37, 46, 79

Fremont Women's Clinic, 87
French, Marilyn, 69, 70
Friedan, Betty, xii, 6, 10, 18, 19, 22, 25, 26, 37, 38–39, 41–42, 43–44, 45, 64, 68, 128, 148, 192, 201, 210n5
friendships, 75, 171–72
Frye, Jerry K., 198
Furies, The, 68
Future Shock (Toffler), 143–44

Galantic, Ivan, 110
Galbraith, John Kenneth, 30
Gallstones, the, 7
Gardner, Jo-Ann Evans, 26
gay liberation movement, 44, 65
Gelles, Richard J., 141
"gender gap," 197, 202, 232n38
ghetto culture, 134–35
Girl Friends, 172
Girl Scouts of America, 119, 191
Glasse, Antonia, 114
Godwin, Gail, 69
Going Down Fast (Piercy), 71
Going Too Far (Morgan), 63
Goldenberg, Naomi, 62
Goldsmith, Judy, 53
Goldwater, Barry, 20
Goldwater Campaign, 178
"Good-bye to All That," (Morgan), 1, 13
Goodman, Ellen, 156, 164
Goodman, Paul, 11
Grasso, Ella, 186
Great Society, 16
Green, Edith, 22, 105–106
Green hearings, 106, 222
Greenfield, Meg, 161
Greer, Germaine, 31
Griffin, Susan, 74, 77, 91, 142, 143
Griffith, Martha, 177, 178, 186, 187
Growing Up Underground (Alpert), 11
Guardian, the, 4
Gyn/Ecology (Daly), 61

Hamilton, Joan, 14
Haney, Eleanor Humes, 61
Harper, Valerie, 170
Hart, Gary, 28, 29, 208n36
Hartmann, Susan, 106

Harvard Graduate School of Design (GSD), 108
Harvard University, 105, 108–109
Hawaii, University of, 107
Hayden, Tom, 172
Healthright Collective, 84
Heckler, Margaret, 186
Heide, Wilma Scott, 26, 42, 45–47, 49, 52, 67, 177, 211n26–27, 213n52
Hellman, Lillian, 171
Helms, Jesse, 185
Hepburn, Katharine, 186
Higher Education Act of 1972, Title IX, 106, 115, 118–19
Hills, Carla, 158
Hoffman, Dustin, 147
Hoff-Wilson, Joan, 198
Hofstadter, Richard, xiv
Hole, Judith, 38, 39, 203n3
Holmes, Dorris, 192
Holtzman, Elizabeth, 35, 165, 166–67, 169
Homemaker Committee, 187
Hooks, Bell, 92
Hopkins, Harry, 162
Hosken, Franziska, 108–109
House Judiciary Committee, 165, 167–68
housework, 144–46
Houston Conference. *See* National Women's Conference
Howe, Florence, 121–22
Hughes, Francine, 140–41
Hughes, Mickey, 140–41
Hurston, Zora Neal, 69, 72, 73
Humphrey, Hubert, 20, 21, 26
Hutar, Pat, 177
Hyde Amendment, 183

In Search of Our Mothers' Gardens (Walker), 73
incest, xiv, 142
Interdepartmental Committee on the Status of Women (ICSW), 18
International Women's Years (IWY), xi, 186
IWY Conference in Mexico City, 186, 187; IWY state meetings, 189–91

"Jane" collective, the, 83–84
Jane Fonda Workout Book, 172
Jeanette Rankin Brigade, 5
Jepson, Roger, 185
John Birch Society, 180, 185
Johnson Administration, 2, 17
Johnson Foundation, Racine, Wisconsin, 106
Johnson, Lady Bird, 159, 192
Johnson, Lyndon B., 20, 39, 104
Johnson, Sonia, 102, 198, 200, 213n4, 221n2, 237n3
Johnston, Jill, 14
Joint Committee of Organizations Concerned with the Status of Women in the Roman Catholic Church, 59
Jones, Ann, 152
Jong, Erica, 70
Joost, Christine, 110
Jordan, Barbara, 165, 166, 167–69, 192

Keaton, Diane, 170
Kempton, Sally, 67
Keniston, Kenneth, 10
Kennedy Administration, xi, 16–17, 20, 206n1
Kennedy, Flo, 10, 14, 67
Kennedy, John F., 155
Kennedy, Robert, 155, 162
Kinds of Love (Sarton), 75
Kinflicks (Alther), 70
King, Billie Jean, 150–54, 192
Kissinger, Henry, 47, 162
Klein, Ethel, 33
Klute, 171
Know Press, 122
Koch, Ed, 164
Koedt, Ann, 5, 63
Kolb, Frances, 52, 203n3, 213n51
Kollias, Karen, 95
Komisar, Lucy, 46
Koontz, Elizabeth, 177
Kramer, Sandra, 34
Kramer vs. Kramer, 147
Kreuter, Gretchen, 123–24
Ku Klux Klan, 180

labor unions, 21, 47
Ladies Home Journal, 169

Lady-Unique-Inclination-of-the-Night, 61
Lamb, Myra, 67
Lange, Ann, 49
Latin America, 160
Lauter, Paul, 122
"lavender herring," 64
"Lavender Menace," 66
Lawrence, D. H., 69
Laver, Rod, 152
Laws, Judith Long, 113–14, 224
League of Women Voters (LWV), xi, 33, 35, 41, 119, 178, 191, 194
"lesbian-baiting," 65, 66, 67
lesbian/separatist, xii–xiii, 96–97, 199–200, 220n53, 221n55
Lesbianism, xiii, 43, 44–45, 53, 64–69, 70, 74, 75, 76–77, 96–97, 126, 182, 188, 189, 194–95, 199–200, 215n43
Lessing, Doris, 69
liberal feminists, xi–xii, xiii, 6, 22, 30, 35, 38–39, 104, 132, 148, 175, 176, 178, 187, 190–91, 199, 201
Liberty Lobby, 180
lifestyles, 3, 9, 42, 54, 55, 64, 67, 68, 76, 77, 95, 96–97, 128, 142–43, 144–45, 156
Lindsay, John, 165
Little, Joanne, 92
Livingston, Jacqueline, 114
Loose Change (Davidson), 70
Lorde, Audre, 74, 217n36
Luce, Clare Boothe, 186
Lucky Jim (Amis), 70

McCarthy, Eugene, 26, 165
McGovern Commission, 20–21, 23, 207n15
McGovern, George, 14, 21, 24, 25, 26–31, 47, 165
MacLaine, Shirley, 27, 28, 29, 30, 170, 171
McNulty, Faith, 140
Made From This Earth (Griffin), 77
Mailer, Norman, 69
Mainardi, Pat, 145
Maine, University of, 42, 117
"Majority Caucus," 51–52
Malcolm X, 74

Manson family murders, 11
march for gay and lesbian rights, 97
Marcuse, Herbert, 11
Marcy, Mildred, 187, 191
marriage, 7, 63, 70, 75, 76, 131–32, 143–45, 202, 238n15
married women workers, 129–30, 227n7
marital status, of women, 129, 133, 135
Marxist Feminists, xii, 45–46
"Mary Tyler Moore Show," 170
Maryland, University of, 104, 117
Matter of Simple Justice, A, 176
Mayo, Edith, 198
Mead, Margaret, 192
media, 43, 51, 67, 97, 128, 148–49, 152–55, 155–56, 173–74, 187, 194, 233n60
Media Report for Women, 97
Meissner, Doris, 23
Melville, Sam, 11, 12, 14
Memoirs of an Ex-Prom Queen (Shulman), 70
men, 1–2, 4, 7, 8, 9–10, 11, 33, 60–61, 62–63, 73, 99, 123, 126, 132–33, 134, 141, 146–47, 169, 201
men's liberation movement, 146
Mermaid and the Minotaur (Dinnerstein), 147
metaphysical feminism, 59, 77–78, 217n74
Michigan, University of, 117
Midler, Bette, 170
Miller, Henry, 69
Millett, Kate, 14, 66, 67, 69, 71
Minnesota Historical Society, 124
Minnesota, University of, 104, 120, 226n80
Minority Task Force (NOW), 53
minority women, 25, 27, 34, 47, 49, 53–54, 71, 90, 116, 126, 192, 199, 225n53, 228n32
Mitchell, Martha, 165
Modern Language Association (MLA), 121, 122
Moral Majority, 29, 142, 186, 209n44
Morgan, Robin, 1–2, 12, 13, 63, 68, 71, 77
Mormon Relief Society, 190

Morrison, Toni, 69, 72, 74
mothering, 143, 147–48
Moynihan, Daniel Patrick, 164
Mrs. Stevens Hears the Mermaid (Sarton), 75
Ms. Magazine, 13, 63, 68, 146, 148, 164, 169, 170, 233n61
Munson, Howard, 114
"Myth of Vaginal Orgasm" the, 5, 63

National Abortion Rights Action League, 191, 194
National Advisory Committee on Women, 195
National Advisory Council on Women's Educational Programs, 119
National Association for the Advancement of Colored People, (NAACP), 26
National Coalition Against Domestic Violence, 141–42
National Coalition for Research in Women's Education and Development (NCRWED), 106
National Coalition for Women and Girls in Education, 107, 119
National Collegiate Athletic Association (NCAA), 118–19
National Commission on the Observance of IWY (IWY Commission), 159, 186, 187–88, 192, 194–95, 198
National Committee to Stop ERA, 180
National Conference for New Politics (NCNP), 2–3
National Conference of Bishops, 59
National Conference of Catholic Bishops, 183
National Council of Catholic Women, 191
National Federation of Business and Professional Women, xi, 33, 41, 176, 191, 194
National Federation of Republican Women, 178–79
National Gay Rights Task Force, 188
National Lawyers Guild, 14

National Organization for Women (NOW), xi, 1, 4, 6, 18, 19, 21, 26, 35, 37–39, 46–49, 55, 64, 65, 67–68, 105, 106, 107, 108, 119, 131, 132, 166, 177, 191, 194, 195, 210
National Right to Life Committee (NRLC), 182, 185
National Task Force on Sexuality and Lesbianism, NOW, 45
National Women's Conference (Houston Conference), x, 159, 162, 175–76, 186, 187–89, 191–96, 198, 236–37
National Women's Educational Fund (NWEF), 34
National Women's Health Conference, 86
National Women's Health Network, 86
National Women's Party, 37
National Women's Political Caucus (NWPC), xi, 22–34, 35, 41, 54, 119, 163, 191
National Women's Studies Association (NWSA), 125
natural child-birth, 89–90
Nelson, Barbara, 36, 210n1
neofeminism, 200–201, 238n13
Neuberger, Maurine, 18
New Democratic Coalitions (NDCS), 21
New Frontier, 16–17, 20
New Left, the, xii, 1–15, 16, 53, 62–63, 71, 81, 164, 204–205n8
New Right, xiii–xiv, 29, 142, 149, 174, 175, 176, 180–81, 185–86, 200, 209n44
New Woman, 169
New York Chapter, NOW, 6, 65, 66
New York Radical Feminists, 8
New York Radical Women, 1, 5
New York State's Right to Life party (RTL), 182
New York Women's School, 14
New York Women's Union, 14
New York Times, 63, 97
Newsweek, 63, 158, 161, 162, 168
Nineteenth Amendment, 36, 44
Nixon Administration, 34, 177
Nixon, Pat, 156–57, 165, 231n19

Nixon, Richard, ix, 21, 29, 30, 32, 47, 165
Norsigian, Judy, 79, 86
no-fault divorce, 131–32
Notes from the First Year, 5
NOW Acts, 48

Oates, Joyce Carol, 69
O'Brien, Larry, 22
occupations, of women, 128–29, 136–37
Oldendorf, Yvette, 33
Old Left, 3, 204–205n8
O'Leary, Jean, 188
On Campus, 107
On Lies, Secrets and Silences (Rich), 76
Onassis, Aristotle, 155
Onassis, Jacqueline Bouvier Kennedy, 155–56
O'Neills, Nena and George, 144
Open Marriage (O'Neills), 144
Ordination of women, Episcopal Church, 58–59
O'Reilly, Jane, 17
Oughton, Diane, 9–10, 11
Our Bodies, Ourselves, 85

Paley, Grace, 14
Parmet, Herbert S., 21
Paul, Alice, 37
patriarchal system, xii, 4, 6–7, 38, 47, 53, 61, 63
peace movement, 81, 163
Pennsylvania NOW, 49
Pentimento (Hellman), 171
People Magazine, 167
Percy, Charles, 186
Petchesky, Rosalind Pollack, 184
Peterson, Esther, 16
Philadelphia Conference, NOW, 51–52
Philadelphia Women's Liberation Center, 90
Phillips, Kevin, 21
Phyllis Schlafly Report, 180, 181
Piercy, Marge, 69, 71
Pittsburg NOW, 49
Playboy, 154, 180
Plitt, Jane, 50–51
Pogrebin, Letty Cottin, 145, 148

politicos, xii, xiii, 4, 5, 13
"Politics of Ego," the, 8
"Politics of Housework," the (Mainardi), 145
"Politics of Rape," the, (Griffin), 91, 142
Polivy, Margot, 34
popular culture, 169, 170–74
pornography, xiv, 37, 142, 202
Porterfield, Amanda, 61
postfeminist, 197, 201–202, 237n1
Pottinger, J. Stanley, 115
Prairie Fire Distributing Committee, 14
Presidential Commission on the Status of Women (PCSW, or Kennedy Commission), xi, 16–17, 18, 186
President's Commission on Mental Health, 160
President's Task Force on Women's Rights and Responsibilities, 176, 177
Pressler, Larry, 185
Priest Forever, A (Carter), 58–59
"prison-guards," 7
Prizzey, Erin, 94–95
profamily movement, 52, 77, 185–86
Pro-Family Rally, 193–94
Professional Women's Caucus, 105
Progressive Labor Organization (PL), 3
Project on the Education and Status of Women, 107–108
Project on Equal Educational Rights (PEER), 106–107
"prowoman" argument, 6, 7, 8
Public Law 95-555, 1978, 129
Public Man, Private Women, (Ehlstain), 201

Quest: A Feminist Quarterly, 14, 95–96

racism, 71, 72, 73, 117–18, 135, 138–39
Radcliffe College, 124
radical feminism, xii, xiii, 2–3, 13, 41–43, 49, 52–53, 54, 55–56, 62–63, 68–69, 71, 74, 77, 78, 95–96, 143, 176, 182, 188–89, 199–200
Radicalesbians, 65
Ramparts Magazine, 91
rape, xii, xiii, xiv, 91–94, 120, 142, 219–220n38

rape crisis centers, 56, 79, 92–94
Rape: The Power of Consciousness (Griffin), 91
Rat, 1, 11, 12
Rayburn, Sam, 20
Reagan Administration, 115
Reagan, Ronald, xiv, 196
Reckitt, Lois Galgay, 42
Reckoning, A (Sarton), 75
Redford, Robert, 171
Redgrave, Vanessa, 171, 172
Redstockings, 1, 5–6, 8
religion, 56–62
Reproduction of Mothering, The (Chodorow), 147
reproductive freedom, x, 29–30, 40, 82, 89–90, 189, 192
Republican Party, 22, 24, 30, 32, 183
Revenue Act of 1978, 129
Rich, Adrienne, 69, 74, 75–77, 125, 142, 143n66
Rigg, Diana, 170
Riggs, Bobby, 150, 153, 154
Rights of Passage, (Hoff-Wilson), 198
right-to-life-movement, 29–30, 182–85, 209n44
right-wing women, xiv, 176
Rising Sun Feminist Health Alliance, 86
Roberts, Joan, 105, 112–13, 114, 121
"Roe vs. Wade," 29, 82, 130, 182, 183, 185, 209n44
Roman Catholic Church, 57–58, 59
Roosevelt (Franklin) coalition, ix
Roosevelt, Eleanor, 16, 158, 161, 162
Rosen, Marjorie, 172
Rossi, Alice, 77, 200–201, 237n10
Rothman, Lorraine, 88
Rubyfruit Jungle (Brown), 70
Ruckelhaus, Jill, 30, 32, 177, 186, 187, 188
Rudd, Mark, 14
Ruether, Rosemary Radford, 57, 58, 61, 62
Russell, Letty M., 61

Safer, Morley, 158
SALT treaties, 179

Saiving, Valerie, 57
Salinger, J. D., 70
Sandler, Bernice, 19, 104 105, 120
Sarah Lawrence College, 72
Sarton, May, 69, 74–75, 217n64
Savvy, 169
Schapiro, Miriam, 98–99
Schlafly, Phyllis, 178–82, 185, 193, 194, 199
Schroeder, Patricia, 35
Schultz, George, 177
Scott, Ann, 46, 47
Scott, Arlie, 53
Scream Quietly or the Neighbors Will Hear (Prizzey), 95
S.E. Portland Women's Health Clinic, 86
Second Vatican Council, 57, 59
Second Wave, The (Friedan), 201
Segal, Phyllis, 24
self-help groups, 87–91
Senate Judiciary Committee, 177
sexism, xiii, 8, 11, 17, 56, 57, 58, 62, 72, 73, 103, 105–106, 222n12
sexual harassment, xiv, 120
Sexual Politics (Millett), 66, 69, 71
sexual preference, x, 44–45, 53, 66, 67, 188, 192
sexuality, 44–45, 47, 62–63, 64, 67, 70, 75, 81, 96, 185
Shafer, Bryon E., 23, 24
Shange, Ntozake, 138
Shelly, Martha, 65
Shulman, Alix Kates, 70
Signs: A Journal of Women in Culture and Society, 122–23
"Sisterhood is powerful," 5
Sita (Millett), 69
Sloane, Margaret, 14
Small Changes (Piercy), 71
"small group" movement, 79–81
Small Room, The, (Sarton), 75
Smeal, Eleanor, 52, 53, 166, 192, 198
Smith, Barbara, 72, 138
social feminism, 201
Social Security Act, 176
Socialist Workers' party (SWP), 3, 14, 45

Solanas, Valerie, 6
Somerville Women's Health Project, 86
Spacek, Sissy, 170
"Spirit of Houston," 195
sports, 47, 118–19, 150–54, 172–73
Sports Illustrated, 150
Sportswoman of the Year, 150
Stapleton, Jean, 170, 186, 191
state commissions on the status of
  women, xi, xii, 17–18, 20, 38, 40, 176
state legislatures, women elected to, 22,
  34
State University of New York, 105, 121
Stearns, Rick, 28
Steinem, Gloria, 13, 14, 22, 26–27, 29,
  67, 164, 165, 169
Stern, Susan, 10–11
Stimpson, Catharine, 122, 125
Stop ERA Campaign, 179–82, 198
Streep, Meryl, 170
Striesand, Barbra, 170
Students for a Democratic Society
  (SDS), 10–11
Student Non-Violent Coordinating
  Committee (SNNC), 2, 3
Sudow, Ellen, 34
"superwoman," 148
Sutherland, Don, 146
Swenson, Norma, 79
Swerd, Sheryl, 188
Syracuse University, 113

"Take Back the Night," 93
Task Force on Family Law and Policy,
  18
Tax Reform Act of 1976, 129
teenage pregnancy, 130, 134, 135
television, 151, 170
Time, 66, 168, 175
Title VI, Civil Rights Act of 1964, 104
Title VII, Civil Rights Act of 1964, 18,
  103, 104, 105
Title IX, Higher Education Act of
  1972, 106, 115, 118–19
Through the Flower (Chicago), 98
. . . *To Form a More Perfect Union* . . .,
  186–87
Tobias, Sheila, 122

Toffler, Alvin, 143–44
Tomlin, Lily, 170
"trashing," 68, 125–26
Truax, Anne, 120–21
Tufts University, 110–11
Turning Point, The, 171–72
Tyson, Cicely, 170

United Auto Workers, 40, 178
U.S. Civil Service Commission, 17
U.S. Department of Health, Education
  and Welfare (HEW), 108, 109, 111,
  115, 117
U.S. Department of Labor, 104, 177
U.S. News and World Report, 168

Vietnam War, 35, 81, 129, 172
Village Voice, 4, 63
Violent Home, The (Gelles), 141
Virginia Slims, 150, 152, 154, 173
vocational education, 119
Vogue, 169

Walker, Alice, 69, 72, 73–74
Walker, Margaret, 72
Wall Street Journal, 168
Wall Street Lawyers Against the
  Vietnam War, 35
Wallace, George, 21, 41
Wallace, Michele, 73, 138, 216–17n61
War on Poverty, 135
Warhol, Andy, 6
Washington, D.C. Area Women's
  Center, 89
Washington Post, 160, 168
Watergate, 150, 157, 166
Watergate hearings, 165
Weal Washington Report, 19, 34
weathermen, the, 1, 2, 3, 9, 10–11
Weitzman, Lenore, 133–34
West Coast Lesbian Feminist
  Conference, 1973, 68
Westwood, Jean, 27
White, Barbara E., 110
White, Theodore, 25
Whitlock, Kay, 53
wife abuse, xiii, xiv, 91, 94–95, 139–42
Wild Patience, A (Rich), 76

Wilkerson, Cathy, 9
Willis, Ellen, 4, 5, 12
Wisconsin, University of,
    104, 112–13, 121
"Womanhouse," 99
"Woman-Identified-Woman," The, 65,
    66
"womanish," 73–74
Woman Spirit, 61
Women Historians of the Midwest
    (WHOM), 124
Women in Transition, 90–91
Women on the Edge of Time (Piercy), 71
women theologians, 57–62
"women on the move," 195
Women's Advocates, 95
Women's Bureau, xi, 16, 18, 177
Women's Campaign Fund, 34
Women's Caucus for the Arts of Central
    New York, 100
women-centered consciousness, 56, 62,
    64, 64–67, 68, 69, 77, 79, 81, 97,
    100–101
women's centers, xii, 56, 79, 80, 88, 120
Women's Clinic, Evergreen State
    College, 86
women's collectives, xii, 56, 79, 80, 83–
    84, 85, 88, 89, 90–91, 218n8
Women's Conference Network, 191
women's continuing education, 106
women's culture, xii, 62, 69–71
Women's Educational Equity Act, 1974,
    129
Women's Educational Equity Act
    Program (WEEAP), 119
Women's Equity Action League
    (WEAL), xi, 19–20, 40, 41, 104–105,
    107, 115, 118, 119
Women's Health Action Movement
    (WHAM), 87

Women's Health Forum, 14
women's health movement, 79, 81–88,
    219n20
Women's International Terrorist
    Conspiracy from Hell (WITCH), 1, 5
Women's Liberation Front, 9, 10, 16,
    37, 41
women's liberation movement, xi, xii,
    xiii, 1–15, 35, 42, 59, 62, 91, 95, 122,
    150, 211n17
women's magazines, 169–70
women's movement, ix–xv, 15, 17, 23,
    32–35, 37, 39, 46, 54, 60, 63, 67, 71–
    72, 80, 91, 100, 102–104, 111, 140,
    143, 154, 156, 158, 167, 173–74, 198–
    99, 200, 202
Women's Page, the, 7
"women's renaissance," 69
women's rights, xiii, 18–19, 23, 31, 36,
    38, 39, 40, 43, 104, 186
Women's Room, The, 70
womenSports, 153
Women's Strike for Equality, 43–44
women's studies, xiii, 56, 59, 102, 112,
    120–26, 225n68–69
women's studies movement, 123–26
Women's Studies Newsletter, 122
Wood, Rosemary, 165
working-class women, 71, 191, 227n11
Working Woman, 169

Yale University, 108
Young Americans for Freedom, 185
Young Socialist Alliance, 3, 45
YWCA, xi

Zahorik, Donna, 114
Zami (Lorde), 74
Zarker, John, 110